RULES OF ORIGIN IN ASEAN

Rules of Origin in ASEAN is the first in-depth exploration of the complex rules of origin in ASEAN's trade agreements. Written by two leading practitioners, it explains with clarity the existing ASEAN Rules of Origin (RoO) practices and their administration regimes in a comparative context and provides a recommendation for reform. The ASEAN RoOs can be simplified by imparting transparency and predictability to the legal drafting, focusing on a calculation method based on value of materials and lowering the regional value content required to qualify as ASEAN origin. The administration of ASEAN RoOs can be improved by expanding the use of self-certification, moving away from document-based verification to more modern post-entry audit and trade facilitation approaches. This is a timely and important topic that will be insightful to practitioners, policymakers and businesses in understanding how commerce and trade are conducted in Southeast Asia.

STEFANO INAMA is a Chief and trade lawyer at UNCTAD. He has been responsible for the preferences and trade laws section in UNCTAD and is Coordinator of the UNCTAD commercial diplomacy programme. He has provided trade policy advice for the last twenty years to governments during the WTO negotiations and the implementation aspects of WTO agreements, as well as during negotiations of Free Trade Agreements such as the ASEAN–China, EU–South Africa, SADC area and the Tripartite Free Trade Area as well as FTA negotiations by Latin American and Caribbean countries with the EU. He is the author of *Rules of Origin in International Trade* (Cambridge University Press, 2009).

The views expressed are those of this author and do not necessarily reflect the views of UNCTAD or any other UN institutions or agencies.

EDMUND W. SIM is a partner at Appleton Luff, Singapore and an adjunct associate professor at the National University of Singapore Law School, where he created the world's first course on ASEAN Economic Community (AEC) law. He has participated in more than 200 trade remedy proceedings and has advised government ministries on anti-dumping and countervailing duty laws, rules of origin, Free Trade Agreements and investment laws and their consistency with the WTO agreements.

INTEGRATION THROUGH LAW

The Role of Law and the Rule of Law in ASEAN Integration

General Editors

J. H. H. Weiler, European University Institute
Tan Hsien-Li, National University of Singapore
Michael Ewing-Chow, National University of Singapore

The Association of Southeast Asian Nations (ASEAN), comprising the ten member states of Brunei Darussalam, Cambodia, Indonesia, Lao PDR, Malaysia, Myanmar, Philippines, Singapore, Thailand and Vietnam, has undertaken intensified integration into the ASEAN Community through the Rule of Law and Institutions in its 2007 Charter. This innovative book series evaluates the community-building processes of ASEAN to date and offers a conceptual and policy toolkit for broader Asian thinking and planning of different legal and institutional models of economic and political regional integration in the region. Participating scholars have been divided up into six separate thematic strands. The books combine a mix of Asian and Western scholars.

Centre for International Law, National University of Singapore (CIL-NUS)

The Centre for International Law (CIL) was established in 2009 at the National University of Singapore's Bukit Timah Campus in response to the growing need for international law expertise and capacity building in the Asia-Pacific region. CIL is a university-wide research center that focuses on multidisciplinary research and works with other NUS or external centers of research and academic excellence. In particular, CIL collaborates very closely with the NUS Faculty of Law.

INTEGRATION THROUGH LAW
The Role of Law and the Rule of Law in ASEAN Integration
General Editors: J. H. H. Weiler, Tan Hsien-Li and Michael Ewing-Chow

RULES OF ORIGIN IN ASEAN
A Way Forward

STEFANO INAMA AND EDMUND W. SIM

CAMBRIDGE
UNIVERSITY PRESS

University Printing House, Cambridge CB2 8BS, United Kingdom

Cambridge University Press is part of the University of Cambridge.

It furthers the University's mission by disseminating knowledge in the pursuit of education, learning and research at the highest international levels of excellence.

www.cambridge.org
Information on this title: www.cambridge.org/9781107472440

© Centre for International Law 2015

This publication is in copyright. Subject to statutory exception and to the provisions of relevant collective licensing agreements, no reproduction of any part may take place without the written permission of Cambridge University Press.

First published 2015

A catalogue record for this publication is available from the British Library

Library of Congress Cataloguing in Publication data
Rules of origin in ASEAN : a way forward / edited by Stefano Inama, Edmund W. Sim.
  pages cm. – (Integration through law:the role of law and the rule of law in asean integration ; 1)
ISBN 978-1-107-47244-0 (Paperback)
1. Certificates of origin–Southeast Asia. 2. Tariff–Law and legislation–Southeast Asia. 3. ASEAN. I. Inama, Stefano, editor. II. Sim, Edmund W., editor.
KNC947.R85 2014
343.25908′7–dc23   2014038361

ISBN 978-1-107-47244-0 Paperback

Cambridge University Press has no responsibility for the persistence or accuracy of URLs for external or third-party internet websites referred to in this publication, and does not guarantee that any content on such websites is, or will remain, accurate or appropriate.

CONTENTS

List of tables page ix
General editors' preface x
Preface xvi
List of abbreviations xxi

1. Introduction 1
2. The initial set of ASEAN rules of origin: the lack of clarity and transparency masquerading as simplicity 1992–1995 12
   2.1 The value-based calculation 12
   2.2 Cumulation 19
   2.3 Absorption/roll-up 21
   2.4 Introduction of alternative rules of origin 1995–2000 24
      2.4.1 Fixing a hole by digging deeper: introduction of the substantial transformation test 24
      2.4.2 Adding on confusion to a final consolidation phase in ATIGA: the introduction of alternative product-specific rules of origin (PSRO) 2000–2009 27
3. Externalizing the confusion: the proliferation of rules in the ASEAN FTAs with dialogue partners 40
   3.1 Main features of the various FTAs' rules of origin contained in FTAs with ASEAN Dialogue partners 40
   3.2 Ancillary rules 40
   3.3 ASEAN–China FTA 40
   3.4 ASEAN–Australia–New Zealand FTA (AANZFTA) 48
   3.5 ASEAN–India FTA 49

CONTENTS

    3.6 ASEAN–Korea FTA   51
    3.7 ASEAN–Japan FTA   52

4. The silent cost: the cumbersome administration of ASEAN rules of origin   57
    4.1 Form D over substance   57
    4.2 Customs administration   72
    4.3 Preventing loss of origin   73

5. The possible way forward: self-certification   76

6. Conclusion and recommendations   86

    Executive summary   93
    Appendices   96
    Bibliography   399
    Index   401

TABLES

Table 1.1	Utilization of FTAs	*page* 4
Table 1.2	Utilization rates of ASEAN FTA	8
Table 3.1	A comparison of the main features of the various FTAs' rules of origin	41
Table 3.2	Comparison table of cumulation and other provisions in ASEAN FTAs with dialogue partners	44
Table 4.1	Form D	59
Table 4.2	The matrix of decisions on RoO implementation issues (endorsed at the 5th SCAROO (July 19, 2011)	62
Table 5.1	Corporate income tax rates within ASEAN	81
Table 6.1	Calculation of the ASEAN RVC in the ATIGA formulae	90

GENERAL EDITORS' PREFACE

This monograph is published within the context of a wide-ranging research project entitled, Integration Through Law: The Role of Law and the Rule of Law in ASEAN Integration (ITL), undertaken by the Centre for International Law at the National University of Singapore and directed by J. H. H. Weiler, Michael Ewing-Chow and Tan Hsien-Li.

The Preamble to the ASEAN Charter concludes with a single decision: "We, the Peoples of the Member States of the Association of Southeast Asian Nations ... [h]ereby decide to establish, through this Charter, the legal and institutional framework for ASEAN." For the first time in its history of over four decades, the Legal and the Institutional were brought to the forefront of ASEAN discourse.

The gravitas of the medium, a Charter: the substantive ambition of its content, the creation of three interlocking Communities, and the turn to law and institutions as instruments for realization provide ample justification for this wide-ranging project, to which this monograph is one contribution, examining ASEAN in a comparative context.

That same substantive and, indeed, political ambition means that any single study, illuminating as it may be, will cover but a fraction of the phenomena. Our modus operandi in this project was to create teams of researchers from Asia and elsewhere who would contribute individual monographs within an overall framework which we had designed. The project framework, involving several thematic clusters within each monograph, is thus determined by the framework and the place of each monograph within it.

As regards the specific content, however, the authors were free, indeed encouraged, to define their own understanding of the problem and their own methodology and reach their own conclusions. The thematic structure of the entire project may be found at the end of this Preface.

The project as a whole, and each monograph within it, display several methodological sensibilities.

First, law, in our view, can only be understood and evaluated when situated in its political and economic context. Thus, the first studies in the overall project design are intended to provide the political, economic, cultural and historical context against which one must understand ASEAN and are written by specialists in these respective disciplines. This context, to a greater or lesser degree, also informs the sensibility of each monograph. There are no "black letter law" studies to be found in this project and, indeed, even in the most technical of areas we encouraged our authors to make their writing accessible to readers of diverse disciplines.

Comparative experience suggests that the success of achieving some of the more ambitious objectives outlined in Article 1 of the Charter will depend in no small measure on the effectiveness of legal principles, legal rules and legal institutions. This is particularly true as regards the success of establishing "an ASEAN Community comprising the ASEAN Security Community, the ASEAN Economic Community and the ASEAN Socio-Cultural Community as provided for in the Bali Declaration of ASEAN Concord II". Article 2(2)(n) stipulates the commitment of ASEAN Member States to act in accordance with the principle of "adherence to multilateral trade rules and ASEAN's rules-based regimes for effective implementation of economic commitments and progressive reduction towards elimination of all barriers to regional economic integration." The ASEAN Member States therefore envisage that rules of law and the Rule of Law will become a major feature in the future of ASEAN.

Although, as seen, the Charter understands itself as providing an institutional and legal framework for ASEAN, the question of the "role of law and the rule of law" is not advocacy but a genuine enquiry in the various substantive areas of the project as to:

- the substantive legal principles and substantive rules of the various ASEAN communities;
- the procedural legal principles and rules governing institutional structures and decision-making processes;
- implementation, enforcement and dispute settlement.

One should not expect a mechanical application of this scheme in each study; rather, a sensibility that refuses to content itself with legal enactments as such and looks to a "living" notion of law and institutions is ubiquitous in all the studies. Likewise, the project is sensitive to "non Law." It variously attempts to locate the appropriate province of the law in this experience. That is, not only the role of law, but also the areas that are and should remain outside the reach of legal institutionalization with due sensitivity to ASEAN and Asian particularism and political and cultural identities.

GENERAL EDITORS' PREFACE

The project, and the monographs of which it is made, are not normatively thick. They do not advocate. They are designed, for the most part, to offer reflection, discuss the pros and cons, and in this way enrich public awareness, deepen understanding of different options and in that respect contribute indirectly to policymaking.

This decisive development of ASEAN has been accompanied by a growing Asian interest in various legal and institutional forms of transnational economic and political cooperation, notably the various voices discussing and showing an interest in an East Asia Integration project. The number of Free Trade Agreements (FTAs) and Regional Trade Agreements (RTAs) has increased from six in 1991 to 166 in 2013, with a further 62 in various stages of negotiations.

Methodologically, the project and many of the monographs are comparative in their orientation. Comparative law is one of the few real-life laboratories that we have in which to assess and understand the operation of different legal and institutional models designed to tackle similar objectives and problems. One should not need to put one's own hand in the fire to learn that it scorches. With that in mind a couple of monographs offer both conceptual reflection and pragmatic "tool boxing" on some of the key elements featuring in all regional integration systems.

Comparative law is in part about divergence: it is a potent tool and means to understand one's own uniqueness. One understands better the uniqueness of Apples by comparing them to Oranges. You understand better the specialness of a Toyota by comparing it to a Ford.

GENERAL EDITORS' PREFACE

Comparative law is also about convergence: it is a potent tool and means to understand how what are seemingly different phenomena are part of a broader trend, an insight which may enhance both self-understanding and policy potentialities.

Although many studies in the project could have almost immediate policy implications, as would the project as a whole, this is not its only or even principal purpose. There is a rich theory of federalism which covers many countries around the world. There is an equally rich theory of European integration, which has been associated with the advent Union. There is also considerable learning on Free Trade Areas and the like.

To date, the study of the legal aspects of ASEAN specifically and other forms of Asian legal integration has been derivative of, and dependent on, theoretical and conceptual insight which were developed in different contexts.

One principal objective of ITL and these monographs will be to put in place the building blocks for an authentic body of ASEAN and Asian integration theory developed in, and with sensitivity to, the particularities and peculiarities of the region and continent. A theory and conceptual framework of Asian legal integration will signal the coming of age of research of and in the region itself.

Although the monographs form part of an overarching project, we asked our authors to write each as a "standalone" – not assuming that their readers would have consulted any of the other titles. Indeed, the project is rich and few will read all monographs. We encourage readers to pick and choose from the various monographs and design their own

GENERAL EDITORS' PREFACE

menu. There is, on occasion, some overlap in providing, for example, background information on ASEAN in different studies. That is not only inevitable but desirable in a project of this amplitude.

The world is increasingly witnessing a phenomenon of interlocking regional organization where the experience of one feeds on the others. In some way, the intellectual, disciplinary and comparative sensibility of this project is a microcosm of the world it describes.

The range of topics covered in this series comprises:

The General Architecture and Aspirations of ASEAN
The Governance and Management of ASEAN: Instruments, Institutions, Monitoring, Compliance and Dispute Resolution
Legal Regimes in ASEAN
The ASEAN Economic Community
ASEAN and the World
The Substantive Law of ASEAN

PREFACE

The rules of origin (RoOs) constitute a fundamental foundation for any preferential trade agreement (PTA) involving trade in goods. RoOs are similar to nationality and citizenship rules for natural persons in a nation-state, in that both sets of rules establish the rights and privileges applicable to qualifying persons or goods. Nationality and citizenship rules determine who may enjoy the benefits of citizenship, such as freedom of movement, permanent residency and the like. Similarly, RoOs determine the applicable duty rate and other treatment for goods in the PTA.

RoOs generally fall into three types:

a. RoOs based on the "wholly originating" principle apply to goods which are naturally occurring (such as minerals) or grown/harvested (such as agricultural products). Human involvement in the production of such goods is limited to extracting, cultivating and/or harvesting the goods. In such circumstances, the country of origin is where the extraction, cultivation or harvest has taken place, i.e., the product "wholly originates" in that country.
b. RoOs based on qualitative analysis examine the extent to which a good has been further processed into another good, with an emphasis on the processing that has taken place in that country. In the "substantial transformation" standard, the relevant authorities examine the nature of the

processing and whether the product has been fundamentally changed into another product. Another approach is the "change in tariff classification," which examines whether the initial product and the processed products are classified differently under the Harmonized Tariff Schedule (HTS); sufficient deviation in HTS classification confers origin under this type of RoO. Finally, there are special product-specific RoOs that provide for specific processes as conferring origin on the product; these product-specific rules are commonly used for textiles.
c. RoOs based on quantitative analysis examine the value added by the processing in the country. This approach is known as "regional value content," under which the relevant authorities examine the value of the goods input into the production process, labor, overheads, and other costs. If after processing the resulting product meets a specified criterion, that product will satisfy the RoO.

The authors note that these are broad generalizations and that some RoOs may involve both qualitative and quantitative criteria. However, maintaining a broad view will guide readers as they parse our specific, critical approach to the RoOs used in ASEAN. Wholly originating goods usually do not cause controversy in the operation of PTAs, except where they are wrongly used for non-natural products (e.g., for products which are not extracted, cultivated or harvested) or where the products may be mobile (e.g., fish swimming across maritime boundaries). Qualitative RoOs have their own complications, as the "substantial transformation" standard tends to be very product specific and difficult to administer consistently, and the "change in tariff classification" approach is heavily dependent on a customs classification system that was not developed for determining origin. Quantitative RoOs require that manufacturers maintain detailed accounting and financial records, which may be difficult for small and medium-sized enterprises (SMEs).

Taken in this context, the ASEAN RoOs, originating in the ASEAN Preferential Trade Agreement (APTA), developed in the ASEAN Free Trade Area (AFTA) agreement and purportedly refined in the ASEAN Trade in Goods Agreement (ATIGA), have created a relatively muddled and confused trading situation in trade in goods within the ASEAN Economic Community (AEC).

The poor definition of ASEAN RoOs dates back to the APTA and AFTA. The APTA and AFTA generally applied quantitative RoOs that conferred origin on products which met a specified regional value content (RVC) of ASEAN-related inputs. The RVC rules were not clearly articulated or administered, resulting in much confusion, particularly among ASEAN SMEs, which do not have the capability to comply with the accounting and financial requirements of the RVC approach. Nor did ASEAN customs authorities have sufficient training to administer the RVC approach consistently, with ASEAN customs authorities and practitioners having to fill out the details through trial and error, often to the detriment of the business sector. As a result, use of the APTA and AFTA trade preferences was relatively limited, with only those industries with sufficient institutional resources and regionalization (e.g., the Japanese automobile industry) making full use of the RoOs.

PREFACE

Continued underutilization of the ASEAN trade preferences led to further tinkering with RoOs by ASEAN authorities, such as the introduction of product-specific RoOs as well as the alternative rule of change in tariff classification, a qualitative approach. Yet despite these revisions, implemented in their latest form in the ATIGA, the ASEAN RoOs remain relatively ill-defined and difficult to administer, and utilization rates of the ASEAN trade preferences also remain relatively low.

Further compounding the confusion have been the inconsistent RoOs used in ASEAN's FTAs with its main dialogue partners of Australia-New Zealand, China, India, Japan and Korea. Not only are the RoOs for the ASEAN FTAs mutually inconsistent, but they are inconsistent with the RoOs currently applied by the ATIGA.

The poor administration of ASEAN RoOs also has been a persistent problem. Despite repeated attempts to ease administrative burdens on importers and exporters, and thereby expand use of the ASEAN trade preferences, ASEAN customs authorities remain wedded to the verification and authentication of Form D certificate of origin (CO) documents rather than using modern trade facilitation approaches that would focus on the data contained in those documents instead of the documents themselves.

This book surveys all of these problems in the context of the APTA, AFTA, ATIGA and ASEAN FTAs. After surveying both the ASEAN RoOs and their administration, the authors recommend that ASEAN leaders reform both.

The RoOs in the ATIGA and ASEAN FTAs can be simplified by focusing on (1) an overall improvement of the legal texts in terms of transparency and predictability; (2) applying a percentage criterion based on value of materials; (3) lowering the RVC required to qualify as ASEAN origin; and (4) clarifying the text of product-specific rules of origin (PSROs).

The administration of ASEAN RoOs can be improved by (1) expanding the use of self-certification; (2) moving away from document-based verification; and (3) shifting to modern post-entry audit and trade facilitation approaches.

By imposing greater clarity in the RoOs and their administration, ASEAN authorities can encourage the use of the ASEAN trade preferences by all segments of the business community, including the SMEs. This reform should take place in conjunction with Regional Comprehensive Economic Partnership talks taking place among ASEAN and its FTA partners to harmonize the terms of its FTAs. Only with more effective and simplified RoOs can all sectors participate in the AEC and enjoy its benefits.

ABBREVIATIONS

AANZFTA	ASEAN–Australia–New Zealand Free Trade Agreement
ACFTA	ASEAN–China Free Trade Agreement
AEC	ASEAN Economic Community
AFTA	ASEAN Free Trade Area
AICO	ASEAN Industrial Cooperation
APTA	ASEAN Preferential Trade Agreement
ASEC	ASEAN Secretariat
ASEAN	Association of Southeast Asian Nations
ATIGA	ASEAN Trade in Goods Agreement
BOI	Binding Origin Information
CCCA	The Coordinating Committee on the Implementation of the CEPT Scheme for AFTA
CIF	Cost Insurance Freight (INCOTERMS)
CEPT	Common Effective Preferential Tariff
CO	Certificate of Origin
CTC	Change in Tariff Chapter
CTH	Change in Chapter
CTSH	Change in Tariff Sub-heading
FOB	Free-On-Board (INCOTERMS)
FTA	Free Trade Agreement
GSP	Generalized System of Preferences
HLTF	High Level Task Force on Economic Integration

ABBREVIATIONS

HS	Harmonized System
HTF	Harmonized Tariff Schedule
ITA	Information Technology Agreement
MFN	Most Favored Nation
MS	Member States
NAFTA	North American Free Trade Agreement
OCP	Operational Certification Procedures
PSRO	Product-Specific Rule of Origin
PTA	Preferential Trade Agreement
RoO	Rule of Origin
ROOTF	Rules of Origin Task Force
RVC	Regional value content
SCAROO	ASEAN Sub-committee on Rules of Origin
SEOM	Senior Economic Officials Meeting
SME	small and medium-sized enterprise
TOR	Terms of Reference
UNCTAD	United Nations Conference on Trade and Development
WTO	World Trade Organization

Chapter 1

Introduction

ASEAN Rules of Origin (RoOs) have often been branded as an example of simplicity, including by ASEAN's own leaders. However a number of reports and the increased calls by the same leaders to further simplify the ASEAN RoOs tell a different story.

In reality, the RoOs contained in the AFTA implementing the Common Effective Preferential Tariff (CEPT) Scheme have been systematically revisited for more than two decades by the ASEAN negotiating machinery in a perpetual quest to improve them. The results have been less than meager. Such failure is the result from, on the one hand, a consistent allergy to drawing from the lessons learned in ASEAN and in other regions, and, on the other hand, lack of capacity or simple inability to draft predictable and transparent legal texts on RoOs. All of this has been complicated by the "ASEAN Way" of consensus and non-confrontation; the "ASEAN Way" prevents problems from being raised or addressed.

In the face of its domestic failures, ASEAN has tried to export its model of RoOs when negotiating bilateral or plurilateral FTAs with, again, meager results. So far, the FTAs with China and India still reflect the shortcomings of the ASEAN RoOs, while the other FTAs negotiated by ASEAN

INTRODUCTION

with Japan, Korea and Australia/New Zealand reflect the RoOs models of these respective ASEAN partners.[1]

In this book the successive evolution of the ASEAN RoOs from their inception in the early ASEAN trading agreements to the later formulation in the ATIGA will be analyzed. This survey will include efforts now ongoing for more than twenty years to improve such RoOs as well as the flourishing of different sets of RoOs that ASEAN is confronting today in the FTAs entered with its trading partners.

For firms and products the tariff liberalization emerging from FTAs takes place at the time of customs clearance and it is subject to compliance with RoOs requirements. These requirements are both of a *substantive* nature, i.e., whether the imported product complies with the specific RoOs requirements in the partner country and of a *formal* nature, i.e., whether there is documentary evidence such as a CO demonstrating that a product is originating. Unless these requirements are met the products will be charged the full Most Favored Nation (MFN) rate of customs duty instead of the duty-free or reduced rate of customs duty.

Recent studies have shown that stringent RoOs and cumbersome administrative procedures have a decisive impact on utilization of trade preferences.[2] The recent reform

---

[1] To the extent that, as one ASEAN Member State official described it to one of the authors, ASEAN officials were "brainwashed" during the negotiations of the FTA agreement with Australia and New Zealand on the use of change of tariff classification as a preferred method of drafting rules of origin.

[2] See, for an analysis of the utilization rates in unilateral trade preferences and effects of restrictive rules of origin, "Erosion of Trade Preferences in

INTRODUCTION

of RoOs in the EU has been driven by studies that identified a strict and direct correlation between stringency of RoOs and underutilization of trade preferences.[3] As a result the EU has significantly liberalized its RoOs under the EU Generalised System of Preferences program.[4]

A stream of studies have also been carried out specifically in East Asia on the utilization of ASEAN FTAs by Asian firms, in particular by Japanese firms.[5] The result of these studies summarized in a recent publication shows that particularly in East Asia, the rate of FTA utilization remains at a fairly low level for a number of reasons.[6] A study pointed out that Japanese firms and their affiliates operating in ASEAN are not well aware of FTAs.[7] Under this study, the utilization of the AFTA measured by the ratio of the AFTA

---

the Post Hong Kong (China) Framework" in UNCTAD, Trade is Better than Aid to Aid for Trade (2008); UNCTAD, Trade Preferences for LDCs: An Early Assessment of Benefits and Possible Improvements (2003); UNCTAD, Market Access for Least Developed Countries (2001).

[3] See European Commission, *Impact Assessment on Rules of Origin for the Generalized System of Preference (GSP)* (2007).

[4] See S. Inama, "The Reform of the EC GSP Rules of Origin: Per Aspera Ad Astra?" *Journal of World Trade*, 45 (2011) 577–603.

[5] K. Hayakawa, D. Hiratsuka, S. Shiino and S. Sukegama, *Who Uses Free Trade Agreements?* (JETRO, 2007); E. M. Medalla and J. Balboa, *ASEAN Rules of Origin: Lessons and Recommendations for Best Practice* (PIDS, 2009).

[6] Ibid.

[7] D. Hiratsuka, I. Isono, H. Sato and S. Umezaki, "Escaping from FTA Trap and Spaghetti Bowl Problem in East Asia: An Insight from the Enterprise Survey in Japan" in Soesastro, H. (ed.), *Deepening Economic Integration in East Asia: The ASEAN Economic Community and Beyond* (ERIA, 2007), pp. 304–327.

Table 1.1 *Utilization of FTAs*

	Use by exporters	Intend to use	No intention to use	Use by importers	Intend to use	No intention to use
ASEAN	27%	27%	46%	23%	27%	50%
Indonesia	43%	22%	35%	33%	34%	33%
Malaysia	26%	19%	55%	20%	34%	59%
Philippines	14%	29%	57%	8%	21%	71%
Singapore	46%	17%	37%			
Thailand	26%	31%	43%	28%	29%	43%
Vietnam	12%	35%	53%	14%	28%	58%

Source: Survey of Japanese-Affiliated Firms in ASEAN, India, and Oceania.
Note: "Use" refers to the share of affiliates that are already using FTAs, "Intend to use" refers to the share of affiliates that are now not using but are considering the use of FTAs, and "No intention to use" refers to the share of affiliates that are now not using and are not going to use FTAs. The figures for Singaporean imports are not available since the general tariff rates are already zero or quite low in Singapore.

administrative records to total exports was low, at around 15 to 20 percent, during the period 2003–2006. The utilization rate on the import side was around 11 to 16 percent, lower than the corresponding rate for the export side.

Table 1.1, excerpted from a recent study and drawn from data collected from a questionnaire, corroborates the findings of these studies about low utilization of the trade preferences under FTAs.[8] In the context of these results it has to be noted that the higher utilization rates are achieved by exporters from Singapore, perhaps due to a better

---

[8] See Hayakawa *et al.*, "Who Uses Free Trade Agreements?" 245–264.

management of exports procedures and issuance of COs. The lowest utilization is recorded by Philippines (14 percent for exporters) and Vietnam (12 percent for exporters) and for importers the same countries show an utilization rate as low as 8 per cent for Philippines and 14 per cent for Vietnam.

The authors of the above-mentioned study conclude that the reasons why FTA utilization in East Asia is low by international standards is mainly due to the following:

(1) The use of investment incentive schemes in ASEAN obviating the use of the FTA preferences. According to the authors Japanese affiliates established in ASEAN countries do not need to use FTA schemes in order to import inputs at zero tariff rates since they benefit from investment schemes such as the ASEAN Industrial Cooperation (AICO) scheme, which allowed for application of fully liberalized tariff rates ahead of the region-wide application of such rates in 2010.
(2) The major trade in ASEAN for Japanese firms is in the electrical machinery industry, where MFN tariff rates are already low.
(3) The costs of complying with RoOs requirements are prohibitive, e.g., the administrative costs resulting from the cumbersome procedures for obtaining a CO.

Concerning the main reason under (1) above it has to be noted that while this could be the case for Japanese affiliates, investment schemes often do not apply to local firms that may be penalized in this respect. At the same time such benefits are allowed for imported inputs and not on exports and are often tied up with a limited time frame. In any event, the

INTRODUCTION

AICO scheme lost its practical significance when the CEPT rates went into full effect in 2010 and the AICO scheme was terminated in 2011.

Concerning the second reason under (2) above, this may be true for electronics but not in sectors such as the automotive industry for instance. A recent study of the ASEAN automotive industry showed that based on ASEAN intra-trade the maximum duty cost applying MFN rates to intra-ASEAN trade is about US$1.9 billion while applying the CEPT rate the minimum duty cost would be reduced to about US$165 million per annum.[9] This finding shows that MFN rates of duties in certain industrial sectors remain quite high and the scope of potential preferential tariff treatment and savings is therefore significant.

The fact that ASEAN preferences are consistently underutilized is further corroborated by ASEAN official reports. The most compelling evidence and official recognition of the underutilization of ASEAN preferences come from the record of the Senior Economic Officials Meeting (SEOM) Chairman's Report to the AEM-25th AFTA Council Meeting held in August 2011.[10] Table 1.2 provides a significant insight into the utilization rate of ASEAN preferences contained in an offficial ASEAN document. At that meeting ASEAN Member States submitted their data on

---

[9] See "ASEAN-EU Programme for Regional Integration Support Phase II, Pilot Sector Study on Rules of Origin to Facilitate the Integration of ASEAN Production Networks", unpublished report (2010).

[10] SEOM Chairman's Report to the AEM-25th AFTA Council Meeting of August 10, 2011, Manado, Indonesia

INTRODUCTION

Form D imports for the period of 2010, which was summarized as follows in the report:

> Based on the available data for the year 2010, it was found that the shares of Form D imports in intra-ASEAN are 3.34%, 47.1%, 18.98%, 3.44%, 11.89%, 0.49%, 41.15%, 22.6% and 13.44% for Brunei Darussalam, Cambodia, Indonesia, Lao PDR, Malaysia, Myanmar, Philippines, Thailand and Vietnam, respectively.

This extremely low utilization average of ASEAN, with major ASEAN trading Member States like Indonesia, Malaysia and Thailand recording utilization rates as low as 19 percent, 11 percent and 23 percent after more than eighteen years of existence of the CEPT, did not make a headline on the policy part of the SEOM Report.

This utilization of the AFTA is extremely low by any international standard. By comparison, the North American Free Trade Agreement (NAFTA) utilization rate by Mexican exports to the United States was around 60 percent in 2004–2005. Even utilization rates by Less Developed Countries, the poorest countries of the world, of trade preferences in the period 1994–2001 were found to exceed an average of 50 percent utilization, which is significantly higher than those of the AFTA.[11]

Yet the SEOM in the same report discussed how to improve the notification procedures of the specimen signatures of customs officials in charge of signing in the ATIGA

---

[11] See UNCTAD, *Trade Preferences for LDCs*.

Table 1.2 Utilization rates of ASEAN FTA

Ctry		Import From										Total
		BRN	KHM	IDN	LAO	MYS	MMR	PHL	SGP	THA	VNM	
BRN (Jan–Jun)	Form D			5,973		6,717		371	2,927	3,088	448	19,523
	Intra-ASEAN	7		25,420		260,819	77	2,671	235,309	57,844	2,398	584,545
	Share (%)	0.00		23.50		2.58	0.00	13.90	1.24	5.34	18.67	3.34
KHM (Jan–Dec)	Form D											792,323
	Intra-ASEAN	666,184	4,726									1,682,043
	Share (%)		10.27									47.10
IDN (Jan–Dec)	Form D	486			189	1,652,923	27,617	234,103	997,932	4,184,024	287,879	7,385,151
	Intra-ASEAN				616	8,648,721	31,847	706,243	20,240,831	7,470,735	1,142,267	38,912,170
	Share (%)				30.67	19.11	86.72	33.15	4.93	56.01	25.20	18.98
LAO (Jan–Dec)	Form D		65						8	13,816	25	13,913
	Intra-ASEAN		10	4,792		282		108	4,900	364,649	29,429	404,170
	Share (%)		0.00	1.35		0.00		0.00	0.16	3.79	0.09	3.44

MYS (Jan–Dec)	Form D														4,975,795
	Intra-ASEAN														44,907,211
	Share (%)														**11.08**
MMR (Jan–Dec)	Form D	981		1,445				534		6,704		152		9,815	
	Intra-ASEAN	203,332	15	135,153	489	14,041		1,126,095		475,806		38,081		1,993,171	
	Share (%)	0.48	0.00	1.07	0.00	0.00		0.05		1.41		0.40		**0.49**	
PHL (Jan–Dec)	Form D	1,695,214		951,403	10,338			1,038,971		2,782,749		210,320		6,694,417	
	Intra-ASEAN	2,399,713	12	2,562,475	13,378			5,439,478		4,098,377		1,750,771		16,269,811	
	Share (%)	70.64	0.00	37.13	77.27			19.10		67.90		12.01		**41.15**	
THA (Jan–Sep)	Form D	1,733,451	241,198	1,272,193	29,531	798,228		670,579				349,944		5,125,741	
	Intra-ASEAN	4,182,901	531,836	8,059,766	2,076,921	1,741,809		4,835,424				1,034,432		22,680,671	
	Share (%)	41.44	45.35	15.78	1.42	45.83		13.87				33.83		**22.60**	
VNM (Jan–Jun)	Form D	168,447		199,751	2,286	35,533		85,372		502,639				1,019,413	
	Intra-ASEAN	794,350	121,891	1,573,008	52,354	328,249		2,046,370		2,535,664				7,586,635	
	Share (%)	21.21	0.00	12.70	4.37	10.83		4.17		19.82				**13.44**	

Source: SEOM Chairman's Report to the AEM-25th AFTA Council Meeting, August 10, 2011, Manado, Indonesia.

Form D certificates of origin – an archaic and obsolete procedure that was eliminated in the Generalized System of Preferences (GSP) Form A in the mid 1980s and which is not even requested anymore in other unilateral preferences. This issue is discussed further below.

From the above analysis the importance for ASEAN to examine ways and means to streamline the existing overlapping sets of RoOs and administrative procedures emerges clearly. Efforts should be devised at the ASEAN level to seek a cohesive strategy toward other partners and internally within ASEAN to introduce reforms in RoOs aimed at facilitating compliance of production networks in the East Asian region. The absence of clear and unambiguous RoOs has frustrated the intra-industry trade flows of the fastest trade-growing region of the world for more than three decades.[12]

A factor that makes negotiation of RoOs difficult in ASEAN is that customs authorities do not play significant roles during the negotiations on the substantive aspects of RoOs, and the trade ministries assume the major negotiation roles. As a result, the substantive requirements of the RoOs are negotiated among trade officials, with inputs, in some cases, from the private sector but with much less input from the customs authorities. This might be one of the reasons for the poor technical quality of the substantive RoOs in ASEAN.

Practical experience and exchange of views indicate that many customs authorities' focus in Asia was on the

---

[12] See S. Inama, "ASEAN–China Free Trade Area: Negotiating Beyond Eternity With Little Trade Liberalization?", *Journal of World Trade* (2005) 39(3), 559–579.

verification of COs and other rather mechanical aspects of the agreements. Little interest was shown, until recently, in the substantive aspects of the rules and how to shape and draft PSROs. However, the implementation problems encountered seem to have generated an evolution of ASEAN's RoOs as described above.

Nevertheless, much remains to be done to increase transparency and predictability. The status and working methods of the ASEAN negotiations on RoOs seem to be far from transparent and the results of the negotiations are not widely available – not even to the private sector. In addition, and as described above, when progress is made there is little effort to align the results of the negotiations with previous legislation.

Chapter 2

The initial set of ASEAN rules of origin: the lack of clarity and transparency masquerading as simplicity 1992–1995

This section will discuss the apparently straightforward features of the ASEAN RoOs, the direct and indirect methods and their inconsistency, and the initial set of administrative rules with comments on their lack of flexibility.

2.1 The value-based calculation

The original AFTA RoOs consisted of eight main rules (i.e., articles) and two annexes detailing some calculation methods and twenty-three separate rules concerning operational certification procedures for the RoOs of the CEPT Scheme for the AFTA. The overall result was that the original AFTA rules focused more on the administrative aspects of the rules than on the substantive RoOs requirements per se.

RULES OF ORIGIN FOR THE CEPT SCHEME FOR AFTA

RULE 3 Not Wholly Produced or Obtained

(a) (i) A product shall be deemed to be originating from ASEAN Member States, if at least 40% of its content originates from any Member States.

   (ii) Locally-procured materials produced by established licensed manufacturers, in compliance with

2.1 THE VALUE-BASED CALCULATION

domestic regulations, will be deemed to have fulfilled the CEPT origin requirement; locally-procured materials from other sources will be subjected to the CEPT origin test for the purpose of origin determination.

(iii) Subject to sub-paragraph (i) above, for the purpose of implementing the provisions of Rule I(b), products worked on and processed as a result of which the total value of the materials, parts or produce originating from non-ASEAN countries or of undetermined origin used does not exceed 60% of the FOB value of the product produced or obtained and the final process of the manufacture is performed within the territory of the exporting Member State.

(b) The value of the non-originating materials, parts or produce shall be:
  (i) The CIF value at the time of importation of the products or importation can be proven; or
  (ii) The earliest ascertained price paid for the products of undetermined origin in the territory of the Member State where the working or processing takes place.

The formula for 40% ASEAN Content is as follows:

$$\frac{\text{Value of Imported Non − ASEAN Materials, Parts or Produce} \pm \text{Value of Undetermined Origin Materials, Parts Produce}}{\text{FOB Price}} \times 100\% \leq 60\%$$

(c) The method of calculating local/ASEAN content is as set out in Annex A of this Rules. The principles to determine cost for ASEAN origin and the guidelines for costing methodologies in Annex B shall also be closely adhered to.

THE INITIAL SET OF ASEAN RULES OF ORIGIN

As contained in Rule 3 above the drafting of the original AFTA rules was rather ambiguous and contained a number of provisions and wording leaving too much space to interpretation and little guidance to the various actors that had to implement this rule, e.g., customs authorities and the private sector. Neither the various elements nor the definitions of the rules were laid down in a sequential manner.

For instance, the first paragraph (a)(i) stipulated that a product is originating if at least 40 percent of its content originates from any Member States. This provision in paragraph (a)(i) did not further specify the criteria for determining and calculating such 40 percent local content since it did not provide a denominator. Moreover the clause "from any Member States" suggested a situation where the local content might originate in different Members and could be added up together to reach the required figure of 40 percent. However, there was no definition of what could be considered local content, which is a very vague concept unless properly defined.

The formula contained in paragraph (b)(ii) does not provide any clarification of the definition of local content since it is expressed indirectly: it requires that the amount of third country material or undetermined origin not exceed 60 percent of the free-on-board (FOB) price.

Annexes A and B mentioned in paragraph (c) and attached to the AFTA rules shed some partial light on the definitions of some of the elements and method of calculation of the ASEAN RoOs. Only from the wording of Annex A (reproduced on the next page) is the reader made aware of the existence of two ways of calculating the required local/ ASEAN content: *the direct and indirect methods.* The direct

2.1 THE VALUE-BASED CALCULATION

method is an *addition* method, whereby qualifying content is added up to determine whether the 40 percent threshold is met. Singapore, Indonesia, Laos and Myanmar had used this method.[1]

The indirect method is a deductive method, whereby non-qualifying content is deducted from the value of the finished good; the finished good qualified as ASEAN origin if the total of the non-qualifying content did not exceed 60 percent. Thailand, Malaysia, the Philippines, Brunei and Vietnam had used this method.

Annex A further stipulates that ASEAN member countries should adhere to only one method of calculation: either direct or indirect. However the same Annex A does not contain the formula or additional elements that are needed for the calculations of the direct method.

In fact, Annex A did not expressly provide a method of calculation of local content and it is limited to defining the elements of the FOB price, ex-factory price and production costs.

Thus one may wonder whether under this definition of local content in paragraph (A)(i) labor incurred in one or more ASEAN countries could be counted as numerator to reach the 40 percent requirement or whether only material inputs obtained in different ASEAN countries may be cumulated.

---

[1] This different method of calculations among different ASEAN Member States was only known in ASEAN circles and was not made publicly available for years, nor has it appeared in official legislation.

ANNEX A METHOD OF CALCULATION OF LOCAL/ ASEAN CONTENT

1. Member Countries shall adhere to only one method of calculating local/ASEAN content, i.e. whether it is the direct or indirect method, although Member Countries shall not be prevented from changing their method, if deemed necessary. Any change in the calculation method shall be notified to the AFTA Council Meeting.
2. FOB price shall be calculated as follows:
   a. **FOB Price = Ex-Factory Price + Other Costs**
   b. **Other Costs** in the calculation of the FOB price shall refer to the costs incurred in placing the goods in the ship for export, including but not limited to, domestic transport costs, storage and warehousing, port handling, brokerage fees, service charges, etc.
3. Formula for ex-factory price:
   a. **Ex-Factory Price = Production Cost + Profit**
   b. Formula for production cost,
      i. **Production Cost = Cost of Raw Materials + Labor Cost + Overhead Cost**
      ii. **Raw Materials** shall consist of:
         - Cost of raw materials
         - Freight and insurance
      iii. **Labor Cost** shall include:
         - Wages
         - Remuneration
         - Other employee benefits associated with the manufacturing process
      iv. **Overhead Costs**, (non exhaustive list) shall include, but not limited to:

2.1 THE VALUE-BASED CALCULATION

- real property items associated with the production process (insurance, factory rent and leasing, depreciation on buildings, repair and maintenance, taxes, interests on mortgage)
- leasing of and interest payments for plant and equipment
- factory security

Annex B, reproduced below, does not provide additional guidance on defining the numerator for the direct method but rather provides some principles and guidelines. In the absence of clear rules defining the numerators it is only by interpretation that one may get to the conclusion that the applicable formula for the direct method could be as follows:

ASEAN RM + Labor + Overhead + Profit + Other Costs × 100 % > 40 % FOB

ANNEX B PRINCIPLES AND GUIDELINES ON THE CEPT-AFTA RULES OF ORIGIN

A. **Principles to Determine Cost for ASEAN Origin**
   i. **Materiality** – all cost material to the evaluation, assessment and determination of origin;
   ii. **Consistency** – costing allocation method should be consistent unless justified by commercial reality;
   iii. **Reliability** – costing information must be reliability and supported by appropriate information;
   iv. **Relevance** – costs must be allocated based on objective and quantifiable data;
   v. **Accuracy** – costing methodology should provide an accurate representation of the cost element in question;

vi. **Application of GAAP of the exporting country** – costing information must be prepared based in accordance with the general accepted accounting principles and this includes the avoidance of double-counting of cost items;
vii. **Currency** – updated costing information from existing accounting and costing records of companies should be used to calculate origin.

B. **Guidelines for Costing Methodologies**
   i. **Actual Costs** – basis for actual costs should be defined by the company. Actual costs should include all direct and indirect costs incurred in producing the product.
   ii. **Projected and Budgeted Costs** – projected costs may be used if it is justified. Companies should provide variance analysis and proof during the period origin is claimed to indicate accuracy of projections.
   iii. **Standards Costs** – the basis for standards costs should be indicated. Companies should provide evidence that the costs are used for accounting purposes.
   iv. **Average/Moving Average Costs** – average costs may be used if justified; the basis for calculating average costs, including time, etc. should be highlighted. Companies should provide variance analysis and proof during the period origin is claimed to indicate accuracy of average costs.
   v. **Fixed Costs** – fixed costs should be apportioned according to sound cost accounting principles. They should be a representative reflection of unit costs for the company in the particular period in question. The method for apportionment should be indicated.

At the same time, there was no definition for the "locally-procured materials" mentioned under Rule 4 paragraph (a)(ii). Should this provision be interpreted as meaning that any material locally sourced will be deemed to be originating? How can this provision be reconciled with the concept of origin? Apparently this provision was meant to be accompanied by a list of ASEAN companies nominated by the respective ASEAN Member States producing inputs and intermediate inputs deemed to be *locally produced materials*. However such list was not public or at least not posted in the ASEAN website.

2.2 Cumulation

Experience has shown that implementation of the calculation guidelines laid down in these two annexes has not been an easy task in ASEAN. The cumulation rules as contained in Rule 4 (reproduced in the following section) were not any easier to administer given the uncertain drafting:

> **RULE 4 Cumulative Rule of Origin**
>
> (a) Products which comply with origin requirements provided for in Rule 1 and which are used in a Member State as inputs for a finished product eligible for preferential treatment in another Member States shall be considered as products originating in the Member State where working or processing of the finished product has taken place provided that the aggregate ASEAN content of the final product is not less than 40%.
>
> (b) If the material has less than 40 percent ASEAN content, the qualifying ASEAN national content shall be in direct

proportion to the actual domestic content provided that it is equal to or more than the agreed threshold of 20%.

It is quite evident that it was difficult to define the methodology of the calculation for cumulation purposes. In fact there was no definition of what could be counted toward the 40 percent aggregate ASEAN content.

Paragraph (b) of Rule 4 did not provide any further guidance because it was not clear what was the "qualifying ASEAN national content" in respect of the "actual domestic content". An explanatory note was added to Rule 4 to better explain the functioning of cumulation in the ASEAN context:

> To be considered for partial cumulation, the local/ASEAN content of the materials, parts or produce originating from the country of last manufacture should not be less than 20 percent;
>
> (b) the formula to be used in the calculation would be similar to the formula for calculating the 40 percent local/ASEAN content;
>
> (c) no CEPT preference shall be extended by the importing member country for that particular intermediate good;

Considering this drafting of the AFTA RoOs it was not surprising that there have been bitter disputes among ASEAN Member States over the interpretation and implementation of the AFTA rules. These disputes were never made public (as is the typical ASEAN way) but the Thailand/Singapore discussions over the application of the percentage criterion to flour and the issue of whisky from Philippines were widely known to practitioners.

2.3 Absorption/roll-up

Rule 4 of the AFTA RoOs provided for cumulation when an ASEAN good crossed the border for incorporation into the finished product in another ASEAN Member State. This concept of cumulation, being conditional upon crossing national borders, was brought forward into Article 30 of the ATIGA:

> **ARTICLE 30. ACCUMULATION**
>
> 1. Unless otherwise provided in this Agreement, goods originating in a Member State, which are used in another Member State as materials for finished goods eligible for preferential tariff treatment, shall be considered to be originating in the latter Member State where working or processing of the finished goods has taken place.

On a related note, the vast majority of EU and US FTAs (in the case of the EU, all FTAs) include the notion of "intermediate products" (US jargon), also known as "roll-up" or the "absorption principle" (EU jargon). This notion covers the principle that once a non-originating product has acquired originating status by fulfilling the applicable origin criteria, any non-originating materials used in its production will not be taken into account when the product is used as a material in the manufacture of another product.

The AFTA did not explicitly incorporate roll-up, but it was an ASEAN practice to accept the principle although the concept was often confused with cumulation. Yet whether or not such a principle is applied has substantial consequences for the outcome of an origin determination process, as illustrated below:

THE INITIAL SET OF ASEAN RULES OF ORIGIN

Assume that 40 percent ASEAN value is sufficient to confer ASEAN origin for a final product, and assume that the final product consists of three components: A, B and C.

Item	% ASEAN origin	Value
Component A	50%	$100
Component B	40%	$200
Component C	0%	$200
Total		$500

With a roll-up rule, A and B items would be considered ASEAN origin, as they met the 40 percent value added rule. This would mean that for purposes of determining the origin of the final product, components A and B would be considered of 100 percent ASEAN origin – the assumption would be that qualifying for ASEAN origin at the component level would have the effect of absorbing component C conferring ASEAN origin on the overall finished product:

Item	% ASEAN origin	Value	After roll-up
Component A	50%	$100	$100 ASEAN origin
Component B	40%	$200	$200 ASEAN origin
Component C	0%	$200	$0 ASEAN origin
Total		$500	$300 ASEAN origin, or 60% ($300/$500)

Hence the final product would be considered as ASEAN origin.

However, without a roll-up rule, the final product would be considered not of ASEAN origin according to the calculation below:

2.3 ABSORPTION/ROLL-UP

Item	% ASEAN origin	Value	NO roll-up
Component A	50%	$100	$50 ASEAN origin (50% * $100)
Component B	40%	$200	$80 ASEAN origin (40% * $200)
Component C	0%	$200	$0 ASEAN origin
Total		$500	$130 ASEAN origin, or 26% ($130/$500)

Hence the roll-up concept has a significant effect on the origin calculation. Note that the roll-up rules cannot be equated to cumulation since the roll-up rule does not require that the goods cross a border. Rather, the application of the roll-up rule depends on when a good becomes incorporated into the production of a further processed good, which can take place even within the same production facility. ASEAN customs officials have indicated to the authors that the roll-up concept (without requiring crossing a border) is incorporated into the ATIGA by way of Article 54.2, which is a general article stating that "Customs procedures of Member States shall, where possible and to the extent permitted by their respective customs law, conform to standards and recommended practices of the World Customs Organisation and other international organisations as relevant to customs." However, recommended practices of the World Customs Organization do not contain any guidelines on the roll-up text and practices by major trading powers such as the US and EU, which differ in the method and substance of application of the roll-up rule.

The fact that the ATIGA does not contain any specific rules on the issue of roll-up leaves a conspicuous loophole in the ATIGA RoOs, which ASEAN national customs officers can interpret at will. This tendency of ASEAN officials to leave important issues unsettled is revealing of the reluctance to provide transparent and predictable RoOs aimed at ensuring legal certainty and a better utilization of the ATIGA.

2.4 Introduction of alternative rules of origin 1995–2000

2.4.1 *Fixing a hole by digging deeper: introduction of the substantial transformation test*

In an apparent recognition of the inadequacy of an across-the-board percentage criterion based on the direct and indirect method discussed in section 2.1, ASEAN introduced a set of requirements based on a "substantial transformation text." However it was never sufficiently clear how these rules applied in relation to the main across-the-board percentage criterion.

As a conspicuous sign of the difficulties in determining origin according to the vaguely defined ASEAN percentage criterion in the above section, ancillary product-specific rules were adopted in the area of textile and textile products by the 7th AFTA Council held in 1995:

> Recognizing that the existing percentage criterion of the CEPT Rules of Origin may not be conducive towards the objective of increasing intra-ASEAN trade in textiles and textile products, the 7th AFTA Council at its meeting on 6th September 1995 decided that for the purpose of origin determination of textiles and textile products either the percentage or the substantial transformation criterion can be used by the exporting country. The 7th AFTA Council also decided that an ASEAN Single List identifying the

2.4 INTRODUCTION OF ALTERNATIVE RULES OF ORIGIN

processes for each of the textile and textile products shall be formulated to administer the substantial transformation criterion.

2. When an exporting country chooses to apply the substantial transformation criterion, the following rules of origin shall apply. The rules of origin should be read in conjunction with the attached **ASEAN Single List**.

It must be observed that according to the ASEAN Single List and unlike the EU RoOs model, the across-the-board general percentage rules continued to apply together with the product-specific rules contained in the single list. In fact, the above text explicitly mentioned that the percentage or the substantial transformation criterion could be adopted. This implied that the exporting country had the option to choose to adopt the percentage or the substantial transformation criterion.

The introduction of the substantial transformation criterion provided an illuminating example of the muddled state of affairs in the ASEAN RoOs. In fact, ASEAN officials and official documents referred to the rules on textile and clothing as adopting the substantial transformation criterion as an alternative to the percentage transformation criterion.

However, the rest of the world – as contained in the WTO Agreement on Rules of Origin and Annex K of the revised Kyoto Convention – consider the term "substantial transformation" to mean a general criterion that has to be further technically defined and expressed by the adoption of different methodologies to determine origin that could be

(a) the change of tariff classification or (b) *ad valorem* percentages under the revised Annex K of the Kyoto Convention 2000.

In addition, Article 9(2)(c)(iii) of the WTO Agreement also provides for specific manufacturing or processing operations as additional methodology to express the substantial transformation criterion.

Thus it is multilaterally accepted that the substantial transformation criterion is not an alternative to the *ad valorem* percentage but rather is one of the methodologies, together with the change of tariff classification criteria and specific working or processing requirements, that may be used to express the substantial transformation criterion.

This terminology problem was so deeply rooted in ASEAN that even the ASEAN Framework Agreement for the Integration of Priority Sectors still refers in its Article 7(b) to "adopting substantial transformation as alternative criterion for conferring origin status."

In fairness the introduction of the product-specific rules on textiles and clothing represented a trade liberalization effort in so far as these rules provided for a single-stage transformation criterion for textiles and clothing, basically one stage – from yarn to fabric by weaving or knitting – and one stage – by cutting and making-up from fabrics to finished garments. These rules were at that time far more liberal than the comparable rules in the EU demanding a double transformation – spinning and weaving for fabrics and weaving and making-up for finished products and those under the NAFTA demanding a triple transformation requirement. In addition they compared favorably with the

2.4 INTRODUCTION OF ALTERNATIVE RULES OF ORIGIN

40 percent percentage requirements of ASEAN rules since they were more predictable and easier to comply with.

2.4.2 Adding on confusion to a final consolidation phase in ATIGA: the introduction of alternative product-specific rules of origin (PSRO) 2000–2009

2.4.2.1 From 2000 to the ATIGA (2009)
As a result of industry complaints about the inaccessibility of the AFTA benefits because of the RoOs, ASEAN began studying alternative RoOs in the early 2000s. This resulted in the decision by the AFTA Council in 2003 to adopt "substantial transformation" as an alternative RoO.

After several years of study, the ASEAN task force on RoOs proposed that a dual RoOs approach be used for certain products, e.g., both RVC[2] and substantial transformation through change in tariff chapter (CTC), change in chapter (CTH) or change in tariff sub-heading (CTSH). The results of these efforts were consolidated in a large annex of product-specific rules of 166 pages and implemented in the second half of 2007 after adoption by the AFTA Council.

These were additional PSROs to those for textiles and clothing adopted earlier. The 2007 revision subjected to PSROs products in nine priority sectors designated by the

---

[2] According to some ASEAN officials, the main reason the RVC content of 40 percent was retained was because it used to be the main rule of origin of ASEAN in the ASEAN Preferential Trade Agreement of 1977 and its successor agreements.

THE INITIAL SET OF ASEAN RULES OF ORIGIN

ASEAN Framework Agreement for the Integration of Priority Sectors, namely: (i) agro-based products; (ii) automotive products; (iii) e-ASEAN; (iv) electronics; (v) fisheries; (vi) healthcare; (vii) rubber-based products; (viii) textiles and apparels; and (ix) wood-based products.

Product-specific rules were also adopted for aluminum products of HS (Harmonized System) Chapter 76 (CTH with or without exceptions); steel products of HS Chapter 72 (CTH with exceptions, change of chapter); wheat flour (change of chapter); and wood products of HS Chapter 44; HS 94.01–94.03 and HS 94.06 (CTSH six digits).

In the case of wheat flour and wood products the product-specific rules were accompanied by a text explaining that these product-specific rules apply at the choice of the exporting country when *the substantial transformation criterion* is applied.

The techniques used in drafting these PSROs followed somewhat of a default pattern. Almost all rules provide for an RVC and as an alternative a change of tariff classification that could take the form of change from another chapter: "A regional value content of not less than 40 percent of the FOB value of the good; or Change to Subheading 1605.30 from any other Chapter;" a change from another heading: "A regional value content of not less than 40 percent of the FOB value of the good; or Change to Subheading 2304.00 from any other Heading;" or a change from another sub-heading: "A regional value content of not less than 40 percent of the FOB value of the good; or Change to Subheading 4409.10 from any other Subheading."

2.4 INTRODUCTION OF ALTERNATIVE RULES OF ORIGIN

In the case of textile and clothing from Chapters 50 to 63, a series of alternatives among the RVC, the change of tariff classification and a specific working or processing are provided as shown in the example below:

> A regional value content of not less than 40 percent of the FOB value of the good; or Change to Subheading 6105.10 from any other Chapter provided that the good is both cut and sewn in the territory of any Member State; or Process Rules for Textile and Textile Products as set out in Attachment 1.

Attachment 1 provided for specific one-stage working or processing operations such as the following:

> Working or Processing Carried Out on Non-Originating Materials that Confers Originating Status: Manufacture through the processes of cutting and assembly of parts into a complete article (for apparel and tents) and incorporating embroidery or embellishment or printing (for made-up articles) from:
>
> d. raw or unbleached fabric
>
> e. finished fabric

Attachment 2 contained definitions of RVC and substantial transformation. The formula of RVC was defined as follows:

> 1. RVC of a good specified in Product Specific Rules shall be calculated in accordance with the following formula
>   (a) *Direct Method*

$$RVC = \frac{\text{ASEAN Material Cost} + \text{Direct Labour Cost} + \text{Direct Overhead Cost} + \text{Other Cost} + \text{Profit}}{\text{FOB Price}} \times 100\%$$

THE INITIAL SET OF ASEAN RULES OF ORIGIN

(b) *Indirect Method*

$$RVC = \frac{\text{FOB Price} - \text{Value of Non Originating Materials, Parts or Produce}}{\text{FOB Price}} \times 100\%$$

For the purpose of calculating the regional value content provided in paragraph 1:

(a) The value of imported non-ASEAN materials, parts or produce shall be:
   (i) The CIF value at the time of importation of the products or importation can be proven; or
   (ii) The earliest ascertained price paid for the products of undetermined origin in the territory of the Member State where the working or processing takes place.

(b) Labour cost shall include wages, remuneration and other employee benefits associated with the manufacturing process;

(c) The calculation of overhead cost shall include, but not limited to real property items associated with the production process (insurance, factory rent and leasing, depreciation on buildings, repair and maintenance, taxes, interests on mortgage); leasing of and interest payments for plant and equipment; factory security; insurance (plant, equipment and materials used in the manufacture of the goods); utilities (energy, electricity, water and other utilities directly attributable to the production of the good); research, development, design and engineering; dies, moulds, tooling and the depreciation, maintenance and repair of plant and equipment; royalties or licenses

2.4 INTRODUCTION OF ALTERNATIVE RULES OF ORIGIN

(in connection with patented machines or processes used in the manufacture of the good or the right to manufacture the good); inspection and testing of materials and the goods; storage and handling in the factory; disposal of recyclable wastes; and cost elements in computing the value of raw materials, i.e. port and clearance charges and import duties paid for dutiable component; and

(d) FOB price means the free-on-board value of the good, inclusive of the cost of transport to the port or site of final shipment abroad. FOB price shall be determined by adding the value of materials, production cost, profit and other costs.

(e) Other costs shall refer to the costs incurred in placing the goods in the ship for export, including but not limited to, domestic transport costs, storage and warehousing, port handling, brokerage fees, service charges, etc.

The definition of substantial transformation contained in Attachment 2 was described as follows:

B. Substantial Transformation Criterion

1. A country of origin is that in which the last substantial transformation or process was performed resulting in a new product. Thus, materials which underwent a substantial transformation in a country shall be a product of that country.
2. A product in the production of which two or more countries are involved shall be regarded as originating in the country in which the last substantial transformation or process was performed, resulting in a new product.

3. A product will be considered to have undergone a substantial transformation or process if it has been transformed by means of substantial manufacturing or processing into a new and different article of commerce.
4. A new and different article of commerce will usually result from manufacturing or processing operations if there is a change in:
    i. Commercial designation or identity,
    ii. Fundamental character, or
    iii. Commercial use.
5. In determining whether a product has been subjected to substantial manufacturing or processing operations, the following will be considered:
    i. The physical change in the material or article as a result of the manufacturing or processing operations;
    ii. The time involved in the manufacturing or processing operations in the country in which they are performed;
    iii. The complexity of the manufacturing or processing operations in the country in which they are performed;
    iv. The level or degree of skill and/or technology required in the manufacturing or processing operations.

C. Specific Rules Applicable for Textile and Textile Products

1. Textile and Textile Products covered under this Rules are set out in Attachment 1.
2. Textile material or article shall be deemed to be originating in a Member State, when it has undergone,

2.4 INTRODUCTION OF ALTERNATIVE RULES OF ORIGIN

prior to the importation to another Member Sate, any of the following:
  i. Petrochemicals which have undergone the process of polymerization or polycondensation or any chemicals or physical processes to form a polymer;
  ii. Polymer which has undergone the process of melt spinning or extrusion to form a synthetic fiber;
  iii. Spinning fiber into yarn;
  iv. Weaving, knitting or otherwise forming fabric;
  v. Cutting fabric into parts and the assembly of those parts into a completed article;
  vi. Dyeing of fabric, if it is accompanied by any finishing operation which has the effect of rendering the dyed good directly;
  vii. Printing of fabric, if it is accompanied by any finishing operation which has the effect of rendering the printed good directly usable;
  viii. Impregnation or coating when such treatment leads to the manufacture of a new product falling within certain headings of customs tariffs;
  ix. Embroidery which represents at least five percent of the total area of the embroidered good.
3. Notwithstanding any provisions in the CEPT Rules of Origin, an article or material shall not be considered to be originating in the territory of a Member State by virtue of merely having undergone any of the following:
  i. Simple combining operations, labelling, pressing, cleaning or dry cleaning or packaging operations, or any combination thereof;
  ii. Cutting to length or width and hemming, stitching or over-locking fabrics which are readily identifiable as being intended for a particular commercial use;

iii. Trimming and/or joining together by sewing, looping, linking, attaching of accessory articles such as straps, bands, beads, cords, rings and eyelets;
iv. One or more finishing operations on yarns, fabrics or other textile articles, such as bleaching, waterproofing, decating, shrinking, mercerizing, or similar operations; or
v. Dyeing or printing of fabrics or yarns.

Overall, the period from 2000 to 2009[3] was marked by a series of texts on new versions of PSROs that appeared on the ASEAN website with no clear indication of their legal status. This demonstrated once again the unpredictability of ASEAN RoOs.

2.4.2.2 ATIGA and beyond

The ATIGA represents the culmination of the ASEAN revision of RoOs, which lasted almost a decade. While efforts have undeniably been deployed and improvements are present, the ATIGA still contains loopholes and drafting ambiguities.

The key RoO provisions of the ATIGA are contained in Article 28. Paragraph 1 of Article 28 reproduced below contains across-the-board RoOs with two alternatives: an RVC of 40 percent and a CTH.

---

[3] Check, for instance, a Singapore Ministry of Trade and Industry website still quoting one of these earlier versions of rules of origin of 2008 at www.fta.gov.sg/fta_afta.asp?hl=1 (accessed on 20 January 2014).

2.4 INTRODUCTION OF ALTERNATIVE RULES OF ORIGIN

A spontaneous comment arises on the significance of this rule since an RVC of 40 percent and CTH are not coequal. Therefore, depending on the product, the exporter will always choose the most lenient to the exclusion of the other, i.e., an exporter of fish fillets of Heading 03.04 carrying out filleting on imported fresh fish will not opt for the RVC of 40 percent since a CTH from Heading 03.03 to 03.04 is sufficient to acquire origin. Thus one alternative makes obsolete the other alternative since they are not coequal in terms of stringency.

Paragraph (b) is a welcome insertion in the main text since it clarifies that the exporter Member State should leave the exporter free to choose between the alternatives. However it would have been advisable to complement this provision by adding also that the importer Member States should accept the choice made by the exporter.

Article 12 ATIGA

1. (a) For the purposes of Article 26(b), goods shall be deemed to be originating in the Member State where working or processing of the goods has taken place:
    (i) if the goods have a regional value content (hereinafter referred to as "ASEAN Value Content" or the "Regional Value Content (RVC)") of not less than forty percent (40%) calculated using the formula set out in Article 29; or
    (ii) if all non-originating materials used in the production of the goods have undergone a change in tariff classification (hereinafter

referred to as "CTC") at four-digit level (i.e. a change in tariff heading) of the Harmonized System.
(b) Each Member State shall permit the exporter of the good to decide whether to use paragraph 1(a)(i) or 1(a)(ii) of this Article when determining whether the goods qualify as originating goods of the Member State.
2. (a) Notwithstanding paragraph 1 of this Article, goods listed in Annex 3 shall qualify as originating goods if the goods satisfy the product specific rules set out therein.
(b) Where a product specific rule provides a choice of rules from a RVC-based rule of origin, a CTC-based rule of origin, a specific manufacturing or processing operation, or a combination of any of these, each Member State shall permit the exporter of the goods to decide which rule to use in determining whether the goods qualify as originating goods of the Member State.
(c) Where product specific rules specify a certain RVC, it is required that the RVC of a good is calculated using the formula set out in Article 29.
(d) Where product specific rules requiring that the materials used have undergone CTC or a specific manufacturing or processing operation, the rules shall apply only to non-originating materials.

Paragraph 2 above introduces the PSRO exceptions to the general rule of paragraph 1. Once again, and as pointed out in a previous analysis of the ASEAN legal texts, it is not entirely clear from the text under (a) if the PSROs under

2.4 INTRODUCTION OF ALTERNATIVE RULES OF ORIGIN

Annex 3 are to be applied as an exception to the general rule and therefore as the only applicable criteria or if they are to be understood as criteria additional to the general rule.[4] This loophole is enough to seriously question the overall efforts of consolidation of the ATIGA.

Adding to the proliferation of alternative rules for the same products, paragraph 3 of Article 28 of the ATIGA (reproduced below) provides that for products covered by the WTO Information Technology Agreement (ITA) assembly operations carried out on materials covered by the same ITA are origin conferring.

> 3. Notwithstanding paragraphs 1 and 2 of this Article, a good which is covered by Attachment A or B of the Ministerial Declaration on Trade in Information Technology Products adopted in the Ministerial Conference of the WTO on 13 December 1996, set out as Annex 4, shall be deemed to be originating in a Member State if it is assembled from materials covered under the same Annex.

The definition of what could be considered assembly is not further defined in the ATIGA. Not all ASEAN countries are signatories of the ITA since Laos, Cambodia and Myanmar have yet to accede.

---

[4] In the absence of a clear direction from the legal text, different answers are provided depending on the websites consulted. The Malaysian Ministry of Trade and Industry suggests that the PSROs are additional to the general rules: www.miti.gov.my/cms/content.jsp?id=com.tms.cms.section.Section_a788349e-c0a81573-6e076e07-bdac91ac.

Article 29 of the ATIGA provides for the calculation method of the RVC and is basically a replica of what was contained in previous texts circulated in the period 2000–2009 and reproduced above under Attachment 2 of the previous RoOs. As further outlined later in this book, the drafting of ATIGA Article 29 provided an excellent opportunity to impart clarity to the percentage calculation of ASEAN RoOs by eliminating the direct calculation method, which has proved to be difficult to administer.

Article 30 of the ATIGA deals with cumulation adding more clarity in the text by incorporating the Implementing Guidelines.

ARTICLE 30. ACCUMULATION

1. Unless otherwise provided in this Agreement, goods originating in a Member State, which are used in another Member State as materials for finished goods eligible for preferential tariff treatment, shall be considered to be originating in the latter Member State where working or processing of the finished goods has taken place.
2. If the RVC of the material is less than forty percent (40%), the qualifying ASEAN Value Content to be cumulated using the RVC criterion shall be in direct proportion to the actual domestic content provided that it is equal to or more than twenty percent (20%). The Implementing Guidelines are set out in Annex 6.

A thorough evaluation of the ATIGA and its functioning has yet to be carried out. However, the comments raised above

2.4 INTRODUCTION OF ALTERNATIVE RULES OF ORIGIN

cast serious doubts over the ability of the present ATIGA text to fill the previous gaps of the AFTA-CEPT RoOs and subsequent developments.

As outlined in the following pages, questions have already arisen and implementation issues are still to be solved in ASEAN internal meetings.

Chapter 3

Externalizing the confusion: the proliferation of rules in the ASEAN FTAs with dialogue partners

3.1 Main features of the various FTAs' rules of origin contained in FTAs with ASEAN Dialogue partners

ASEAN failed to modernize its own RoOs and externalized its own problems by advocating the use of ASEAN RoOs in the FTAs entered into with different dialogue partners. This strategy did not bear much fruit as dialogue partners wanted to stick to their rules as well. The result is a Pandora's box of different requirements as each ASEAN dialogue partner brought in its own view and experience on RoOs and no attempt was made to set at least some best practices. Table 3.1 shows a comparison of the main features of the different FTAs entered into by ASEAN with dialogue partners.

3.2 Ancillary rules

Table 3.2 shows a brief comparison of the Cumulation and other provisions in ASEAN FTAs with dialogue partners.

3.3 ASEAN–China FTA

The RoOs contained in the ASEAN–China FTA (ACFTA) are the result of the insistence of ASEAN in proposing the adoption of the ASEAN RoOs and the Chinese acceptance of the

Table 3.1 A comparison of the main features of the various FTAs' rules of origin

	Main origin criteria	Numerator	Denominator	Percentage level	Method of percentage calculation	Product-specific rules of origin	Administrative requirements
ASEAN	40% RVC, or CTC at four-digit level	*Direct method:* Value of originating materials + cost of direct working or processing. *Indirect method:* A subtraction from the FOB price of the value of non-originating materials.	FOB price	Not less than 40% RVC	*Direct and indirect* calculation based in the case of direct method of a value added calculation adding cost of processing and local materials. Indirect method is a subtraction from the FOB price of the value of the non-originating materials	Contained in Annex 3 of 288 pages of PSROs. They apply to the majority of HS chapters including textiles and clothing, steel products, electronics and automotive products. Requirements vary from Wholly Obtained, RVC, CTSH with or without exceptions, specific working or processing requirements.	CO required. Certified exporters initiative underway.
ASEAN–China	Percentage criteria of 40% according to a direct formula and not exceeding 60% according to indirect formula.	The legal text provides for an unclear direct formula plus an indirect formula based on maximum allowance of non-originating inputs.	FOB price	Not less than 40% or according to the direct formula and not to exceed 60% of non-originating inputs according to the indirect formula.	The direct calculation is based on a 40% requirement of "ACFTA content." The indirect calculation is based on a formula requiring products not to exceed 60% of non-originating inputs (non-ACFTA or unknown origin inputs).	Contained in Attachment B of Annex 3 of 23 pages. PSROs apply mostly to leather and leather products, textiles and clothing.	CO required.

Table 3.1 (cont.)

	Main origin criteria	Numerator	Denominator	Percentage level	Method of percentage calculation	Product-specific rules of origin	Administrative requirements
ASEAN–Australia–New Zealand (AANZ)	40% RVC, or CTC at four-digit level.	The legal texts provide for direct and indirect methods similar to ATIGA.	FOB price	Not less than 40% RVC	The direct and indirect calculations are similar to the ones used under ATIGA.	Contained in Annex 3 of 240 pages of PSROs. They apply to all HS chapters. Requirements vary from Wholly Obtained, RVC, CTSH with or without exceptions, specific working or processing requirements or alternative rules.	CO required.
ASEAN–India	35% RVC, or CTH at six-digit level.	In the *direct method*, the cost of processing and values of originating materials. In the *indirect method*, the value of non-originating materials, similar to ACFTA.	FOB price	35% in the case of *direct method*, 65% in the case of *indirect method*.	The *direct method*, is a value added calculation method similar to ASEAN. The *indirect method* is a calculation based on a maximum allowance of non-originating inputs similar to ACFTA.	To be negotiated.	CO required.

ASEAN–Japan	40% RVC, or CTC at 4-digit level.	The ASEAN–Japan FTA provides only for an *indirect method*: A subtraction from the FOB price of the value of non-originating materials similar to ASEAN.	FOB price	40% RVC	Only one method of calculation based on a subtraction from the FOB price of the value of non-originating inputs.	Contained in Annex 3 of 63 pages of PSROs. They apply to all HS chapters. Requirements vary from Wholly Obtained, RVC, CTSH with or without exceptions, specific working or processing requirements and alternative rules. In the case of the Japan–Vietnam Economic Partnership Agreement, the PSROs are contained in Annex 2 of around 100 pages.	CO issued by designated authority. Requirement of notifications of seals and name signature of authorized officials.
ASEAN–Korea	40% RVC, or CTC at four-digit level.	The ASEAN–Korea FTA provides for a value of materials calculation.	FOB price	40% RVC	Two methods of calculation: build-up based on the value of originating materials and build-down based on the amount of non-originating materials.	Contained in Annex 3 of 63 pages of PSROs. They apply to all HS chapters. Requirements vary from Wholly Obtained, RVC, CTSH with or without exceptions, specific working or processing requirements and alternative rules.	CO required. Each has to provide the names, addresses, specimen signatures and specimen of official seals of its issuing authorities to all the other parties, through the ASEAN Secretariat.

Table 3.2 *Comparison table of cumulation and other provisions in ASEAN FTAs with dialogue partners*

	Kind of cumulation	De minimis	Absorption
ASEAN	Cumulation of originating materials. Special provision for "partial cumulation" where a good not meeting the 40% RVC may nevertheless be eligible for cumulation.	10% in the case of CTC criteria.	Not specifically mentioned.
ASEAN-China	Not clear. The legal text mentions cumulation of originating goods and "full cumulation."	Not applicable.	Not specifically mentioned.
ASEAN-Australia-New Zealand (AANZ)	Cumulation of originating materials.	10% with qualifications for some products.	Not specifically mentioned.
ASEAN-India	Cumulation of originating materials.	Not applicable.	Not specifically mentioned.
ASEAN-Japan	Cumulation of originating materials.	10% with qualifications for some products.	Not specifically mentioned.
ASEAN-Korea	Cumulation of originating materials.	10% with qualifications for some products.	Not specifically mentioned.

3.3 ASEAN–CHINA FTA

proposal. This acceptance by the Chinese side was, however, accompanied by a request to strengthen the administrative rules related to the issuance and administration of COs.

The main substantive origin criteria in the ACFTA closely resembled those of the AFTA and contained similar shortcomings. The ACFTA Rule 4 shown in Box 2 raises a similar critique to the one raised above in the context of the AFTA rules:

ARTICLE 4 OF RULES OF ORIGIN UNDER THE ASEAN–CHINA FTA

Similarly to the AFTA, 22 rules of the ACFTA RoOs contained in Annex 3 of the Vientiane Agreement (this annex is subdivided into rules rather than more appropriately into articles) are dedicated to administrative aspects of RoOs. The substantive rules are confined to the definition of wholly obtained goods and Rule 4's determining origin requirement for goods not wholly obtained or produced.

The ACFTA RoOs are very similar in architecture and design to the AFTA RoOs and unfortunately replicate their shortcomings. In certain cases, some ACFTA rules clearly inspired by the original AFTA rules are even less precise and transparent, ultimately resulting in a worsening of the whole text.

Thus the core of the ACFTA rules is a rather simple percentage criterion as shown in Article 4 below.

Article 4

 (a) For the purposes of Rule 2(b), a product shall be deemed to be originating if:
   (i) Not less than 40% of its content originates from any Party; or

(ii) If the total value of the materials, part or produce originating from outside of the territory of a Party (i.e. non-ACFTA) does not exceed 60% of the FOB value of the product so produced or obtained provided that the final process of the manufacture is performed within the territory of the Party.

(b) For the purposes of this Annex, the originating criteria set out in Rule 4(a)

(ii) shall be referred to as the "ACFTA content". The formula for the 40% ACFTA content is calculated as follows:

$$\frac{\text{Value of Undetermined Materials} + \text{Value of materials of Non-ACFTA origin}}{\text{FOB Price}} \times 100\% < 60\%$$

Therefore, the ACFTA content: 100% − non-ACFTA material = at least 40%

(c) The value of the non-originating materials shall be:
  (i) the CIF value at the time of importation of the materials; or
  (ii) the earliest ascertained price paid for the materials of undetermined origin in the territory of the Party where the working or processing takes place.
(d) For the purpose of this Rule, "originating material" shall be deemed to be a material whose country of origin, as determined under these rules, is the same country as the country in which the material is used in production.

The Article 4(a)(i) definition of "*40% of its content originates from any Party*" is unclear.

3.3 ASEAN–CHINA FTA

- Article 4(b) may be interpreted as an effort to clarify the ACFTA content but it does not refer to paragraph (a)(i) but to paragraph (a)(ii).
- As a result, we have two alternative rules under Article 4: one under paragraph (a)(i); and another under paragraph (a)(ii), further specified in paragraph (b).

In order to give some sense to the provision in (a)(i), one may read it as a provision allowing cumulation to reach the 40 percent local content requirement.

However, Article 5 of the ACFTA Annex on RoOs on cumulation raises additional questions rather than clarifying the provision of Article 4(a)(i):

> Unless otherwise provided for, products which comply with origin requirements provided for in Rule 2 and which are used in the territory of a Party as materials for a finished product eligible for preferential treatment under the Agreement shall be considered as products originating in the territory of the Party where working or processing of the finished product has taken place provided that the aggregate ACFTA content (i.e. full cumulation, applicable among all Parties) on the final product is not less than 40%.

In fact, there are contradictory statements in this provision. In the first part, it refers to "products that comply with origin requirements provided for in Rule 2." Because Rule 2 of Annex 3 of the Vientiane Agreement determines the rules for originating products it follows that only material already originating may be cumulated. This means that a partial or diagonal cumulation is applied under the ACFTA. However, the last sentence of Article 5 expressly provides for "full cumulation, applicable among all Parties," leaving a lot of uncertainty about the scope and the implementation of this cumulation provision.

Finally, Article 6 of Annex 3 of the Vientiane Agreement provides for the elaboration of PSROs that were negotiated in the period 2004–2005.[1] PSROs have been established as an alternative to the general rule for 565 items for products such as processed fish, plastics, leather items, textile items, footwear, and iron and steel products and for nine items such as edible oil, ice cream, animal hair and cultured pearls.

On one side, the elaboration of PSROs may be an opportunity to impart clear and predictable rules, easy to implement and administer. On the other hand, if badly drafted or excessively stringent, these product-specific rules could potentially become another formidable obstacle to the effective functioning of the ACFTA.

3.4 ASEAN–Australia–New Zealand FTA (AANZFTA)

As in the case of other FTAs, the AANZFTA provides for a general rule of origin set out in Article 4.1 of the Rules of Origin Chapter providing that a good will be considered as an originating good if it meets either of the following:

- The good has an RVC of not less than 40 percent of the FOB (free on board) value and the final process of production is performed within a Party.

---

[1] See www.thaifta.com/trade/china/seom_%20letter.pdf.

- All non-originating materials used in the production of the good have undergone a CTC change at the four-digit level (i.e., a change in tariff heading).

As contained in an ASEAN publication, originating goods status can be determined in the case of 83 percent of all AANZFTA tariff lines through either the CTC approach or through an RVC calculation.[2] Another 1 percent of tariff sub-headings require an RVC-only approach.

AANZFTA inherits the ASEAN approaches in calculating the RVC: the "Direct Formula" calculation; and the "Indirect/Build-Down Formula" calculation. In most cases, the RVC must equal at least 40 percent of the FOB value of the good before it can be considered as an originating good under the AANZFTA RoOs.

For those products covered by the tariff sub-headings listed in Annex 2 on Product-specific Rules (PSR), the RoOs applicable to them is set out in that Annex. For products covered by tariff sub-headings not listed in Annex 2, the "general rule" applies. As in most cases most of the products fall under Annex 2, which numbers around 240 pages.

3.5 ASEAN–India FTA

The results of the FTA with India below in Rule 4 clearly show in the first part of the rule the influence of the ASEAN RoOs in the method of calculation while the Indian influence can be

---

[2] ASEAN Secretariat, *Primer on Rules of Origin: ASEAN-Australia-New Zealand Free Trade Area* (2009).

identified in the inclusion of CTSH at the six-digit level, which is indeed a quite liberal rule if taken by itself but in the specific case is an additional requirement to the 35 percent requirement.

RULE 4 Not Wholly Produced or Obtained Products

(a) For the purposes of Rule 2(b), a product shall be deemed to be originating if:
  (i) the AIFTA content is not less than 35 per cent of the FOB value; and
  (ii) the non-originating materials have undergone at least a change in tariff sub-heading (CTSH) level of the Harmonized System,

provided that the final process of the manufacture is performed within the territory of the exporting Party.

(b) For the purposes of this Rule, the formula for the 35 per cent AIFTA content is calculated respectively as follows:
  (i) Direct Method

$$\frac{Material\ Cost + Direct\ Labour\ Cost + Direct\ Overhead\ Cost + Other\ Cost + Profit}{FOB\ Price} \times 100\% \geq 35$$

  (ii) Indirect method

$$\frac{Value\ of\ Imported\ Non\text{-}AIFTA\ Materials, + Value\ of\ Undetermined\ origin}{FOB\ Price} \times 100\% \leq 65\%$$

(c) The value of the non-originating materials shall be:
  (i) the CIF value at the time of importation of the materials, parts or produce; or
  (ii) the earliest ascertained price paid for the materials, parts or produce of undetermined origin in the territory of the Party where the working or processing takes place.

(d) The method of calculating the AIFTA content is as set out in Appendix A.

In addition, Rule 6 reproduced below establishes a list of PSROs that have yet to be developed.

> **RULE 6 Product Specific Rules**
> Notwithstanding the provisions of Rule 4, products which satisfy the Product Specific Rules shall be considered as originating from that Party where working or processing of the product has taken place. The list of Product Specific Rules shall be appended as Appendix B.

3.6 ASEAN–Korea FTA

The core of the RoOs in the ASEAN–Korea FTA is based on an alternative across-the-board percentage rule or CTH RoOs. The formulation of the percentage criterion or RVC is based on a formulation largely inherited from the US-Central America Free Trade Area or other US FTAs based on a value of material calculation.

> **RULE 4 Not Wholly Obtained or Produced Goods**
> 1. For the purposes of paragraph 1(b) of Rule 2, a good, except those covered under Rule 5 as provided for in Appendix 2, shall be deemed to be originating if the regional value content (hereinafter referred to as the "RVC") is not less than 40% of the FOB value or if a good has undergone a change in tariff classification at four digit-level (change of tariff heading) of the Harmonized System.
> 2. The formula for calculating the RVC shall be
>   (a) Build-Up Method

$$RVC = \frac{VOM}{FOB} \times 100\%$$

VOM means value of originating materials, which includes the value of originating materials, direct labour cost, direct overhead cost, transportation cost and profit

(b) Build-Down Method

$$RVC = \frac{FOB-VNM}{FOB} \times 100\%$$

VNM means value of non-originating materials, which shall be: (i) the CIF value at the time of importation of the materials, parts or goods; or (ii) the earliest ascertained price paid for the materials, parts or goods of undetermined origin in the territory of the Party where the working or processing has taken place.

However, most of the goods are subject to PSROs contained in Appendix 2 of the FTA as stipulated in Rule 5 of the ASEAN–Korea FTA:

RULE 5 Product Specific Rules

For the purposes of Rule 2, goods which satisfy the Product Specific Rules provided in Appendix 2 shall be considered to be originating in the territory of the Party where working or processing of the goods has taken place.

3.7 ASEAN–Japan FTA

The relevant articles of the ASEAN–Japan FTA are reproduced below. The main criterion for the RoOs for these two FTAs is an RVC of 40 percent or a change of tariff heading at the four-digit level. However, most of the RoOs requirements are set at the product-specific level and contained in a specific annex of PSROs.

Article 26 Goods Not Wholly Obtained or Produced

1. For the purposes of paragraph (b) of Article 24, a good shall qualify as an originating good of a Party if:
   (a) the good has a regional value content (hereinafter referred to as "RVC"), calculated using the formula set out in Article 27, of not less than forty (40) per cent, and the final process of production has been performed in the Party; or
   (b) all non-originating materials used in the production of the good have undergone in the Party a change in tariff classification (hereinafter referred to as "CTC") at the 4-digit level (i.e. a change in tariff heading) of Harmonized System.

Note: For the purposes of this subparagraph, "Harmonized System" is that on which the product specific rules set out in Annex 2 are based. Each Party shall permit the exporter of the good to decide whether to use subparagraph (a) or (b) when determining whether the good qualifies as an originating good of the Party.

2. Notwithstanding paragraph 1, a good subject to product specific rules shall qualify as an originating good if it satisfies the applicable product specific rules set out in Annex 2. Where a product specific rule provides a choice of rules from a RVC-based rule of origin, a CTC-based rule of origin, a specific manufacturing or processing operation, or a combination of any of these, each Party shall permit the exporter of the good to

decide which rule to use in determining whether the good qualifies as an originating good of the Party.
3. For the purposes of subparagraph 1(a) and the relevant product specific rules set out in Annex 2 which specify a certain RVC, it is required that the RVC of a good, calculated using the formula set out in Article 27, is not less than the percentage specified by the rule for the good.
4. For the purposes of subparagraph 1(b) and the relevant product specific rules set out in Annex 2, the rules requiring that the materials used have undergone CTC, or a specific manufacturing or processing operation, shall apply only to non-originating materials.
5. For the purposes of this Chapter, Annex 3 shall apply.

Article 27 below defines the calculation methodology to be used for the RVC. It must be noted in the case of both agreements that the requirements for the calculations of the RVC are based on an indirect calculation, and do not provide, as in the case of the ATIGA, for the possibility of using a direct calculation method.

Article 27 Calculation of Regional Value Content

1. For the purposes of calculating the RVC of a good, the following formula shall be used:

$$RVC = \frac{FOB - VNM}{FOB} \times 100\%$$

2. For the purposes of this Article:
    (a) "FOB" is, except as provided for in paragraph 3, the free-on-board value of a good, inclusive of the cost of transport from the producer to the port or site of final shipment abroad;

(b) "RVC" is the RVC of a good, expressed as a percentage; and

(c) "VNM" is the value of non-originating materials used in the production of a good.

3. FOB referred to in subparagraph 2(a) shall be the value:

   (a) adjusted to the first ascertainable price paid for a good from the buyer to the producer of the good, if there is free-on-board value of the good, but it is unknown and cannot be ascertained; or

   (b) determined in accordance with Articles 1 through 8 of the Agreement on Customs Valuation, if there is no free-on-board value of a good.

4. For the purposes of paragraph 1, the value of non originating materials used in the production of a good in a Party:

   (a) shall be determined in accordance with the Agreement on Customs Valuation and shall include freight, insurance, and where appropriate, packing and all other costs incurred in transporting the material to the importation port in the Party where the producer of the good is located; or

   (b) if such value is unknown and cannot be ascertained, shall be the first ascertainable price paid for the material in the Party, but may exclude all the costs incurred in the Party in transporting the material from the warehouse of the supplier of the material to the place where the producer is located such as freight, insurance and packing as well as any other known and ascertainable cost incurred in the Party.

5. For the purposes of paragraph 1, the VNM of a good shall not include the value of non-originating materials used in the production of originating materials of the Party which are used in the production of the good.
6. For the purposes of subparagraph 3(b) or 4(a), in applying the Agreement on Customs Valuation to determine the value of a good or non-originating material, the Agreement on Customs Valuation shall apply, mutatis mutandis, to domestic transactions or to the cases where there is no domestic transaction of the good or non originating material.

Chapter 4

The silent cost: the cumbersome administration of ASEAN rules of origin

4.1 Form D over SUBSTANCE

The "Form D" CO is the documentary foundation of the ATIGA and AFTA. Companies wishing to claim the zero tariff rate applicable under the ATIGA must demonstrate that their goods qualify as ASEAN origin either by achieving 40 percent value added from ASEAN inputs and processing, or by a CTC at the four-digit harmonized tariff system level through processing in ASEAN (there are some special product-specific rules for automotive, steel, chemical and other products as discussed earlier).

The Form D is issued – on application by the exporter – by designated authorities in ASEAN Member States on the basis of pre-export examination of the goods in question and submission of relevant documents by the exporter for each and every export consignment. The procedure includes pre-export examination of the relevant records (including sourcing and cost accounting) and – where relevant – production processes. A 2009 ERIA paper[1] reviewed the relevant processes in two ASEAN Member States and concluded that compliance with the rules can be "costly and

---

[1] ERIA, *ASEAN Rules of Origin: Lessons and Recommendations for Best Practice* (2009).

administratively burdensome." However, the situation differs from country to country between full manual and personal treatment to a high degree of computerization.

The Form D process would probably score relatively high on reliability, but much less highly (and in some cases quite poorly) on simplicity and cost effectiveness, for both ASEAN Member States and exporters. This could be a major contributing factor to the severe underutilization of the ATIGA duty preferences.

Form D is established in the ATIGA as follows:

> **ARTICLE 38. CERTIFICATE OF ORIGIN**
>
> A claim that a good shall be accepted as eligible for preferential tariff treatment shall be supported by a Certificate of Origin (Form D), as set out in Annex 7 issued by a Government authority designated by the exporting Member State and notified to the other Member States in accordance with the Operational Certification Procedures, as set out in Annex 8.

A copy of Form D is reproduced in Table 4.1. It is issued by the authorized authority in the ASEAN Member State, usually the ministry of trade or the chamber of commerce:

Unfortunately, there have been recurring documentary problems that have plagued Form D processing in ASEAN since its inception. The AFTA had explicit requirements for the Form D documents, which were laid out as follows:[2]

---

[2] Operational Certification Procedures (OCP) for the Rules of Origin of the ASEAN Common Effective Preferential Tariff Scheme for ASEAN Free Trade Area.

Table 4.1 *Form D*

1. Goods consigned from (Exporter's business name, address, country)	Reference No. ASEAN TRADE IN GOODS AGREEMENT/ ASEAN INDUSTRIAL COOPERATION SCHEME CERTIFICATE OF ORIGIN (Combined Declaration and Certificate) Issued in $\dfrac{\text{FORM D}}{\text{(Country)}}$ See Overleaf Notes
2. Goods consigned to (Consignee's name, address, country)	
3. Means of transport and route (as far as known) Departure date Vessel's name/Aircraft etc. Port of Discharge	4. For Official Use Preferential Treatment Given Under ASEAN Trade in Goods Agreement Preferential Treatment Given Under ASEAN Industrial Cooperation Scheme Preferential Treatment Not Given (Please state reason/s) .... Signature of Authorised Signatory of the Importing Country

5. Item number	6. Marks and numbers on packages	7. Number and type of packages, description of goods (including quantity where appropriate and HS number of the importing country)	8. Origin criterion (see Overleaf Notes)	9. Gross weight or other quantity and value (FOB)	10. Number and date of invoices

11. Declaration by the exporter The undersigned hereby declares that the above details and statement are correct; that all the goods were produced in .... (Country) and that they comply with the origin requirements specified for these goods in the ASEAN Trade in Goods Agreement for the goods exported to .... (Importing Country) .... Place and date, signature of authorised signatory	12. Certification It is hereby certified, on the basis of control carried out, that the declaration by the exporter is correct. .... Place and date, signature and stamp of certifying authority
13. ☐ Third Country Invoicing ☐ Exhibition ☐ Accumulation ☐ De Minimis ☐ Back-to-Back CO ☐ Issued Retroactively ☐ Partial Cumulation	

ISSUANCE OF CERTIFICATE OF ORIGIN
RULE 7

(a) The Certificate of Origin must be on ISO A4 size paper in conformity to the specimen as shown in Appendix "A". It shall be made in English.

(b) The Certificate of Origin shall comprise one original and three (3) carbon copies of the following colours:
Original – light violet
Duplicate – orange
Triplicate – orange
Quadruplicate – orange

(c) Each Certificate of Origin shall bear a reference number separately given by each place or office of issuance.

(d) The original copy shall be forwarded, together with the triplicate, by the exporter to the importer for submission to the Customs Authority at the port or place of importation. The duplicate shall be retained by the issuing authority in the exporting Member State. The quadruplicate shall be retained by the exporter. After the importation of the products, the triplicate shall be marked accordingly in box 4 and returned to the issuing authority within reasonable period of time.

As a result of these above-mentioned explicit documentary requirements, and also as a result of the overly stringent inspection imposed by ASEAN customs authorities, Form D documentation has been rejected repeatedly for a variety of apparently trivial reasons:

- The paper was 1–2 millimeters too big or too small, e.g., as not being "A4" size.

4.1 FORM D OVER SUBSTANCE

- The paper was the wrong shade of color, e.g., for not being sufficiently "violet" or being too "light."
- The specimen signature was not updated.
- The authorized signatory was not updated. The signature was slightly different from the specimen signature (e.g., a dot was missing from an "i") or in a slightly different location from specimen signature).
- The document used the wrong font type.
- The document used the wrong font size.
- The exporter's name did not match the invoice documentation, or some other typographical error.

ASEAN customs authorities would thus prevent the importer from clearing customs under the CEPT, forcing the importer either to litigate the matter (a time-consuming process) or pay the MFN rate. Even a single error for one item covered by a Form D would result in denial of benefits for the entire shipment. The ASEAN Sub-committee on Rules of Origin (SCAROO) thus had to compile a list of previous ASEAN decisions regarding such discrepancies in order to emphasize to ASEAN national customs authorities the need to review Form D documents in an appropriate manner (Table 4.2).

Yet despite this explicit instruction by ASEAN, ASEAN national customs authorities continue to reject Form D documents. For example, item 5 in the Matrix specifically allows for the submission of appendices to Form D documents, yet Thai customs authorities are known to reject such documents routinely.

This forces companies to fit the often voluminous information needed to support the Form D claim in multiple

Table 4.2 *The matrix of decisions on RoO implementation issues (endorsed at the 5th SCAROO (July 19, 2011)*

No	Issues/options	Decision	Meeting	Remarks
		Minor discrepancy		
1	The size of ticks in Box 13 of the ATIGA Form D	It could be done either by hand or type writing.	28th ROOTF, October 20–22, 2008, Vientiane, Lao PDR	
2	Minor discrepancies in Form Ds that have been rejected at some of the customs authorities of importing Member States	Minor discrepancies such as the size of ticks, uncertainty over signatures, and size of forms, should be resolved quickly and efficiently between focal points, and not through feedback by the companies (importers or exporters).	52nd CCCA, October 23–25, 2008, Vientiane, Lao PDR	
		CO Form D		
3	The issuance of certified true copy of lost or damaged COs	(i) The date of the issuance would be in line with the dates of the original CO and while the reference number would differ, the reference number of the original CO should be referred by stating "REPLACING CO Ref [original reference number]". (ii) In the case Where no original reference number is made, the certified true copy should be rejected.	28th ROOTF, October 20–22, 2008, Vientiane, Lao PDR	

Table 4.2 (cont.)

No	Issues/options	Decision	Meeting	Remarks
4	Erroneous CO	(i) As an alternative to striking out the erroneous information and revise and initial the correction, the issuing authority could issue a new CO with new reference number. However, the validity shall refer to the old CO. (ii) The erroneous COs could then be destroyed by the issuing authority as appropriately.	28th ROOTF, October 20–22, 2008, Vientiane, Lao PDR; 5th SCA–ROO July 18–19, 2011, Jakarta, Indonesia	
5	CO containing multiple products requiring attachments of the list of products in an A4 paper	Each page of the attachment would have to be initialled by the authorized officer and duly stamped and the reference number of the CO be stated.	28th ROOTF, October 20–22, 2008, Vientiane, Lao PDR	
6	Retroactive issuance of CO	(i) The rules that have been agreed by ASEAN, including the need to tick Box 13 for retroactive issuance of CO, should be respected and adhered to by all parties. (ii) Minor issues such as hand written ticks or crossed instead of ticked, should not be the reason for delays in granting the concession and request of verification.	30th ROOTF, March 28–30, 2009, Manila, the Philippines	

Table 4.2 (cont.)

No	Issues/options	Decision	Meeting	Remarks
7	Replacement of old CO with a new CO	Attaching a note from the issuing authority to the new CO that certifies the new CO as replacement of certain CO (citing the reference number of the old CO), would be sufficient.	30th ROOTF, March 28–30, 2009, Manila, the Philippines	
8	CO issued before the Exporting Date	COs issued before the date of shipment should be accepted subject to the completion of all necessary documents required.	32nd ROOTF, Kuala Lumpur, November 14–17, 2009	"the CO shall be issued at the time of exportation or soon thereafter" in the Rule 10 of the OCP, does not mean that the CO can only be issued on the date of shipment.
9	Back-to-back CO issued beyond the validity period of the Origin CO	Back-to-back CO Form D issued beyond the validity period of the Origin CO could not be accepted. Back-to-back CO would need to be issued by the intermediate exporting Member State and presented to the final importing Member State within the validity period of the original CO.	32nd ROOTF, Kuala Lumpur, November 14–17, 2009	
10	Reference number on the new Form D	The reference number of the new Form D would be subject to the exporting Party's domestic regulations.	28th ROOTF, October 20–22, 2008, Vientiane, Lao PDR; 5th SCAROO: changed "their respective" to "the exporting Party."	

Table 4.2 *(cont.)*

No	Issues/options	Decision	Meeting	Remarks
11	Issuance of a Form D for products classified under the same tariff classification sub-heading	*Case*: Issuance of a Form D for several products in a commercial invoice. They are similar in nature, classified in the same tariff sub-heading and are only different in colours *Resolution*: The issuing authorities would issue one ATIGA Form D for these similar products. This ATIGA Form D specifies the same total quantity as indicated in the commercial invoice.	33rd ROOTF, 11–13 January 2010, Hoi An, Vietnam	
		Specimen signatures		
12	High frequency of requests by some Member States for verification of specimen signatures	(i) Member States were urged to ensure dissemination of any updates on specimen signatures to all entry points as soon as possible. (ii) For efficiency, there would be a need to establish a website in which the specimen signatures could be uploaded and easily accessible by the authorised importing authorities. (iii) One possible option is to include specimen signatures in the trade repository currently deliberated by the CCA.	28th ROOTF, October 20–22, 2008, Vientiane, Lao PDR	

Table 4.2 *(cont.)*

No	Issues/options	Decision	Meeting	Remarks
13	To confirm/verify specimen signature	Emails should be accepted to confirm/verify the specimen signature in question.	30th ROOTF, March 28–30, 2009, Manila, the Philippines	
14	Verification of specimen signatures	Difficulties in verifying the signatures that appear in the CO should not be the basis to reject a CO.	30th ROOTF, March 28–30, 2009, Manila, the Philippines	
15	Confidentiality of specimen signature and official seals	Specimen signature and official seals should be treated as confidential documents and only be exchanged between the respective government authorities and should not be disclosed to unauthorised persons.	32nd ROOTF, Kuala Lumpur, November 14–17, 2009	Article 7(5) of the OCP: any rejection by the customs authorities, the subject CO shall be marked accordingly in Box 4 and be returned to the issuing authority directly and not through any other Party such as the importer. The grounds of the denial preference should also be notified to the issuing authority
16	Mechanisms for provision of specimen signatures	Each focal point in each Member State must ensure that the specimen signatures received by and communicated from the ASEAN Secretariat would be communicated to the appropriate Customs authorities.	33rd ROOTF, January 11–13, 2010, Hoi An, Vietnam	
17	Information on specimen signatures	All Member States to update contacts of the focal points and information on specimen signatures to facilitate the circulation of specimen signatures.	33rd ROOTF, January 11–13, 2010, Hoi An, Vietnam	

Table 4.2 *(cont.)*

No	Issues/options	Decision	Meeting	Remarks
		Third party invoicing		
18	Implementation of third party invoicing	A third party invoice issued by an ASEAN Member State would be accepted.	30th ROOTF, March 28–30, 2009, Manila, the Philippines	
19	Third party invoice arrangement (reaffirmed by 55th CCCA, July 9–11, 2009, Singapore)	A third party invoice issued by an ASEAN Member State would be accepted. The principles of its implementation are: Exporter should indicate his/her intention to use third party invoicing arrangement when applying for Form D to the issuing authority; The third party invoice should be presented to the issuing authority, if any; In the absence of information on the invoice reference number and the FOB price of the third party, the invoice reference of the manufacturer may be reflected in the relevant box of Form D; and A component of "third party invoice" in Box 13 (of Form D) should then be ticked and used as an indication and justification to the receiving authority on any discrepancies found between information reflected in the Form D and the actual invoices attached to the said Form D.	31st ROOTF, July 4–6, 2009, Singapore	

Table 4.2 *(cont.)*

No	Issues/options	Decision	Meeting	Remarks
	Supporting documents			
20	The understanding of Rule 21(d) of the OCP, particularly on the types of other documents required for the purpose of the Article and the agency to issue such other additional documents	The intention of the Article is to provide flexibility for the traders to present suitable supporting documents issued by a competent party as long as the documents provide sufficient evidence to the receiving authorities that the shipment meet the requirements of the Article.	29th ROOTF, 12–14 January 2009, Siem Reap, Cambodia	
	Direct/indirect consignment			
21	Direct/indirect consignment	*Case*: Goods produced in Malaysia, sent to Vietnam using multimodal transportation, e.g., by train to Singapore and by vessel to Vietnam. In this arrangement, Malaysia only issues the transportation document sending the goods to Singapore, and B/L would be issued by a Singaporean company to ship the goods to Vietnam. *Resolution*: For this case, the bill of lading should be issued by the exporting country, describing all transportation modes required at the exportation.	33rd ROOTF, 11–13 January 2010, Hoi An, Vietnam	

Table 4.2 *(cont.)*

No	Issues/options	Decision	Meeting	Remarks
22		*Case*: whether only one RVC criterion could be attributed for the origin status of several items declared in a single CO Form D. *Resolution*: Multiple items declared in one CO Form D shall qualify separately in its own right.	33rd ROOTF, January 11–13, 2010, Hoi An, Vietnam	Rule 6(e) of the OCP

copies of the standard one-page Form D document. This becomes very problematic for complex goods, such as automobiles; submissions involving hundreds of Form D pages are common in the automotive industry.

Appendix 8 of the ATIGA attempts to eliminate these issues by eliminating some of the documentary requirements:

RULE 7 CERTIFICATE OF ORIGIN (FORM D)

1. The Certificate of Origin (Form D) must be on ISO A4 size white paper in conformity to the specimen shown in Annex 7 of this Agreement. It shall be made in the English language.
2. The Certificate of Origin (Form D) shall comprise one (1) original and two (2) carbon copies (Duplicate and Triplicate).
3. Each Certificate of Origin (Form D) shall bear a reference number separately given by each place or office of issuance.
4. Each Certificate of Origin (Form D) shall bear the manually executed signature and seal of the authorised issuing authority.

5. The original copy shall be forwarded by the exporter to the importer for submission to the customs authority at the port or place of importation. The duplicate shall be retained by the issuing authority in the exporting Member State. The triplicate shall be retained by the exporter.

Thus, the ATIGA language regarding Form D does not specify the form of the document: an attempt to place substance over form. Indeed, the ATIGA specifies that minor discrepancies should not prevent the entry of goods under the ATIGA duty preferences:

RULE 16 TREATMENT OF MINOR DISCREPANCIES

1. Where the ASEAN origin of the goods is not in doubt, the discovery of minor discrepancies, such as typographical error in the statements made in the Certificate of Origin (Form D) and those made in the documents submitted to the customs authorities of the importing Member State for the purpose of carrying out the formalities for importing the goods shall not ipso facto invalidate the Certificate of Origin (Form D), if it does in fact correspond to the goods submitted.
2. In cases where the exporting Member State and importing Member State have different tariff classifications for a good subject to preferential tariffs, the goods shall be released at the MFN rates or at the higher preferential rate, subject to the compliance of the applicable ROO, and no penalty or other charges shall be imposed in accordance with relevant laws and regulations of the importing Member State. Once the classification differences have been resolved, the correct rate shall be applied and any overpaid duty shall be

4.1 FORM D OVER SUBSTANCE

> refunded if applicable, in accordance with relevant laws and regulations of the importing Member State, as soon as the issues have been resolved.
>
> 3. For multiple items declared under the same Certificate of Origin (Form D), a problem encountered with one of the items listed shall not affect or delay the granting of preferential treatment and customs clearance of the remaining items listed in the Certificate of Origin (Form D). Rule 18(c) may be applied to the problematic items.

Under the ATIGA, therefore, small discrepancies should not stop customs clearance under the ATIGA preferences. The importer should be allowed to clear the goods under the MFN rate, but also to challenge the decision and be refunded any excess duty should the Form D be found valid (this was not a certainty under the AFTA). An error for one line item should not affect all of the line items involved in the shipment.

However, the directives of the ATIGA do not deal with all of the Form D problems. The previously mentioned issue regarding the rejection of appendices by one ASEAN Member State continues. The model Form D also requires the submission of cost statements and maintenance of the supporting documentation, even if the goods qualify under the CTC standard, for which cost data are completely irrelevant. Nor does the updated Form D deal with the issue of whether the cost statement should be based on the overall operations of the company, or on the precise costs involved in the production of the specified goods involved in the customs entry. Very few exporters maintain such detailed cost information.

Other problems relate to the interaction between the ATIGA and ASEAN's bilateral FTAs with China, India,

Japan, Korea and Australia–New Zealand. Although the ASEAN bilateral FTAs have their own RoOs to determine whether goods qualify for preferential treatment, these rules are mostly consistent with the ATIGA. Thus, 40 percent value added in ASEAN should qualify a product as ASEAN origin in most ASEAN FTAs and the ATIGA itself, regardless of how that is documented, whether under Form D or its equivalent under the ASEAN bilateral FTAs. Yet the current setup of the ATIGA only allows for cumulation of ASEAN value added, which is reported in Form D itself. In other words, a product could have ASEAN value added, which helps it qualify for the ASEAN–China FTA, but because no Form D has been issued for the product, the ASEAN value added cannot be used to qualify that product for the ATIGA! ASEAN can remedy this situation by allowing for data to be used for multiple COs, and not requiring the submission of data on multiple occasions.

In sum, continued reliance on Form D documentation will prevent full usage of the ATIGA preferences, despite any reforms that have been implemented in the agreement. A shift to self-certification, which is used in other FTAs, would help. Although ASEAN has planned to use self-certification, internal disputes, even within the same ASEAN Member State, present major issues in its implementation.

4.2 Customs Administration

Another problem raised by the private sector – concerning the implementation of preferential tariffs in general, and touching on the issues of trade facilitation and utilization of the ATIGA preferences – is the treatment of shipments where the required certificate (or a claim for a preference) is not immediately submitted with the import declaration, but presented at a later time. Not all ASEAN Member States have a legal regime dealing with requests for the repayment or reimbursement of duties in place, and an importer may well end up having to pay the full MFN rate just because the certificate arrived a few days late. At the same time, an ASEAN national customs administration may have the right to recover duties from importers over a period ranging between one and three years when post-import audits show that the amount originally collected was an incorrect one.

This is not a balanced situation. Excluding a claim for preferential treatment after importation seems to be, to say the least, at odds with the OCP, as Rule 14 provides for certificates to be accepted after importation and does not call for the actual claim to have been made upon importation. Furthermore, although Article 60.1 of the ATIGA refers to the decision on claims for repayment, it does not describe the cases in which an importer is entitled to a repayment. This is left to the national legislation. Hence it is imperative that the ASEAN Member States follow up on their ratification of the ATIGA by also ratifying the 2012 ASEAN Customs Agreement and amending their domestic customs legislation to allow for this type of refund procedure.

4.3 Preventing Loss of Origin

Another administrative issue that has arisen in the administration of COs is that sometimes origin is lost. If an ASEAN-originating product from Member State A was declared for importation with a Form D in Member State B, and at a later stage exported to Member State C, it is at present impossible (legally and practically) to obtain a Form D in Member State B, and the full rate of duty will be applied in Member State C. The "loss of origin" issue has been identified in earlier studies as one of the possible causes of underuse of preferences under the CEPT.

Apart from being a possible cause of underutilization, this issue is also felt to stand in the way of a true "free movement of ASEAN originating goods," which, with a view to the AEC objectives, makes finding and introducing/implementing a solution even more important. It should be realized, however, that there is no solution that will solve all cases of "lost origin," as there will always be situations in which an exporter (a trader in particular), is just not able to prove that the goods to be exported were already originating in an ASEAN Member State. "Proof" is an elementary requirement that should not be dropped.

Under Article 31.2 of the ATIGA, the issuing authorities can only issue a certificate (Form D) for goods originating in the country in which the certificate is applied for:

> A good originating in the territory of a Member State shall retain its initial originating status, when exported from another Member State, where operations undertaken have not gone beyond those referred to in paragraph 1 of this Article.

An exception is provided for the issuing of back-to-back COs (Form D): a CO can be issued on the basis of another CO under certain conditions. However, in practice this will only be applicable to goods originating under the ATIGA in another ASEAN Member State, which have not been imported into free circulation in the country in question. The first step toward a solution is therefore to remove the restriction and to allow

4.3 PREVENTING LOSS OF ORIGIN

that COs can also be issued when the ASEAN country of origin of the goods in question is different from the issuing ASEAN Member State. The legal basis for the issuing of COs is laid down in Article 38 of the ATIGA:

> A claim that a good shall be accepted as eligible for preferential tariff treatment shall be supported by a Certificate of Origin (Form D), as set out in Annex 7, issued by a Government authority designated by the exporting Member State and notified to the other Member States in accordance with the Operational Certification Procedures, as set out in Annex 8.

The text of this article does not rule out the issuing of a certificate stating a country of origin different from the country in which the certificate is to be issued, but refers to the OCP. Therefore, Article 38 would not need to be amended. It is Rule 10.1 of the OCP that contains the restriction in question; here the text would require a minor amendment by replacing "... originating in that Member State" with "... originating in a Member State." The OCP text amendments to be developed for the inclusion of a self-certification regime will have to allow for the same. With that, the OCP would allow for certificates to be issued/invoice declarations to be made out for goods originating in an ASEAN Member State different from the exporting ASEAN Member State.

This effort should be undertaken with full implementation of the ASEAN Framework Agreement on Goods in Transit (Hanoi, 1998). The agreement called for a protocol to allow for customs transit between and through ASEAN Member States. However, since 1998, the protocol has not been finalized.

Chapter 5

The possible way forward: self-certification

The Form D process thus involves an emphasis on the verification of paper documentation, rather than the verification of the underlying facts of the transaction. ASEAN government authorities devote more time and resources to confirming whether the Form D document conforms to the ATIGA requirements than to whether the goods actually qualify for the duty preferences.

Self-certification by exporters would move the focus away from the Form D documentation and toward the fundamentals of the transaction. Under certain conditions, trusted traders/exporters could provide a statement/declaration about the origin of the product in question on the invoice. While maintaining a substantial degree of reliability, it would be simpler and more cost-effective and would therefore enhance utilization of the advantages offered by the ATIGA.

Self-certification is based on the assumption that "the exporter knows best" what it is making, how it is made and who supplied the materials to make it; in other words, the exporter is – almost – always in the best position to initially establish whether its goods satisfy the applicable origin criteria. Frankly, the Form D process is also based on the same principle: it is the exporter that declares in the application for a CO that its goods meet the applicable RoO.

The main difference between the two systems is that in the Form D process the ASEAN authorities are in a position to verify the correctness of each and every declaration before they issue the certificate, while under the self-certification regime the exporter sends its declaration – without any interference from the authorities – directly to its customer in the country of importation. That does not mean that under a self-certification system there is no control on the correctness of the declarations made, but only that the pre-export control tools have to be replaced with a different – not necessarily lesser – process. Whereas pre-export examination concentrates on the origin status of a particular product at the time of examination, post-export examination of origin through an exporter's records concentrates on the origin at the time of export. This post-export process provides a more accurate origin profile of the goods and more accurately reflects the dynamic nature of modern manufacturing techniques.

Both the EU and NAFTA use self-certification. The EU operates a dual certification regime in nearly all the FTAs it has concluded: a conventional certification system and a self-certification scheme. Self-certification consists of making out a declaration of a given model on the invoice ("invoice declaration") and is generally available to pre-cleared exporters who have satisfied the authorities in the country of export that their documentation is reliable or to exporters whose shipments are less than 6,000 Euros. The former requirement ensures that only competent, trustworthy exporters use self-certification. Failure to comply would result in the imposition of fines and penalties. The latter requirement ensures that smaller companies are not burdened by CO requirements. In either case, the exporter remains subject to post-shipment inspection by the relevant authorities in the country of export.

Self-certification is the only option under the NAFTA: any exporter in Canada, the United States or Mexico can complete and sign a NAFTA CO and send it to the importer in question. The NAFTA also allows the use of "blanket" COs that can cover up to one year of identical imports. A NAFTA CO is not required for the commercial importation of a good valued at less than US$1,000. However, in that case the invoice accompanying the importation must include a statement by the exporter certifying that the goods qualify as originating goods under the NAFTA RoOs. In either case, the exporter remains subject to post-shipment inspection by the relevant authorities in the country of export.

Accordingly, the ASEAN Member States agreed to adopt self-certification for use in the ATIGA by 2012 (this has been delayed, as will be explained later). Exporters would be allowed to use either self-certification or the Form D process. This "dual regime" approach allows self-certification for those who can, and conventional certification for those who cannot. However, the initial choice for a scheme will be the exporter's. If the exporter were authorized by ASEAN authorities in the exporting country to act as a Certified Exporter, the customs authorities in the importing country would have to accept that and would not be able to insist on a conventional certificate being submitted.

To test how self-certification would work, Brunei, Malaysia and Singapore initiated their pilot program in late 2010, allowing their exporters to obtain approved status and

THE POSSIBLE WAY FORWARD: SELF-CERTIFICATION

self-certify their exports. This included manufacturers and trading companies. Approved companies had to provide the following language in their export documentation:

> The exporter of the product(s) covered by this document (Certified Exporter No . . .) declares that, except where otherwise clearly indicated, the products satisfy the Rules of Origin to be considered as ASEAN Originating Products under ATIGA (ASEAN Trade in Goods: . . . (Exporting Country) with origin criteria: . . . (Eg. 40% RVC).

If the exporter were later found to have contravened this certification, it would be subject to severe penalties.

Thailand joined the pilot program in 2011. The current participants indicate that they believe the program is a great success. The number of transactions covered by the program has increased during its operation, and both companies and governments have been quite happy.

Yet other ASEAN Member States have expressed extreme skepticism about self-certification. Indonesia has publicly stated that it would participate in the pilot program only if participating companies were limited to manufacturers, and if the authorized signatories were limited to three persons per company. This reflects a general suspicion among certain ASEAN customs authorities that companies, and in particular trading companies, could abuse the system to obtain FTA origin wrongly.

Trading companies are particularly suspect, in the view of Indonesia and other ASEAN Member States, because of the difficulty in conducting post-entry audit of documentation. The trading company would not have manufactured the goods, so it would not have direct access to the underlying cost data (for RVC) and manufacturing information (for CTC) to confirm that the goods qualify as ASEAN origin. This would not be the case for the manufacturer. Hence allowing trading companies to self-certify would require the ASEAN authority granting the trading company approved exporter status either to rely on second-hand information obtained by the trading company from the manufacturer, which may not be accurate, or, worse, not to examine any documentation at all when giving the company approved exporter status. These suspicions are particularly prevalent because the authority for conferring approved exporter status would in most cases rest with the trade ministries in the ASEAN Member States whereas the post-entry inspection authority would rest with the customs agencies in the ASEAN Member States. Customs authorities are traditionally suspicious of trade ministries, even those in their own countries!

Furthermore, some of the skepticism about trading companies arises from the different corporate income tax rates within ASEAN, which we reproduce below in Table 5.1 (before credits and deductions).

These tax differentials encourage sales transaction flows, which would benefit the low-tax jurisdictions, and such flows would be exacerbated should trading companies operating in these low-tax jurisdictions be allowed to self-certify. For example, a company located in western Indonesia could elect to sell directly to a customer located in eastern Indonesia. There would be VAT collected, which could be charged off against VAT paid on inputs. More importantly, the profit generated from the sale would be booked in Indonesia and

Table 5.1 *Corporate income tax rates within ASEAN*

ASEAN Member	Maximum rate
Brunei	23.5%
Cambodia	20.0%
Indonesia	25.0%
Laos	35.0%
Malaysia	25.0%
Myanmar	30.0%
Philippines	30.0%
Singapore	17.0%
Thailand	30.0%
Vietnam	25.0%

subject to the 25 percent tax rate. However, the western Indonesian company could elect to transship the goods through Singapore and onwards to eastern Indonesia (for ocean shipments this occurs anyway). Then the western Indonesian company could sell through an affiliated Singaporean trading company, which could self-certify the goods as ASEAN origin and thus qualify the goods for the ATIGA duty preference. The profits from the resulting sale would be booked in Singapore at the 17 percent rate instead of in Indonesia at the 25 percent rate. The eastern Indonesian customer would pay VAT, but that would have been the case under the domestic transaction model as well. In any event, this approach would not be available under the Form D process because either the trading company would be unable to get Form D from the Singapore authorities, or a back-to-back Form D would have been used, which would immediately alert Indonesian customs authorities to the true nature of the sale.

THE POSSIBLE WAY FORWARD: SELF-CERTIFICATION

As a result of the difference of opinion on whether self-certification should be allowed for trading companies, Indonesia, Laos, Philippines and Vietnam implemented their own pilot program to implement self-certification. This would represent an application of the "ASEAN-X" concept contained in Article 21.2 of the ASEAN Charter, which allows a subset of ASEAN to proceed with an economic policy without waiting for participation by other Member States: "In the implementation of economic commitments, a formula for flexible participation, including the ASEAN Minus X formula, may be applied where there is a consensus to do so." ASEAN-X thus allows a sub-group of ASEAN to proceed with an economic policy without waiting for participation by the other Member States. In the context of self-certification ASEAN-X has led to two pilot programs for self-certification, each with four ASEAN Members. In other words, we have two "ASEAN-6" groups operating at the same time.

At first glance, this would appear to be an absurd situation. The self-certification dispute illustrates the potential risks of the ASEAN-X formula. ASEAN-X is intended to allow for a transitional period for the implementation of economic programs in the AEC. A sub-group of Members can experiment with policies, which, if successful, can be adopted by the others in their own time frame. But ASEAN-X should not be used to create a multitude of sub-groups each doing their own thing; that contravenes the entire purpose of establishing a single market. ASEAN-X must be seen instead as a means for experimentation, demonstration and explanation of economic initiatives. This requires continuing dialogue between the sub-group and the others. Otherwise, ASEAN-X risks creating a permanent "two-speed" system or, worse, a "buffet" system whereby Members can pick and choose their programs. ASEAN-X does not work if the "X" is the number "8" or "9." It would be as if the EU had decided to have two "common" currencies, the Euro and the ECU, each competing to be the common currency of the EU. Is this the "buffet" system of selectively picking and choosing economic policies?

The answer is no. A closer examination of the reasons for creating a second pilot program demonstrates that a competition of ideas is not necessarily a bad thing. Indonesia has publicly stated that it would participate in the pilot program only if participating companies were limited to manufacturers, and if the authorized signatories were limited to three persons per company. This reflects a general suspicion among certain ASEAN customs authorities that companies, and in particular trading companies, could abuse the system to obtain FTA origin wrongly. These countries also expressed skepticism about the success of the pilot program.

Hence the Malaysia-Brunei-Singapore-Thailand program allows trading companies to participate whereas the Indonesia-Philippines-Vietnam-Laos program would not allow for this. This issue will need to be resolved for self-certification to be applied universally throughout ASEAN in the ATIGA. However, the authors think that having two pilot programs would allow for that. So long as the pilot programs remain just that – temporary programs to test the merits of a policy – they will be useful.

The Indonesia-Philippines-Vietnam-Laos group is very skeptical about self-certification. Having a pilot program that they can administer on their own terms will give them

THE POSSIBLE WAY FORWARD: SELF-CERTIFICATION

confidence that self-certification can work. They can administer the program in their own way (e.g., for manufacturers only) and review their own data.

Meanwhile, the Malaysia-Brunei-Singapore-Thailand group will have data for comparison purposes, based on both quantitative and qualitative approaches. After the pilot programs have generated sufficient data, a proper debate can be held on which approach is best, given the various policy priorities and administration issues that will have arisen.

Thus, the intent of ASEAN-X, to allow a pathfinder group to move ahead with a policy and letting the others catch up later at their own pace, can be applied properly in this case. However, doing so will require that the pilot programs run their course and that proper policy debate follows. If the pilot programs become entrenched, with each group running them in its own way, then "buffet" style policymaking will also take root in the AEC. Such confusion must not be allowed to happen. The authors still look forward to hearing more good news about the pilot program(s) and the increased use of self-certification.

In any event, the potential for abuse of FTA preferences has always existed, with or without self-certification. The current Form D scheme places too much emphasis on form over substance, as an unscrupulous exporter could obtain a CO using subterfuge anyway. Inspecting individual paper certificates for compliance does not really prevent such abuse. A self-certification scheme, backed by rigorous post-entry audit by customs authorities, will actually target such behavior more efficiently. Trading companies can be subject to additional scrutiny, as they are currently.

THE POSSIBLE WAY FORWARD: SELF-CERTIFICATION

Even with self-certification, the ASEAN Member States could nevertheless frustrate the trade facilitation aims of self-certification if it is not implemented properly. There is apprehension in the private sector that upon importation, self-declared origin by "Certified Exporters" might be subject to more (!) strict controls, more queries and more verification requests than is currently the case with the Form D. If that were to happen, the trade facilitation benefits of the introduction of self-certification would be effectively negated. Therefore, all possible efforts should be made to avoid that happening.

Chapter 6

Conclusion and recommendations

There are more than thirty RTAs in force involving East Asia, and many are led by ASEAN. Among the various methodologies for determining the origin of a good, ASEAN has followed its tradition as in many other trade issues: *the ASEAN way*. For more than two decades ASEAN used a percentage criterion of 40 percent. The drafting of the ASEAN legal texts concerning the calculation methodology of the 40 percent were far from clear and predictable, allowing for different methods used by different ASEAN countries. Recent reforms have introduced the concept of an RVC and the CTC as alternative criteria. An increasing number of products of PSROs are now being given the option to apply CTC as an alternative criterion to the 40 percent calculated as RVC.

The jury is still out on whether the addition of these alternative rules has resulted in a substantial increase of the utilization of ASEAN FTAs, today's ATIGA. Table 1.1 in Chapter 1 indicates that much remains to be done to increase utilization rates.

The consolidation efforts made in the ATIGA made some improvements but they fall short; in sum, they are simply too little too late. An overall overhaul and rejuvenation of the ATIGA RoOs is necessary.

Customs clearance in the East Asia region is still a problem. There are findings indicating that customs managers have been given targets of duty collections. A complex

CONCLUSION AND RECOMMENDATIONS

RoOs regime accompanying an FTA represents to them an opportunity to deny preferential tariff treatment. Along with an improvement of the RoOs in the region, there is an even greater need for the streamlining of customs procedures and simplification of customs clearances, including the introduction of certified exporters.

During negotiations with FTA partners, ASEAN countries have routinely insisted on replicating their own RoOs when negotiating FTA agreements with dialogue partners. However, since the dialogue partners also have their own views on how the RoOs should be drafted, the results of the negotiations have, in certain cases, been the mutual acceptance by both parties of each other's RoOs (as in the case of the FTA with India) or, in other cases (such as the FTAs with Japan and South Korea), the acceptance with some modifications of the RoOs of the partner.

The final outcome of the negotiations on RoOs in the FTAs entered into by ASEAN is that there are few similarities among the various RoOs adopted in the various FTAs. Even if some commonalities may be found, such as the use of an RVC or a CTC, the details of such methodologies differ.

The end result (and the current status) of the RoOs contained in the various FTAs entered into by ASEAN is several rather confusing and overlapping sets of RoOs. If compliance with a given set of RoOs is a cost for a firm, the multiplicity of RoOs also entails a multiplicity of costs.

Differences in RoOs requirements mean obstacles in using FTAs caused by the need to devise and operate an accounting system which differs in the definition of concept, application of accounts, precision, scope and control from its

CONCLUSION AND RECOMMENDATIONS

internal legal requirements. The system must provide the costing information or the CTC to satisfy the rules of the countries of destination, to check the shares of domestic and imported inputs in the unit cost of the exported goods, or the tariff heading of the non-originating inputs, in some cases identifying the country of origin of the inputs and establishing direct and indirect processing costs. This often requires data-processing techniques and customs expertise that are not commonly found in small and medium-size enterprises. It has been found that the willingness of enterprises to change or adopt accounting systems different from normal systems depends on the volume of exports eligible for preferential treatment under the FTA, the share of such exports in total sales, and the cost involved.

In the end, the expenditure incurred in operating a parallel accounting system may outweigh the benefit of preferential rates under an FTA.

Different studies and empirical evidence show that the current proliferation of different sets of RoOs is diminishing the value of the trade liberalization and trade effects expected from FTAs. Harmonization of the RoOs, although in abstract a possible solution, is not realistic. However, there are a number of reforms that could be progressively introduced in the various FTAs entered into by ASEAN to approximate certain aspects of the RoOs among FTAs, both in terms of substance of the RoOs and their administrative requirements:
(a) Conduct an overall revision of the ATIGA, imparting predictability, simplicity and order, especially to the panoply of alternative RoOs, which are confusing and overlapping.
(b) Progressively adopt a value of material calculation of RVC across all FTAs with similar numerator and denominator.

The method of calculating percentages among the different FTAs, although similar, contains differences that could be aligned toward a common standard and best practice. For instance, the calculation of the ASEAN RVC in the ATIGA is carried out using two formulae as shown in Table 6.1.

These calculations of percentages are based on the definition of the numerator and denominator. The direct method above places a minimum limit of value added as in the case of the US GSP represented by cost of local materials + direct cost of processing. The indirect method is a percentage calculation made by subtraction, as in the case of the ASEAN–South Korea FTA formula inspired by the build-down calculation of the US-Central America Free Trade Area.

Lessons learned in preferential RoOs and most recently in the net cost calculations in the NAFTA have amply demonstrated that the formulation of percentage criterion calculations as value added or "domestic content" under formula (a) are overly complex and difficult to administer. The complexities mainly arise from the detailed rules to define what are allowable and non-allowable costs that can be counted as numerator in a value added calculation. In spite of these limitations, such methodologies are still largely replicated in other FTAs to which ASEAN countries are signatories.

The elements of the calculations indicated under formula (a) and further specified in a series of definitions mentioned above in the case of the AFTA RoOs may be familiar only to accountants. As prices, costs and quantities change, recalculations are necessary to ensure compliance. While some of these tasks may form part of the normal accounting procedures required for commercial purposes,

Table 6.1 Calculation of the ASEAN RVC in the ATIGA formulae

RVC of a good specified in Product Specific Rules shall be calculated in accordance with the following formula

(a) Direct Method

$$RVC = \frac{\text{ASEAN Material Cost} + \text{Direct Labour Cost} + \text{Direct Overhead Cost} + \text{Other Cost} + \text{Profit}}{\text{FOB Price}} \times 100\%$$

(b) Indirect Method

$$RVC = \frac{\text{FOB Price} - \text{Value of Non Originating Materials, Parts or Produce}}{\text{FOB Price}} \times 100\%$$

some may not. In such cases, therefore, additional professional expertise may be required. The calculation of the numerator in a value added calculation is complex as:

(i) it entails a distinction of costs, which could be computed as local value added;
(ii) such cost is itemized to the single unit of production; as a consequence it often requires accounting, and discretion may be used in assessing unit costs; additionally, currency fluctuations in beneficiary countries may affect the value of the calculation; and
(iii) low labor costs in developing countries may result in low value added and instead of being a factor of competitiveness may turn out to be a factor penalizing producers based in ASEAN developing countries.

In the light of experience gained in the NAFTA, the US has progressively restricted the use of this kind of calculation to limited items in the automotive sector; and the EU, which initially planned to use such a calculation in its reform of the GSP RoOs, has dropped these plans.

Taking into account the lessons learned by other major players and best practices, ASEAN could adopt and propose to ASEAN dialogue partners a calculation methodology based on a value of materials calculation. This methodology eliminates most of the shortcomings of a value added calculation. The value of material calculation is based on the WTO Customs Valuation Agreement anchoring the rules to a multilateral instrument in use by WTO Members. This method of calculation is similar to the one used by the US in recent FTA agreements with Australia, Singapore, Chile,

CONCLUSION AND RECOMMENDATIONS

Central America and other countries as well as to the EU calculation currently used.

(c) Lower the thresholds of value of materials calculations from the current 40 percent to 30 percent or even less and avoid restrictive PRSOs using the change of tariff classifications criteria combined with exceptions to facilitate compliance by firms. An RVC threshold of 40 percent is too high to match the current level of fragmentation of production where firms delocalize and scatter manufacturing operations across several countries.

(d) Enhance the drafting of the legal texts of certain FTAs in terms of accuracy and precision by aligning them to existing best practices and improve the transparency and predictability of administrative aspects of RoOs.

(e) Adopt clear, transparent and predictable rules for cumulation, *de minimis* and roll-up (absorption) rules in all FTAs.

(f) Streamline and facilitate issuance and verification of COs by progressively adopting self-certification by firms. The current rules for the administration of RoOs are extremely burdensome and cumbersome. An increased use of risk assessment could contribute substantially to simplification and cost reduction. ASEAN should progressively adopt self-certification by exporters under the ATIGA and progressively adopt it in all FTAs entered into with partners.

(g) Government authorities, customs and trade supporting institutions should step up efforts to assist firms and especially SMEs to comply with rules of origin requirements. Modules and templates for value of material calculation and accounting should be developed for SMEs.

EXECUTIVE SUMMARY

The rules of origin (RoO) constitute a fundamental foundation for any preferential trade agreement (PTA). RoOs are similar to nationality and citizenship rules for natural persons in a nation-state. Qualifying persons may enjoy the benefits of citizenship, such as freedom of movement, permanent residency and the like. Similarly, RoOs determine the applicable duty rate and other treatment for goods in the PTA.

Taken in this context, the ASEAN RoOs, originating in the ASEAN Preferential Trade Agreement (APTA), developed in the ASEAN Free Trade Area (AFTA) agreement and purportedly refined in the ASEAN Trade in Goods Agreement (ATIGA), have created a relatively muddled and confused trading situation. The ASEAN RoOs are both ill-defined and ill-administered, resulting in less-than-optimal usage of the ASEAN trade preferences and stunting the growth of the ASEAN Economic Community (AEC). These deficiencies have been carried forward into ASEAN's free trade agreements (FTAs) with its main dialogue partners of Australia–New Zealand, China, India, Japan and Korea.

The poor definition of ASEAN RoOs dates back to the APTA and AFTA. The concept of regional value added as a qualifying RoO was not properly spelled out, with ASEAN customs authorities and practitioners having to fill out the details through trial and error, often to the detriment of the business sector. Continued underuse of the ASEAN trade preferences led to further tinkering with RoOs by ASEAN authorities, such as the introduction of product-specific RoOs as well as the alternative rule of change in tariff classification. Yet despite these revisions, effected in their latest form in the ATIGA, the ASEAN RoOs remain relatively ill-defined and difficult to administer.

The poor administration of ASEAN RoOs has also been a persistent problem. Despite repeated attempts to ease administrative burdens on importers and exporters, and thereby expand use of the ASEAN trade preferences, ASEAN customs authorities remain wedded to the verification and authentication of Form D certificate of origin (CO) documents rather than using modern trade facilitation approaches that would focus on the data contained in those documents instead of the documents themselves.

After surveying both the ASEAN RoOs and their administration, the authors recommend that ASEAN leaders reform both.

The RoOs in the ATIGA and ASEAN FTAs can be simplified by focusing on: (1) an overall improvement of the legal texts in terms of transparency and predictability; (2) applying a percentage criterion based on value of materials; (3) lowering the regional value content (RVC) required to qualify as ASEAN origin; and (4) clarifying the text of product specific rules of origin (PRSOs) by eliminating redundant RoOs.

The administration of ASEAN RoOs can be improved by: (1) expanding the use of self-certification; (2) moving away from document-based verification; and (3) shifting to modern post-entry audit and trade facilitation approaches.

EXECUTIVE SUMMARY

By imposing greater clarity in the RoOs and their administration, ASEAN authorities can encourage the use of the ASEAN trade preferences by all segments of the business community. Only then can all sectors participate in the AEC and enjoy its benefits.

APPENDICES

1. 1992 Agreement on the Common Effective Preferential Tariff Scheme for the ASEAN Free Trade Area (CEPT)   97
2. Rules of Origin for the CEPT (CEPT Origin)   109
3. 2009 ASEAN Trade in Goods Agreement (ATIGA)   114
4. ATIGA Annex 3, Attachment 1 Substantial Transformation Criterion for Textiles and Textile Products (Substantial transformation)   195
5. ATIGA Annex 5 Principles and Guidelines for Calculating Regional Value Content on the ATIGA (ATIGA RVC)   197
6. ATIGA Annex 6 Implementing Guidelines for Partial Cumulation under Article 30(2) on ASEAN Cumulative Rules of Origin (ATIGA Cumulation)   199
7. ATIGA Form D (Form D)   200
8. ATIGA Annex 8 Operational Certification Procedure for the Rules of Origin under Chapter 3 (ATIGA OCP)   206
9. Rules of Origin, ASEAN–Australia–New Zealand Free Trade Agreement (AANZ)   224
10. Rules of Origin, ASEAN–China Free Trade Agreement (ACFTA)   257
11. Rules of Origin, ASEAN–India Free Trade Agreement (AIFTA)   313
12. Rules of Origin, ASEAN–Japan Comprehensive Economic Partnership Agreement (AJFTA)   330
13. Rules of Origin, ASEAN–Korea Free Trade Agreement (AKFTA)   359

Appendix 1

1992 Agreement on the Common Effective Preferential Tariff Scheme for the ASEAN Free Trade Area

Adopted by the Economic Ministers at the 4th ASEAN Summit in Singapore on 28 Jan 1992

ARTICLE 1. DEFINITIONS	99
ARTICLE 2. GENERAL PROVISIONS	100
ARTICLE 3. PRODUCT COVERAGE	101
ARTICLE 4. SCHEDULE OF TARIFF REDUCTION	102
ARTICLE 5. OTHER PROVISIONS	103
A. *Quantitative Restrictions and Non-Tariff Barriers*	103
B. *Foreign Exchange Restrictions*	103
C. *Other Areas of Cooperation*	104
D. *Maintenance of Concessions*	104
ARTICLE 6. EMERGENCY MEASURES	104
ARTICLE 7. INSTITUTIONAL ARRANGEMENTS	105
ARTICLE 8. CONSULTATIONS	106
ARTICLE 9. GENERAL EXCEPTIONS	107
ARTICLE 10. FINAL PROVISIONS	107

The Governments of Brunei Darussalam, the Republic of Indonesia, Malaysia, the Republic of the Philippines, the Republic of Singapore and the Kingdom of Thailand, Member States of the Association of South, East Asian Nations (ASEAN):

MINFUL   of the Declaration of ASEAN Concord signed in Bali, Indonesia on 24 February 1976 which provides that Member States shall cooperate in the field of trade in order to promote development and growth of new production and trade;

APPENDIX 1. CEPT

RECALLING that the ASEAN Heads of Government, at their Third Summit Meeting held in Manila on 13–15 December 1987, declared that Member States shall strengthen intra-ASEAN economic cooperation to maximise the realisation of the region's potential in trade and development;

NOTING that the Agreement on ASEAN Preferential Trading Arrangements (PTA) signed in Manila on 24 February 1977 provides for the adoption of various instruments on trade liberalisation on a preferential basis;

ADHERING to the principles, concepts and ideals of the Framework Agreement on Enhancing ASEAN Economic Cooperation signed in Singapore on 28 January 1992;

CONVINCED that preferential trading arrangements among ASEAN Member States will act as a stimulus to the strengthening of national and ASEAN Economic resilience, and the development of the national economies of Member States by expanding investment and production opportunities, trade, and foreign exchange earnings;

DETERMINED to further cooperate in the economic growth of the region by accelerating the liberalisation of intra-ASEAN trade and investment with the objective of creating the ASEAN Free Trade Area using the Common Effective Preferential Tariff (CEPT) Scheme;

APPENDIX 1. CEPT

DESIRING to effect improvements on the ASEAN PTA in consonance with ASEAN's international commitments;

HAVE AGREED AS FOLLOWS:

Article 1. Definitions

For the purposes of this Agreement:

1. "CEPT" means the Common Effective Preferential Tariff, and it is an agreed effective tariff, preferential to ASEAN, to be applied to goods originating from ASEAN Member States, and which have been identified for inclusion in the CEPT Scheme in accordance with Articles 2 (5) and 3.
2. "Non-Tariff Barriers" mean measures other than tariffs which effectively prohibit or restrict import or export of products within Member States.
3. "Quantitative restrictions" mean prohibitions or restrictions on trade with other Member States, whether made effective through quotas, licences or other measures with equivalent effect, including administrative measures and requirements which restrict trade.
4. "Foreign exchange restrictions" mean measures taken by Member States in the form of restrictions and other administrative procedures in foreign exchange which have the effect of restricting trade.
5. "PTA" means ASEAN Preferential Trading Arrangements stipulated in the Agreement on ASEAN Preferential Trading Arrangements, signed in Manila on 24 February 1977, and

in the Protocol on Improvements on Extension of Tariff Preferences under the ASEAN Preferential Trading Arrangements (PTA), signed in Manila on 15 December 1987.

6. "Exclusion List" means a list containing products that are excluded from the extension of tariff preferences under the CEPT Scheme.

7. "Agricultural products" mean:
   (a) agricultural raw materials/unprocessed products covered under Chapters 1–24 of the Harmonised System (HS), and similar agricultural raw materials/unprocessed products in other related HS Headings; and
   (b) products which have undergone simple processing with minimal change in form from the original products.

Article 2. General Provisions

1. All Member States shall participate in the CEPT Scheme.
2. Identification of products to be included in the CEPT Scheme shall be on a sectoral basis, i.e., at HS 6-digit level.
3. Exclusions at the HS 8/9 digit level for specific products are permitted for those Member States, which are temporarily not ready to include such products in the CEPT Scheme. For specific products, which are sensitive to a Member State, pursuant to Article 1 (3) of the Framework Agreement on Enhancing ASEAN Economic Cooperation, a Member State may exclude products from the CEPT Scheme, subject to a waiver of any concession herein provided for such products. A review of this Agreement

APPENDIX 1. CEPT

shall be carried out in the eighth year to decide on the final Exclusion List or any amendment to this Agreement.
4. A product shall be deemed to be originating from ASEAN Member States, if at least 40% of its content originates from any Member State.
5. All manufactured products, including capital goods, processed agricultural products and those products falling outside the definition of agricultural products, as set out in this Agreement, shall be in the CEPT Scheme. These products shall automatically be subject to the schedule of tariff reduction, as set out in Article 4 of this Agreement. In respect of PTA items, the schedule of tariff reduction provided for in Article 4 of this Agreement shall be applied, taking into account the tariff rate after the application of the existing margin of preference (MOP) as at 31 December 1992.
6. All products under the PTA which are not transferred to the CEPT Scheme shall continue to enjoy the MOP existing as at 31 December 1992.
7. Member States, whose tariffs for the agreed products are reduced from 20% and below to 0%–5%, even though granted on an MFN basis, shall still enjoy concessions. Member States with tariff rates at MFN rates of 0%–5% shall be deemed to have satisfied the obligations under this Agreement and shall also enjoy the concessions.

Article 3. Product Coverage

This Agreement shall apply to all manufactured products, including capital goods, processed agricultural products, and

APPENDIX 1. CEPT

those products failing outside the definition of agricultural products as set out in this Agreement. Agricultural products shall be excluded from the CEPT Scheme.

Article 4. Schedule of Tariff Reduction

1. Member States agree to the following schedule of effective preferential tariff reductions:

    (a) The reduction from existing tariff rates to 20% shall be done within a time frame of 5 years to 8 years, from 1 January 1993, subject to a programme of reduction to be decided by each Member State, which shall be announced at the start of the programme. Member States are encouraged to adopt an annual rate of reduction, which shall be (X-20)%/5 or 8, where X equals the existing tariff rates of individual Member States.

    (b) The subsequent reduction of tariff rates from 20% or below shall be done within a time frame of 7 years. The rate of reduction shall be at a minimum of 5% quantum per reduction. A programme of reduction to be decided by each Member State shall be announced at the start of the programme.

    (c) For products with existing tariff rates of 20% or below as at 1 January 1993, Member States shall decide upon a programme of tariff reductions, and announce at the start, the schedule of tariff reductions. Two or more Member States may enter into arrangements for tariff reduction to 0%–5% on specific products at an accelerated pace to be announced at the start of the programme.

APPENDIX 1. CEPT

2. Subject to Articles 4 (1) (b) and 4 (1) (c) of this Agreement, products which reach, or are at tariff rates of 20% or below, shall automatically enjoy the concessions.
3. The above schedules of tariff reduction shall not prevent Member States from immediately reducing their tariffs to 0%–5% or following an accelerated schedule of tariff reduction.

Article 5. Other Provisions

A. Quantitative Restrictions and Non-Tariff Barriers

1. Member States shall eliminate all quantitative restrictions in respect of products under the CEPT Scheme upon enjoyment of the concessions applicable to those products.
2. Member States shall eliminate other non-tariff barriers on a gradual basis within a period of 5 years after the enjoyment of concessions applicable to those products.

B. Foreign Exchange Restrictions

Member States shall make exceptions to their foreign exchange restrictions relating to payments for the products under the CEPT Scheme, as well as repatriation of such payments without prejudice to their rights under Article XVIII of the General Agreement on Tariff and Trade (GATT) and relevant provisions of the Articles of Agreement of the International Monetary Fund (IMF).

C. Other Areas of Cooperation

Member States shall explore further measures on border and non-border areas of cooperation to supplement and complement the liberalisation of trade. These may include, among others, the harmonisation of standards, reciprocal recognition of tests and certification of products, removal of barriers to foreign investments, macroeconomic consultations, rules for fair competition, and promotion of venture capital.

D. Maintenance of Concessions

Member States shall not nullify or impair any of the concessions as agreed upon through the application of methods of customs valuation, any new charges or measures restricting trade, except in cases provided for in this Agreement.

Article 6. Emergency Measures

1. If, as a result of the implementation of this Agreement, import of a particular product eligible under the CEPT Scheme is increasing in such a manner as to cause or threaten to cause serious injury to sectors producing like or directly competitive products in the importing Member States, the importing Member States may, to the extent and for such time as may be necessary to prevent or to remedy such injury, suspend preferences provisionally and without discrimination, subject to Article 6 (3) of this Agreement. Such suspension of preferences shall be consistent with the GATT.

APPENDIX 1. CEPT

2. Without prejudice to existing international obligations, a Member State, which finds it necessary to create or intensify quantitative restrictions or other measures limiting imports with a view to forestalling the threat of or stopping a serious decline of its monetary reserves, shall endeavour to do so in a manner, which safeguards the value of the concessions agreed upon.
3. Where emergency measures are taken pursuant to this Article, immediate notice of such action shall be given to the Council referred to in Article 7 of this Agreement, and such action may be the subject of consultation as provided for in Article 8 of this Agreement.

Article 7. Institutional Arrangements

1. The ASEAN Economic Ministers (AEM) shall, for the purposes of this Agreement, establish a ministerial-level Council comprising one nominee from each Member State and the Secretary-General of the ASEAN Secretariat. The ASEAN Secretariat shall provide the support to the ministerial-level Council for supervising, coordinating and reviewing the implementation of this Agreement, and assisting the AEM in all matters relating thereto. In the performance of its functions, the ministerial-level Council shall also be supported by the Senior Economic Officials' Meeting (SEOM).
2. Member States which enter into bilateral arrangements on tariff reductions pursuant to Article 4 of this Agreement shall notify all other Member States and the ASEAN Secretariat of such arrangements.

3. The ASEAN Secretariat shall monitor and report to the SEOM on the implementation of the Agreement pursuant to the Article III (2) (8) of the Agreement on the Establishment of the ASEAN Secretariat. Member States shall cooperate with the ASEAN Secretariat in the performance of its duties.

Article 8. Consultations

1. Member States shall accord adequate opportunity for consultations regarding any representations made by other Member States with respect to any matter affecting the implementation of this Agreement. The Council referred to in Article 7 of this Agreement, may seek guidance from the AEM in respect of any matter for which it has not been possible to find a satisfactory solution during previous consultations.
2. Member States, which consider that any other Member State has not carried out its obligations under this Agreement, resulting in the nullifications or impairment of any benefit accruing to them, may, with a view to achieving satisfactory adjustment of the matter, make representations or proposal to the other Member States concerned, which shall give due consideration to the representations or proposal made to it.
3. Any differences between the Member States concerning the interpretation or application of this Agreement shall, as far as possible, be settled amicably between the parties. If such differences cannot be settled amicably, it shall be submitted to the Council referred to in Article 7 of this Agreement, and if necessary, to the AEM.

APPENDIX 1. CEPT

Article 9. General Exceptions

Nothing in this Agreement shall prevent any Member State from taking action and adopting measures, which it considers necessary for the protection of its national security, the protection of public morals, the protection of human, animal or plant life and health, and the protection of articles of artistic, historic and archaeological value.

Article 10. Final Provisions

1. The respective Governments of Member States shall undertake the appropriate measures to fulfil the agreed obligations arising from this Agreement.
2. Any amendment to this Agreement shall be made by consensus and shall become effective upon acceptance by all Member States.
3. This Agreement shall be effective upon signing.
4. This Agreement shall be deposited with the Secretary-General of the ASEAN Secretariat, who shall likewise promptly furnish a certified copy thereof to each Member State.
5. No reservation shall be made with respect to any of the provisions of this Agreement.

IN WITNESS WHEREOF, the undersigned, being duly authorised thereto by their respective Governments, have signed this Agreement on Common Effective Preferential Tariff (CEPT) Scheme for the Free Trade Area (AFTA).

APPENDIX 1. CEPT

DONE at Singapore, this 28th day of January, 1992 in a single copy in the English Language.

For the Government of Brunei Darussalam: ABDUL RAHMAN TAIB, Minister of Industry and Primary Resources

For the Government of the Republic of Indonesia: ARIFIM M SIREGAR, Minister of Trade

For the Government of Malaysia: RAFIDAH AZIZ, Minister of International Trade and Industry

For the Government of the Republic of the Philippines: PETER D GARRUCHO JR, Secretary of Trade and Industry

For the Government of the Republic of Singapore: LEE HSIEN LOONG, Deputy Prime Minister and Minister for Trade and Industry

For the Government of the Kingdom of Thailand: AMARET SILA-OM, Minister of Commerce

Appendix 2

Rules of Origin for the CEPT

In determining the origin of products eligible for the CEPT Scheme under the Agreement on the CEPT, the following Rules shall be applied:

Rule 1 Originating Products

Products under the CEPT imported into the territory of a Member State from another Member State which are consigned directly within the meaning of Rules 5 hereof, shall be eligible for preferential concessions if they conform to the origin requirements under any one of the following conditions:

(a) Products wholly produced or obtained in the exporting Member State as defined in Rule 2; or
(b) Products not wholly produced or obtained in the exporting Member State, provided that the said products are eligible under Rule 3 or Rule 4.

Within the meaning of Rule I (a), the following shall be considered as wholly produced or obtained in the exporting Member State:

Rule 2 Wholly Produced or Obtained

(a) Mineral products extracted from its soil, its water or its Scheme;

APPENDIX 2. CEPT ORIGIN

(b) Agricultural products harvested there;
(c) Animals born and raised there;
(d) Products obtained from animals referred to in paragraph (c) above;
(e) Products obtained by hunting or fishing conducted there;
(f) Products of sea fishing and other marine products taken from the sea by its vessels;
(g) Products processed and/or made on board its factory ships exclusively from products referred to in paragraph (f) above;
(h) Used articles collected here, fit only for the recovery of raw materials;
(i) Waste and scrap resulting from manufacturing operations conducted there; and
(j) Goods produced there exclusively from the products referred to in paragraph (a) to (i) above.

Rule 3 Not Wholly Produced or Obtained

(a)
   (i) A product shall be deemed to be originating from ASEAN Member States, if at least 40% of its content originates from any Member States.
   (ii) Subject to Sub-paragraph (i) above, for the purpose of implementing the provisions of Rule I (b), products worked on and processed as a result of which the total value of the materials, parts or produce originating from non-ASEAN countries or of undetermined origin used does not exceed 60% of the FOB value of the product produced or obtained and the final

APPENDIX 2. CEPT ORIGIN

process of the manufacture is performed within the territory of the exporting Member State.

(b) The value of the non-originating materials, parts or produce shall be:
  (i) The CIF value at the time of importation of the products or importation can be proven; or
  (ii) The earliest ascertained price paid for the products of undetermined origin in the territory of the Member State where the working or processing takes place.

The formula for 40% ASEAN Content is as follows:

$$\frac{\text{Value of Imported Non-ASEAN Materials, Parts or Produce} + \text{Value of Undetermined Origin Materials, Parts Produce}}{\text{FOB Price}} \times 100\% \leq 60\%$$

Rule 4 Cumulative Rule of Origin

Products which comply with origin requirements provided for in Rule 1 and which are used in a Member State as inputs for a finished product eligible for preferential treatment in another Member States shall be considered as products originating in the Member State where working or processing of the finished product has taken place provided that the aggregate ASEAN content of the final product is not less than 40%.

Rule 5 Direct Consignment

The following shall be considered as consigned directly from the exporting Member State to the importing Member State:

APPENDIX 2. CEPT ORIGIN

(a) If the products are transported passing through the territory of any other ASEAN country;
(b) If the products are transported without passing through the territory of any other non-ASEAN country;
(c) The products whose transport involves transit through one or more intermediate non-ASEAN countries with or without transhipment or temporary storage in such countries, provided that:
  (i) The transit entry is justified for geographical reason or by consideration related exclusively to transport requirements;
  (ii) The, products have not entered into trade or consumption there; and
  (iii) The products have not undergone any operation there other than unloading and reloading or any operation required to keep them in good condition.

Rule 6 Treatment of Packing

(a) Where for purposes of assessing customs duties a Member State treats products separately from their packing, it may also, in respect of its imports consigned from another Member State, determine separately the origin of such packing.
(b) Where paragraph (a) above is not applied, packing shall be considered as forming a whole with the products and no part of any packing required for their transport or storage shall be considered as having been imported from outside the ASEAN region when determining the origin of the products as a whole.

APPENDIX 2. CEPT ORIGIN

Rule 7 Certificate of Origin

A claim that products shall be accepted as eligible for preferential concession shall be supported by a Certificate of Origin issued by a government authority designated by the exporting Member State and notified to the other Member States in accordance with the Certification Procedures to be developed and approved by the Senior Economic Officials Meeting (SEOM).

Rule 8 Review

These rules may be reviewed as and when necessary upon request of a Member State and may be open to such modifications as may be agreed upon by the Council of Ministers.

Appendix 3

2009 ASEAN Trade in Goods Agreement
Adopted by the Economic Ministers at the 14th ASEAN Summit in Cha-am Thailand on 26 February 2009

CHAPTER 1. GENERAL PROVISIONS   121
    Article 1. Objective   121
    Article 2. General Definitions   121
    Article 3. Classification of Goods   124
    Article 4. Product Coverage   124
    Article 5. Most Favoured Nation Treatment   124
    Article 6. National Treatment on Internal Taxation
               and Regulation   125
    Article 7. Fees and Charges Connected with
               Importation and Exportation   125
    Article 8. General Exceptions   126
    Article 9. Security Exceptions   127
    Article 10. Measures to Safeguard the Balance
                of Payments   128
    Article 11. Notification Procedures   129
    Article 12. Publication and Administration of Trade
                Regulations   130
    Article 13. ASEAN Trade Repository   131
    Article 14. Confidentiality   131
    Article 15. Communications   132
    Article 16. Participation Enhancement of Member States   132
    Article 17. Capacity Building   132
    Article 18. Regional and Local Government and
                Non-Governmental Bodies   133
CHAPTER 2. TARIFF LIBERALISATION   133
    Article 19. Reduction or Elimination of Import Duties   133
    Article 20. Elimination of Tariff Rate Quotas   137

APPENDIX 3. ATIGA

    Article 21. Issuance of Legal Enactments   137
    Article 22. Enjoyment of Concessions   138
    Article 23. Temporary Modification or Suspension
              of Concessions   138
    Article 24. Special Treatment on Rice and Sugar   141
CHAPTER 3. RULES OF ORIGIN   141
    Article 25. Definitions   141
    Article 26. Origin Criteria   144
    Article 27. Wholly Obtained or Produced Goods   144
    Article 28. Not Wholly Obtained or Produced Goods   146
    Article 29. Calculation of Regional Value Content   148
    Article 30. Accumulation   150
    Article 31. Minimal Operations and Processes   151
    Article 32. Direct Consignment   151
    Article 33. De Minimis   152
    Article 34. Treatment of Packages and Packing Materials   153
    Article 35. Accessories, Spare Parts and Tools   153
    Article 36. Neutral Elements   154
    Article 37. Identical and Interchangeable Materials   155
    Article 38. Certificate of Origin   155
    Article 39. Sub-Committee on Rules of Origin   155
CHAPTER 4. NON-TARIFF MEASURES   157
    Article 40. Application of Non-Tariff Measures   157
    Article 41. General Elimination of Quantitative
              Restrictions   157
    Article 42. Elimination of Other Non-Tariff Barriers   158
    Article 43. Foreign Exchange Restrictions   159
    Article 44. Import Licensing Procedures   160
CHAPTER 5. TRADE FACILITATION   161
    Article 45. Work Programme on Trade Facilitation
              and its Objectives   161
    Article 46. Scope of the ASEAN Trade Facilitation
              Work Programme   161
    Article 47. Principles on Trade Facilitation   161
    Article 48. Progress Monitoring of Trade Facilitation   164
    Article 49. Establishment of the ASEAN Single Window   165
    Article 50. Implementation Arrangement   165

APPENDIX 3. ATIGA

CHAPTER 6. CUSTOMS   165
    Article 51. Objectives   165
    Article 52. Definitions   166
    Article 53. Scope   167
    Article 54. Customs Procedures and Control   168
    Article 55. Pre-arrival Documentation   168
    Article 56. Risk Management   168
    Article 57. Customs Valuation   168
    Article 58. Application of Information Technology   169
    Article 59. Authorised Economic Operators   169
    Article 60. Repayment, Drawback and Security   169
    Article 61. Post Clearance Audit   170
    Article 62. Advance Rulings   170
    Article 63. Temporary Admission   172
    Article 64. Customs Co-operation   172
    Article 65. Transparency   172
    Article 66. Enquiry Points   173
    Article 67. Consultation   173
    Article 68. Confidentiality   173
    Article 69. Review and Appeal   174
    Article 70. Implementation and Institutional Arrangements   174
CHAPTER 7. STANDARDS, TECHNICAL REGULATIONS AND CONFORMITY ASSESSMENT PROCEDURES   175
    Article 71. Objective   175
    Article 72. Terms and Definitions   175
    Article 73. General Provisions   175
    Article 74. Standards   176
    Article 75. Technical Regulations   178
    Article 76. Conformity Assessment Procedures   179
    Article 77. Post Market Surveillance   180
    Article 78. Implementation   181
CHAPTER 8. SANITARY AND PHYTOSANITARY MEASURES   183
    Article 79. Objectives   183
    Article 80. Definitions   183
    Article 81. General Provisions and Obligations   184

APPENDIX 3. ATIGA

  Article 82. Implementation and Institutional
      Arrangements   185
  Article 83. Notification under Emergency Situation 186
  Article 84. Equivalence   187
  Article 85. Co-operation   187
CHAPTER 9. TRADE REMEDY MEASURES   188
  Article 86. Safeguard Measures   188
  Article 87. Anti-dumping and Countervailing Duties 188
CHAPTER 10. INSTITUTIONAL PROVISIONS   189
  Article 88. Advisory and Consultative Mechanism 189
  Article 89. Dispute Settlement   189
  Article 90. Institutional Arrangements   190
CHAPTER 11. FINAL PROVISIONS   191
  Article 91. Relation to Other Agreements   191
  Article 92. Amended or Successor International
      Agreements   191
  Article 93. Annexes, Attachments and Future
      Instruments   191
  Article 94. Amendments   192
  Article 95. Review   192
  Article 96. Entry into Force   192
  Article 97. Reservations   193
  Article 98. Depositary   193

The Governments of Brunei Darussalam, the Kingdom of Cambodia, the Republic of Indonesia, the Lao People's Democratic Republic (Lao PDR), Malaysia, the Union of Myanmar, the Republic of the Philippines, the Republic of Singapore, the Kingdom of Thailand and the Socialist Republic of Viet Nam, Member States of the Association of Southeast Asian Nations (hereinafter collectively referred to as "Member States" or singularly as "Member State"):

RECALLING the Leaders' decision to establish the ASEAN Community, comprising three pillars, namely

APPENDIX 3. ATIGA

	the ASEAN Political-Security Community (APSC), the ASEAN Economic Community (AEC) and the ASEAN Socio-Cultural Community (ASCC), made in the Declaration of ASEAN Concord II signed on 7 October 2003 in Bali, Indonesia, and in the ASEAN Charter signed on 20 November 2007 in Singapore;
DETERMINED	to realise the goals of establishing ASEAN as a single market and production base characterised by free flow of goods, services, investment, skilled labour and freer flow of capital envisaged in the ASEAN Charter and the Declaration on the ASEAN Economic Community Blueprint signed by the Leaders on 20 November 2007 in Singapore;
RECOGNISING	the significant achievements and contribution of the existing ASEAN economic agreements and instruments in various areas in facilitating free flow of goods in the region, including the Agreement on ASEAN Preferential Trading Arrangements (1977), the Agreement on the Common Effective Preferential Tariff Scheme for the ASEAN Free Trade Area (1992), the ASEAN

APPENDIX 3. ATIGA

	Agreement on Customs (1997), the ASEAN Framework Agreement on Mutual Recognition Arrangements (1998), the e-ASEAN Framework Agreement (2000), the Protocol Governing the Implementation of the ASEAN Harmonised Tariff Nomenclature (2003), the ASEAN Framework Agreement for the Integration of Priority Sectors (2004), the Agreement to Establish and Implement the ASEAN Single Window (2005);
DESIRING	to move forward by developing a comprehensive ASEAN Trade in Goods Agreement which is built upon the commitments under the existing ASEAN economic agreements to provide a legal framework to realise free flow of goods in the region;
CONFIDENT	that a comprehensive ASEAN Trade in Goods Agreement would minimise barriers and deepen economic linkages among Member States, lower business costs, increase trade, investment and economic efficiency, create a larger market with greater opportunities and larger economies of scale for the businesses of Member States and create and maintain a competitive investment area;

APPENDIX 3. ATIGA

RECOGNISING the different stages of economic development between and among Member States and the need to address the development gaps and facilitate increasing participation of the Member States, especially Cambodia, Lao PDR, Myanmar and Viet Nam, in the AEC through the provision of flexibility and technical and development co-operation;

RECOGNISING FURTHER the provisions of the ministerial declarations of the World Trade Organization on measures in favour of least-developed countries;

ACKNOWLEDGING the important role and contribution of the business sector in enhancing trade and investment among Member States and the need to further promote and facilitate their participation through the various ASEAN business associations in the realisation of the ASEAN Economic Community; and

RECOGNISING the role of regional trade arrangements as a catalyst in accelerating regional and global trade liberalisation and trade facilitation and as building blocks in the framework of the multilateral trading system;

HAVE AGREED AS FOLLOWS:

APPENDIX 3. ATIGA

Chapter 1 General Provisions

Article 1. Objective

The objective of this Agreement is to achieve free flow of goods in ASEAN as one of the principal means to establish a single market and production base for the deeper economic integration of the region towards the realisation of the AEC by 2015.

Article 2. General Definitions

1. For the purposes of this Agreement, unless the context otherwise requires:

   (a) **ASEAN** means the Association of Southeast Asian Nations, which comprises Brunei Darussalam, the Kingdom of Cambodia, the Republic of Indonesia, Lao PDR, Malaysia, the Union of Myanmar, the Republic of the Philippines, the Republic of Singapore, the Kingdom of Thailand and the Socialist Republic of Viet Nam;
   (b) **customs authorities** means the competent authorities that are responsible under the law of a Member State for the administration of customs laws;
   (c) **customs duties** means any customs or import duty and a charge of any kind imposed in connection with the importation of a good, but does not include any:
      (i) charge equivalent to an internal tax imposed consistently with the provisions of paragraph 2 of

Article III of GATT 1994, in respect of the like domestic goods or in respect of goods from which the imported goods have been manufactured or produced in whole or in part;

    (ii) anti-dumping or countervailing duty applied consistent with the provisions of Article VI of GATT 1994, the Agreement on Implementation of Article VI of GATT 1994, and the Agreement on Subsidies and Countervailing Measures in Annex 1A to the WTO Agreement; or

    (iii) fee or any charge commensurate with the cost of services rendered.

(d) **customs laws** means such laws and regulations administered and enforced by the customs authorities of each Member State concerning the importation, exportation, transit, transhipment, and storage of goods as they relate to customs duties, charges, and other taxes, or to prohibitions, restrictions, and other similar controls with respect to the movement of controlled items across the boundary of the customs territory of each Member State;

(e) **customs value of goods** means the value of goods for the purposes of levying ad valorem customs duties on imported goods;

(f) **days** means calendar days, including weekends and holidays;

(g) **foreign exchange restrictions** means measures taken by Member States in the form of restrictions and other administrative procedures in foreign exchange which have the effect of restricting trade;

(h) **GATT 1994** means the General Agreement on Tariffs and Trade 1994, including its Notes and Supplementary Provisions, contained in Annex 1A to the WTO Agreement;
(i) **Harmonized System or HS** means the Harmonized Commodity Description and Coding System set out in the Annex to the International Convention on the Harmonized Commodity Description and Coding System, including any amendments adopted and implemented by the Member States in their respective laws;
(j) **MFN** means Most-Favoured-Nation treatment in the WTO;
(k) **non-tariff barriers** means measures other than tariffs which effectively prohibit or restrict imports or exports of goods within Member States;
(l) **originating goods** means goods that qualify as originating in a Member State in accordance with the provisions of Chapter 3;
(m) **preferential tariff treatment** means tariff concessions granted to originating goods as reflected by the tariff rates applicable under this Agreement;
(n) **quantitative restrictions** means measures intended to prohibit or restrict quantity of trade with other Member States, whether made effective through quotas, licences or other measures with equivalent effect, including administrative measures and requirements which restrict trade;
(o) **this Agreement** or **ATIGA** means the ASEAN Trade in Goods Agreement;

APPENDIX 3. ATIGA

(p) **WTO** means the World Trade Organization; and
(q) **WTO Agreement** means the Marrakesh Agreement Establishing the World Trade Organization, done on 15 April 1994 and the other agreements negotiated thereunder.

2. In this Agreement, all words in the singular shall include the plural and all words in the plural shall include the singular, unless otherwise indicated in the context.

Article 3. Classification of Goods

For the purposes of this Agreement, the classification of goods in trade between and among Member States shall be in accordance with the ASEAN Harmonised Tariff Nomenclature (AHTN) as set out in the Protocol Governing the Implementation of the ASEAN Harmonised Tariff Nomenclature signed on 7 August 2003 and any amendments thereto.

Article 4. Product Coverage

This Agreement shall apply to all products under the ASEAN Harmonised Tariff Nomenclature (AHTN).

Article 5. Most Favoured Nation Treatment

With respect to import duties, after this Agreement enters into force, if a Member State enters into any agreement with a non-Member State where commitments are more favourable than that accorded under this Agreement, the other Member States have the right to request for negotiations with that Member State to request for the incorporation herein of treatment no less favourable than that provided under the aforesaid agreement. The decision to extend such tariff preference will be on a unilateral basis. The extension of such tariff preference shall be accorded to all Member States.

Article 6. National Treatment on Internal Taxation and Regulation

Each Member State shall accord national treatment to the goods of the other Member States in accordance with Article III of GATT 1994. To this end, Article III of GATT 1994 is incorporated into and shall form part of this Agreement, *mutatis mutandis*.

Article 7. Fees and Charges Connected with Importation and Exportation

1. Each Member State shall ensure, in accordance with Article VIII.1 of GATT 1994, that all fees and charges of whatever character (other than import or export duties, charges equivalent to an internal tax or other internal charge applied consistently with Article III.2 of GATT 1994, and anti-dumping and countervailing duties) imposed on or in connection with import or export are limited in amount to the approximate cost of services rendered and do not represent an indirect protection to domestic goods or a taxation on imports or exports for fiscal purposes.

2. Each Member State shall promptly publish details of the fees and charges that it imposes in connection with importation or exportation, and shall make such information available on the internet.

Article 8. General Exceptions

Subject to the requirement that such measures are not applied in a manner which would constitute a means of arbitrary or unjustifiable discrimination among Member States where the same conditions prevail, or a disguised restriction on international trade, nothing in this Agreement shall be construed to prevent the adoption or enforcement by a Member State of measures:

(a) necessary to protect public morals;
(b) necessary to protect human, animal or plant life or health;
(c) relating to the importations or exportations of gold or silver;
(d) necessary to secure compliance with laws or regulations which are not inconsistent with the provisions of this Agreement, including those relating to customs enforcement, the enforcement of monopolies operated under paragraph 4 of Article II and Article XVII of GATT 1994, the protection of patents, trademarks and copyrights, and the prevention of deceptive practices;
(e) relating to the products of prison labour;
(f) imposed for the protection of national treasures of artistic, historic or archaeological value;
(g) relating to the conservation of exhaustible natural resources if such measures are made effective in conjunction with restrictions on domestic production or consumption;

(h) undertaken in pursuance of the obligations under any intergovernmental commodity agreement which conforms to criteria submitted to the WTO and not disapproved by it or which is itself so submitted and not so disapproved;
(i) involving restrictions on exports of domestic materials necessary to ensure essential quantities of such materials to a domestic processing industry during periods when the domestic price of such materials is held below the world price as part of a governmental stabilisation plan, provided that such restrictions shall not operate to increase the exports of or the protection afforded to such domestic industry, and shall not depart from the provisions of this Agreement relating to nondiscrimination; and
(j) essential to the acquisition or distribution of products in general or local short supply, provided that any such measures shall be consistent with the principle that all Member States are entitled to an equitable share of the international supply of such products, and that any such measures, which are inconsistent with the other provisions of this Agreement shall be discontinued as soon as the conditions giving rise to them have ceased to exist.

Article 9. Security Exceptions

Nothing in this Agreement shall be construed:

(a) to require any Member State to furnish any information, the disclosure of which it considers contrary to its essential security interests; or

(b) to prevent any Member State from taking any action which it considers necessary for the protection of its essential security interests:
  (i) relating to fissionable materials or the materials from which they are derived;
  (ii) relating to the traffic in arms, ammunition and implements of war and to such traffic in other goods and materials as is carried on directly or indirectly for the purpose of supplying a military establishment;
  (iii) taken so as to protect critical public infrastructure, including communications, power and water infrastructures, from deliberate attempts intended to disable or degrade such infrastructure;
  (iv) taken in time of domestic emergency, or war or other emergency in international relations; or
(c) to prevent any Member State from taking any action in pursuance of its obligations under the United Nations Charter for the maintenance of international peace and security.

Article 10. Measures to Safeguard the Balance of Payments

Nothing in this Agreement shall be construed to prevent a Member State from taking any measure for balance-of-payments purposes. A Member State taking such measure shall do so in accordance with the conditions established under Article XII of GATT 1994 and the Understanding on Balance-of-Payments Provisions of the General Agreement on Tariffs and Trade 1994 in Annex 1A to the WTO Agreement.

APPENDIX 3. ATIGA

Article 11. Notification Procedures

1. Unless otherwise provided in this Agreement, Member States shall notify any action or measure that they intend to take:

    (a) which may nullify or impair any benefit to other Member States, directly or indirectly under this Agreement; or
    (b) when the action or measure may impede the attainment of any objective of this Agreement.

2. Without affecting the generality of the obligations of Member States under paragraph 1 of this Article, the notification procedures shall apply, but need not be limited, to changes in the measures as listed in Annex 1 and amendments thereto.

3. A Member State shall make a notification to Senior Economic Officials Meeting (SEOM) and the ASEAN Secretariat before effecting such action or measure referred to in paragraph 1 of this Article. Unless otherwise provided in this Agreement, notification shall be made at least sixty (60) days before such an action or measure is to take effect. A Member State proposing to apply an action or measure shall provide adequate opportunity for prior discussion with those Member States having an interest in the action or measure concerned.

4. The notification of the intended action or measure submitted by a Member State shall include:

    (a) a description of the action or measure to be taken;
    (b) the reasons for undertaking the action or measure; and
    (c) the intended date of implementation and the duration of the action or measure.

5. The contents of the notification and all information relating to it shall be treated with confidentiality.
6. The ASEAN Secretariat shall act as the central registry of notifications, including written comments and results of discussions. The Member State concerned shall furnish the ASEAN Secretariat with a copy of the comments received. The ASEAN Secretariat shall draw the attention of individual Member States to notification requirements, such as those stipulated in paragraph 4 of this Article, which remain incomplete. The ASEAN Secretariat shall make available information regarding individual notifications on request to any Member State.
7. The Member State concerned shall, without discrimination, allow adequate opportunities for other Member States to present their comments in writing and discuss these comments upon request. Discussions entered into by the Member State concerned with other Member States shall be for the purpose of seeking further clarification about the action or measure. The Member State may give due consideration to these written comments and the discussion in the implementation of the action or measure.
8. Other Member States shall present their comments within fifteen (15) days of the notification. Failure of a Member State to provide comments within the stipulated time shall not affect its right to seek recourse under Article 88.

Article 12. Publication and Administration of Trade Regulations

1. Article X of GATT 1994 shall be incorporated into and form an integral part of this Agreement, *mutatis mutandis*.

2. To the extent possible, each Member State shall make laws, regulations, decisions and rulings of the kind referred to in Article X of GATT 1994 available on the internet.

Article 13. ASEAN Trade Repository

1. An ASEAN Trade Repository containing trade and customs laws and procedures of all Member States shall be established and made accessible to the public through the internet.
2. The ASEAN Trade Repository shall contain trade related information such as (i) tariff nomenclature; (ii) MFN tariffs, preferential tariffs offered under this Agreement and other Agreements of ASEAN with its Dialogue Partners; (iii) Rules of Origin; (iv) non-tariff measures; (v) national trade and customs laws and rules; (vi) procedures and documentary requirements; (vii) administrative rulings; (viii) best practices in trade facilitation applied by each Member State; and (ix) list of authorised traders of Member States.
3. The ASEAN Secretariat shall maintain and update the ASEAN Trade Repository based on the notifications submitted by Member States as set out in Article 11.

Article 14. Confidentiality

1. Nothing in this Agreement shall require a Member State to provide confidential information, the disclosure of which would impede law enforcement of the Member State, or otherwise be contrary to the public interest, or which would prejudice legitimate commercial interests of any particular enterprise, public or private.

2. Nothing in this Agreement shall be construed to require a Member State to provide information relating to the affairs and accounts of customers of financial institutions.
3. Each Member State shall, in accordance with its laws and regulations, maintain the confidentiality of information provided as confidential by another Member State pursuant to this Agreement.
4. Notwithstanding the above, paragraphs 1, 2 and 3 of this Article shall not apply to Chapter 6.

Article 15. Communications

All official communications and documentation exchanged among the Member States relating to the implementation of this Agreement shall be in writing and in the English language.

Article 16. Participation Enhancement of Member States

Enhancing participation of Member States shall be facilitated through a negotiated pre-agreed flexibility on provisions under this Agreement. Such pre-agreed flexibility shall be captured in the respective provisions hereunder.

Article 17. Capacity Building

Capacity building shall be provided through effective implementation of programmes to strengthen individual Member States' domestic capacity, efficiency and competitiveness, such as the Work Programme under the Initiative for ASEAN Integration (IAI) and other capacity building initiatives.

Article 18. Regional and Local Government and Non-Governmental Bodies

1. Each Member State shall take such reasonable measures as may be available to it to ensure observance of provisions of this Agreement by the regional and local government and authorities within its territories.
2. In fulfilling its obligations and commitments under this Agreement, each Member State shall endeavour to ensure their observance by non-governmental bodies in the exercise of powers delegated by central, regional or local governments or authorities within its territory.

Chapter 2 Tariff Liberalisation

Article 19. Reduction or Elimination of Import Duties

1. Except as otherwise provided in this Agreement, Member States shall eliminate import duties on all products traded between the Member States by 2010 for ASEAN-6[1] and by 2015, with flexibility to 2018, for CLMV[2].

---

[1] "ASEAN-6" refers to Brunei Darussalam, Indonesia, Malaysia, the Philippines, Singapore and Thailand.
[2] "CLMV" refers to Cambodia, Lao PDR, Myanmar and Viet Nam.

APPENDIX 3. ATIGA

2. Each Member State shall reduce and/or eliminate import duties on originating goods of the other Member States in accordance with the following modalities:

(a) Import duties on the products listed in Schedule A of each Member State's tariff liberalisation schedule shall be eliminated by 2010 for ASEAN-6 and 2015 for CLMV, in accordance with the schedule set out therein. Schedule A of each Member State shall ensure the following conditions are met:

(i) For ASEAN-6, by 1 January 2009:
- Import duties of at least eighty percent (80%) tariff lines are eliminated;
- Import duties on all Information and Communications Technology (ICT) products, as defined in the e-ASEAN Framework Agreement, are eliminated;
- Import duties on all Priority Integration Sectors (PIS) products are at zero percent (0%), except those listed in the accompanying negative lists to the Protocols of the ASEAN Framework Agreement for the Integration of Priority Sectors and any amendments thereto; and
- Import duties on all products are equal to or less than five percent (5%);

(ii) For Lao PDR, Myanmar and Viet Nam, import duties on all products are equal to or less than five percent (5%) by 1 January 2009;

(iii) For Cambodia, import duties of at least eighty percent (80%) tariff lines are equal to or less than five percent (5%) by 1 January 2009; and

APPENDIX 3. ATIGA

(iv) Import duties on some products of CLMV, not exceeding seven percent (7%) of tariff lines, shall be eliminated by 2018. The list of the products and schedule of import duties reduction of these products shall be identified by CLMV no later than 1 January 2014;

(b) Import duties on ICT products listed in Schedule B of each CLMV Member State shall be eliminated in three (3) tranches by 2008, 2009 and 2010 in accordance with the schedule set out therein;

(c) Import duties on PIS products listed in Schedule C of each CLMV Member State shall be eliminated by 2012 in accordance with the schedule set out therein;

(d) Import duties on unprocessed agricultural products listed in Schedule D of each Member State on its own accord shall be reduced or eliminated to zero to five percent (0–5%) by 2010 for ASEAN-6; 2013 for Viet Nam; 2015 for Lao PDR and Myanmar; and 2017 for Cambodia, in accordance with the schedule set out therein. Notwithstanding this, import duties on sugar products of Viet Nam shall be reduced to zero to five percent (0–5%) by 2010;

(e) Unprocessed agricultural products placed in Schedule E of each Member State on its own accord shall have their respective applied MFN import duties reduced in accordance with the schedule set out therein;

(f) The products listed in Schedule F of Thailand and Viet Nam, respectively, shall have their out-quota tariff rates reduced in accordance with the tariff reduction schedules corresponding to their respective product classification;

APPENDIX 3. ATIGA

   (g) Import duties on petroleum products listed in Schedule G of Cambodia and Viet Nam, respectively, shall be reduced in accordance with the schedule as mutually agreed by all Member States and set out therein;
   (h) The products placed in Schedule H of each Member State shall not be subject to import duties reduction or elimination for the reasons as provided in Article 8;
   (i) Reduction and elimination of import duties shall be implemented on 1 January of each year; and
   (j) The base rates from which import duties are to be reduced or eliminated shall be the Common Effective Preferential Tariffs (CEPT) rates at the time of entry into force of this Agreement.

3. Except as otherwise provided in this Agreement, no Member State shall nullify or impair any tariff concessions applied in accordance with the tariff schedules in Annex 2 referred to in paragraph 5 of this Article.
4. Except as otherwise provided in this Agreement, no Member State may increase an existing duty specified in the schedules made pursuant to the provisions of paragraph 2 of this Article on imports of an originating good.
5. Except as provided in paragraph 2(a)(iv) of this Article, the detailed tariff schedules to implement the modalities of reduction and/or elimination of import duties set out in paragraph 2 of this Article shall be finalised before the entry into force of this Agreement for ASEAN-6 and six (6) months after the entry into force of this Agreement for CLMV, and form an integral part of this Agreement as Annex 2.

APPENDIX 3. ATIGA

Article 20. Elimination of Tariff Rate Quotas

1. Unless otherwise provided in this Agreement, each Member State undertakes not to introduce Tariff Rate Quotas (TRQs) on the importation of any goods originating in other Member States or on the exportation of any goods destined for the territory of the other Member States.
2. Viet Nam and Thailand shall eliminate the existing TRQs as follows:

    (a) Thailand shall eliminate in three (3) tranches by 1 January 2008, 2009 and 2010;
    (b) Viet Nam shall eliminate in three (3) tranches by 1 January 2013, 2014 and 2015, with flexibility up to 2018.

Article 21. Issuance of Legal Enactments

1.

    (a) Each Member State shall, no later than ninety (90) days for ASEAN-6 and six (6) months for CLMV after the entry into force of this Agreement, issue a legal enactment in accordance with its laws and regulations to give effect to the implementation of the tariff liberalisation schedules committed under Article 19.
    (b) The legal enactments issued pursuant to paragraph 1 (a) of this Article shall have retroactive implementation with effect from 1 January of the year of the entry into force of this Agreement.
    (c) In the case where a single legal enactment could not be issued, the legal enactments to give effect to the implementation of tariff reduction or elimination of each

year shall be issued at least three (3) months before the date of its effective implementation.

2. Member States may decide to conduct reviews of the products in **Schedules D** and **E** with a view to improving the market access for these products. If a product subject to the review is agreed to be phased out of the said Schedules, it will be placed in **Schedule A** of the respective Member State(s) and be subjected to the import duty elimination of that Schedule.

Article 22. Enjoyment of Concessions

1. Products on which tariffs of the exporting Member State have reached or are at the rate of twenty percent (20%) or below, and satisfy the requirements on rules of origin as set out in Chapter 3 shall automatically enjoy the concessions offered by importing Member States as stated in accordance with the provisions of Article 19.
2. Products listed in **Schedule H** shall not be entitled for tariff concessions offered under this Agreement.

Article 23. Temporary Modification or Suspension of Concessions

1. In exceptional circumstances other than those covered under Article 10, Article 24 and Article 86 where a Member State faces unforeseen difficulties in implementing its tariff commitments, that Member State may temporarily modify or suspend a concession contained in its Schedules under Article 19.

APPENDIX 3. ATIGA

2. A Member State which seeks to invoke the provision of paragraph 1 of this Article (hereinafter referred to as the "applicant Member State"), shall notify in writing of such temporary modification or suspension of concessions to the ASEAN Free Trade Area (AFTA) Council at least one hundred and eighty (180) days prior to the date when the temporary modification or suspension of concessions is to take effect.

3. Member States who are interested in engaging in consultations or negotiations with the applicant Member State, pursuant to paragraph 4 of this Article, shall notify all ASEAN Member States of this interest within ninety (90) days following the applicant Member State's notification of the temporary modification or suspension of concessions.

4. After making the notification pursuant to paragraph 2 of this Article, the applicant Member State shall engage in consultations or negotiations with the Member States who have made notification pursuant to paragraph 3 of this Article. In negotiations with Member States with substantial supplying interest[3], the applicant Member State shall maintain a level of reciprocal and mutually advantageous concessions no less favourable to the trade of all other Member States of substantial supplying interest than that provided in this Agreement prior to such negotiations,

---

[3] A Member State shall be deemed to have "substantial supplying interest" if it has, or because of the tariff concessions, it is to be reasonably expected to have, a significant share of at least twenty percent (20%) of the total import from ASEAN of such products during the past three (3) years in average in the market of the applicant Member State.

which may include compensatory adjustments with respect to other goods. Compensatory adjustment measures in form of tariffs shall be extended to all Member States on a non-discriminatory basis.

5. The AFTA Council shall be notified of the outcome of the consultations or negotiations pursuant to paragraphs 3 and 4 of this Article at least forty-five (45) days before the applicant Member State intends to effect the temporary modification or suspension of concessions. The notification shall include the applicant Member State's justifications for needing to adopt such measures and shall provide the Member State's intended schedule pertaining to the modification or suspension of concessions and the time period for which the Member State intends to apply the measures.

6. In the event that no agreement is reached after the consultations or negotiations pursuant to paragraphs 3 and 4 of this Article, the notification to the AFTA Council shall also include the request for the AFTA Council's recommendation.

7. The AFTA Council shall issue its approval or recommendation within thirty (30) days upon receipt of the notification pursuant to paragraph 5 of this Article.

8. In the event that the circumstances giving rise to the request for the temporary modification or suspension of concessions cease to exist, the applicant Member State shall immediately restore the tariff concessions and notify the AFTA Council accordingly. Upon restoration of tariff concessions or termination of the suspension, the applicant Member State shall apply the rate which it would have

applied according to the scheduled commitments as if the delay or suspension had not occurred.

9. In the event that there is no approval or recommendation by the AFTA Council pursuant to paragraph 7 of this Article, and the applicant Member State nevertheless proceeds with the temporary modification or suspension of the concession, Member States with substantial supplying interest shall be free to take action after thirty (30) days, but not later than ninety (90) days after the applicant Member State effects its modification or suspension of concessions, to modify or suspend substantially equivalent concessions from the applicant Member State. The concerned Member States shall immediately notify the AFTA Council of such actions.

Article 24. Special Treatment on Rice and Sugar

The Protocol to Provide Special Consideration for Rice and Sugar signed on 23 August 2007 shall form an integral part of this Agreement.

Chapter 3 Rules of Origin

Article 25. Definitions

For the purposes of this Chapter:

(a) **aquaculture** means the farming of aquatic organisms including fish, molluscs, crustaceans, other aquatic

APPENDIX 3. ATIGA

invertebrates and aquatic plants, from feedstock such as eggs, fry, fingerlings and larvae, by intervention in the rearing or growth processes to enhance production such as regular stocking, feeding, or protection from predators;

(b) **Costs, Insurance and Freight (CIF)** means the value of the goods imported, and includes the costs of freight and insurance up to the port or place of entry into the country of importation. The valuation shall be made in accordance with Article VII of GATT 1994 and the Agreement on the Implementation of Article VII of GATT 1994 as contained in Annex 1A to the WTO Agreement;

(c) **FOB** means the free-on-board value of the goods, inclusive of the costs of transport to the port or site of final shipment abroad. The valuation shall be made in accordance with Article VII of GATT 1994 and the Agreement on the Implementation of Article VII of GATT 1994 as contained in Annex 1A to the WTO Agreement;

(d) **generally accepted accounting principles (GAAP)** means the recognised consensus or substantial authoritative support in the territory of a Member State, with respect to the recording of revenues, expenses, costs, assets and liabilities; the disclosure of information; and the preparation of financial statements. These standards may encompass broad guidelines of general application as well as detailed standards, practices and procedures;

(e) **goods** shall include materials and/or products, which can be wholly obtained or produced, even if they are intended for later use as materials in another production process.

For the purposes of this Chapter, the terms "goods" and "products" can be used interchangeably;

(f) **identical and interchangeable materials** means materials being of the same kind and commercial quality, possessing the same technical and physical characteristics, and which after being incorporated into the finished product cannot be distinguished from one another for origin purposes by virtue of any markings, etc.;

(g) **materials** means any matter or substance used or consumed in the production of goods or physically incorporated into another good or are subject to a process in the production of another good;

(h) **originating goods** or **originating material** means goods or material that qualifies as originating in accordance with the provisions of this Chapter;

(i) **packing materials and containers for transportation** means the goods used to protect a good during its transportation, different from those containers or materials used for its retail sale;

(j) **production** means methods of obtaining goods, including growing, mining, harvesting, raising, breeding, extracting, gathering, collecting, capturing, fishing, trapping, hunting, manufacturing, producing, processing or assembling goods; and

(k) **product specific rules** means rules that specify that the materials have undergone a change in tariff classification or a specific manufacturing or processing operation, or satisfy a Regional Value Content criterion or a combination of any of these criteria.

Article 26. Origin Criteria

For the purposes of this Agreement, a good imported into the territory of a Member State from another Member State shall be treated as an originating good if it conforms to the origin requirements under any one of the following conditions:

(a) a good which is wholly obtained or produced in the exporting Member State as set out and defined in Article 27; or
(b) a good not wholly obtained or produced in the exporting Member State, provided that the said goods are eligible under Article 28 or Article 30.

Article 27. Wholly Obtained or Produced Goods

Within the meaning of Article 26(a), the following shall be considered as wholly obtained or produced in the exporting Member State:

(a) Plant and plant products, including fruit, flowers, vegetables, trees, seaweed, fungi and live plants, grown and harvested, picked or gathered in the exporting Member State;
(b) Live animals, including mammals, birds, fish, crustaceans, molluscs, reptiles, bacteria and viruses, born and raised in the exporting Member State;
(c) Goods obtained from live animals in the exporting Member State;

(d) Goods obtained from hunting, trapping, fishing, farming, aquaculture, gathering or capturing conducted in the exporting Member State;

(e) Minerals and other naturally occurring substances, not included in paragraphs (a) to (d) of this Article, extracted or taken from its soil, waters, seabed or beneath its seabed;

(f) Products of sea-fishing taken by vessels registered with a Member State and entitled to fly its flag and other products[4] taken from the waters, seabed or beneath the seabed outside the territorial waters[5] of that Member State, provided that that Member State has the rights to exploit such waters, seabed and beneath the seabed in accordance with international law[6];

(g) Products of sea-fishing and other marine products taken from the high seas by vessels registered with a Member State and entitled to fly the flag of that Member State;

(h) Products processed and/or made on board factory ships registered with a Member State and entitled to fly the flag

---

[4] "Other products" refers to minerals and other naturally occurring substances extracted from the waters, seabed or beneath the seabed outside the territorial waters.

[5] For products of sea-fishing obtained from outside the territorial waters (e.g. Exclusive Economic Zone), originating status would be conferred to that Member State with whom the vessels used to obtain such products are registered with and whose flag is flown in the said vessel, and provided that that Member State has the rights to exploit it under international law.

[6] In accordance with international law, registration of vessels could only be made in one Member State.

of that Member State, exclusively from products referred to in paragraph (g) of this Article;
(i) Articles collected there which can no longer perform their original purpose nor are capable of being restored or repaired and are fit only for disposal or recovery of parts of raw materials, or for recycling purposes;
(j) Waste and scrap derived from:
   (i) production in the exporting Member State; or
   (ii) used goods collected in the exporting Member State, provided that such goods are fit only for the recovery of raw materials; and
(k) Goods obtained or produced in the exporting Member State from products referred to in paragraphs (a) to (j) of this Article.

Article 28. Not Wholly Obtained or Produced Goods

1.

(a) For the purposes of Article 26(b), goods shall be deemed to be originating in the Member State where working or processing of the goods has taken place:
   (i) if the goods have a regional value content (hereinafter referred to as "ASEAN Value Content" or the "Regional Value Content (RVC)") of not less than forty percent (40%) calculated using the formula set out in Article 29; or
   (ii) if all non-originating materials used in the production of the goods have undergone a change in tariff

APPENDIX 3. ATIGA

classification (hereinafter referred to as "CTC") at four-digit level (i.e. a change in tariff heading) of the Harmonized System.
(b) Each Member State shall permit the exporter of the good to decide whether to use paragraph 1(a)(i) or 1(a)(ii) of this Article when determining whether the goods qualify as originating goods of the Member State.

2.

(a) Notwithstanding paragraph 1 of this Article, goods listed in Annex 3 shall qualify as originating goods if the goods satisfy the product specific rules set out therein.
(b) Where a product specific rule provides a choice of rules from a RVC-based rule of origin, a CTC-based rule of origin, a specific manufacturing or processing operation, or a combination of any of these, each Member State shall permit the exporter of the goods to decide which rule to use in determining whether the goods qualify as originating goods of the Member State.
(c) Where product specific rules specify a certain RVC, it is required that the RVC of a good is calculated using the formula set out in Article 29.
(d) Where product specific rules requiring that the materials used have undergone CTC or a specific manufacturing or processing operation, the rules shall apply only to non-originating materials.

3. Notwithstanding paragraphs 1 and 2 of this Article, a good which is covered by Attachment A or B of the *Ministerial Declaration on Trade in Information Technology Products*

adopted in the Ministerial Conference of the WTO on 13 December 1996, set out as Annex 4, shall be deemed to be originating in a Member State if it is assembled from materials covered under the same Annex.

Article 29. Calculation of Regional Value Content

1. For the purposes of Article 28, the formula for calculating ASEAN Value Content or RVC is as follows:

   (a) Direct Method

$$RVC = \frac{\text{ASEAN Material Cost} + \text{Direct Labour Cost} + \text{Direct overhead Cost} + \text{Other Cost} + \text{Profit}}{\text{FOB Price}} \times 100\%$$

or

   (b) Indirect Method

$$RVC = \frac{\text{FOB Price} - \text{Value of Non-originating Materials, Parts of Goods}}{\text{FOB Price}} \times 100\%$$

2. For the purposes of calculating the RVC provided in paragraph 1 of this Article:

   (a) **ASEAN Material Cost** is the CIF value of originating materials, parts or goods that are acquired or self-produced by the producer in the production of the good;

   (b) **Value of Non-Originating Materials, Parts or Goods** shall be:

   (i) The CIF value at the time of importation of the goods or importation can be proven; or

   (ii) The earliest ascertained price paid for the goods of undetermined origin in the territory of the Member State where the working or processing takes place;

(c) **Direct labour cost** shall include wages, remuneration and other employee benefits associated with the manufacturing process;

(d) **The calculation of direct overhead cost** shall include, but is not limited to, real property items associated with the production process (insurance, factory rent and leasing, depreciation on buildings, repair and maintenance, taxes, interests on mortgage); leasing of and interest payments for plant and equipment; factory security; insurance (plant, equipment and materials used in the manufacture of the goods); utilities (energy, electricity, water and other utilities directly attributable to the production of the goods); research, development, design and engineering; dies, moulds, tooling and the depreciation, maintenance and repair of plant and equipment; royalties or licences (in connection with patented machines or processes used in the manufacture of the goods or the right to manufacture the goods); inspection and testing of materials and the goods; storage and handling in the factory; disposal of recyclable wastes; and cost elements in computing the value of raw materials, i.e. port and clearance charges and import duties paid for dutiable component; and

(e) **FOB price** means the free-on-board value of the goods as defined in Article 25. FOB price shall be determined by adding the value of materials, production cost, profit and other costs.

3. Member States shall determine and adhere to only one (1) method of calculating the RVC. Member States shall be

given the flexibility to change their calculation method provided that such change is notified to the AFTA Council at least six (6) months prior to the adoption of the new method. Any verification to the ASEAN Value Content calculation by the importing Member State shall be done on the basis of the method used by the exporting Member State.

4. In determining the ASEAN Value Content, Member States shall closely adhere to the guidelines for costing methodologies set out in Annex 5.
5. Locally-procured materials produced by established licensed manufacturers, in compliance with domestic regulations, shall be deemed to have fulfilled the origin requirement of this Agreement; locally-procured materials from other sources shall be subjected to the origin verification pursuant to Article 57 for the purpose of origin determination.
6. The value of goods under this Chapter shall be determined in accordance with the provisions of Article 57.

Article 30. Accumulation

1. Unless otherwise provided in this Agreement, goods originating in a Member State, which are used in another Member State as materials for finished goods eligible for preferential tariff treatment, shall be considered to be originating in the latter Member State where working or processing of the finished goods has taken place.
2. If the RVC of the material is less than forty percent (40%), the qualifying ASEAN Value Content to be cumulated

using the RVC criterion shall be in direct proportion to the actual domestic content provided that it is equal to or more than twenty percent (20%). The Implementing Guidelines are set out in Annex 6.

Article 31. Minimal Operations and Processes

1. Operations or processes undertaken, by themselves or in combination with each other for the purposes listed below, are considered to be minimal and shall not be taken into account in determining whether a good has been originating in one Member State:

    (a) ensuring preservation of goods in good condition for the purposes of transport or storage;
    (b) facilitating shipment or transportation; and
    (c) packaging or presenting goods for sale.

2. A good originating in the territory of a Member State shall retain its initial originating status, when exported from another Member State, where operations undertaken have not gone beyond those referred to in paragraph 1 of this Article.

Article 32. Direct Consignment

1. Preferential tariff treatment shall be applied to goods satisfying the requirements of this Chapter and which are consigned directly between the territories of the exporting Member State and the importing Member State.
2. The following shall be considered as consigned directly from the exporting Member State to the importing Member State:

(a) goods transported from an exporting Member State to the importing Member State; or
(b) goods transported through one or more Member States, other than the exporting Member State and the importing Member State, or through a non-Member State, provided that:
   (i) the transit entry is justified for geographical reason or by consideration related exclusively to transport requirements;
   (ii) the goods have not entered into trade or consumption there; and
   (iii) the goods have not undergone any operation there other than unloading and reloading or any other operation to preserve them in good condition.

Article 33. De Minimis

1. A good that does not undergo a change in tariff classification shall be considered as originating if the value of all non-originating materials used in its production that do not undergo the required change in tariff classification does not exceed ten percent (10%) of the FOB value of the good and the good meets all other applicable criteria set forth in this Agreement for qualifying as an originating good.
2. The value of non-originating materials referred to in paragraph 1 of this Article shall, however, be included in the value of non-originating materials for any applicable RVC requirement for the good.

Article 34. Treatment of Packages and Packing Materials

1. Packaging and Packing Materials for retail sale:

   (a) If a good is subject to the RVC-based rule of origin, the value of the packaging and packing materials for retail sale shall be taken into account in its origin assessment, where the packaging and packing materials for retail sale are considered to be forming a whole with the good.

   (b) Where paragraph 1(a) of this Article is not applicable, the packaging and packing materials for retail sale, when classified together with the packaged good shall not be taken into account in considering whether all non-originating materials used in the manufacture of a product fulfils the criterion corresponding to a change of tariff classification of the said good.

2. The containers and packing materials exclusively used for the transport of a good shall not be taken into account for determining the origin of the said good.

Article 35. Accessories, Spare Parts and Tools

1. If a good is subject to the requirements of CTC or specific manufacturing or processing operation, the origin of accessories, spare parts, tools and instructional or other information materials presented with the good shall not be taken into account in determining whether the good qualifies as an originating good, provided that:

(a) the accessories, spare parts, tools and instructional or other information materials are not invoiced separately from the good; and
(b) the quantities and value of the accessories, spare parts, tools and instructional or other information materials are customary for the good.

2. If a good is subject to the RVC-based rule of origin, the value of the accessories, spare parts, tools and instructional or other information materials shall be taken into account as the value of the originating or non-originating materials, as the case may be, in calculating the RVC of the originating good.

Article 36. Neutral Elements

In order to determine whether a good originates, it shall not be necessary to determine the origin of the following which might be used in its production and not incorporated into the good:

(a) fuel and energy;
(b) tools, dies and moulds;
(c) spare parts and materials used in the maintenance of equipment and buildings;
(d) lubricants, greases, compounding materials and other materials used in production or used to operate equipment and buildings;
(e) gloves, glasses, footwear, clothing, safety equipment and supplies;
(f) equipment, devices and supplies used for testing or inspecting the good;

(g) catalyst and solvent; and
(h) any other goods that are not incorporated into the good but of which use in the production of the good can reasonably be demonstrated to be a part of that production.

Article 37. Identical and Interchangeable Materials

1. The determination of whether identical and interchangeable materials are originating materials shall be made either by physical segregation of each of the materials or by the use of generally accepted accounting principles of stock control applicable, or inventory management practice, in the exporting Member States.
2. Once a decision has been taken on the inventory management method, that method shall be used throughout the fiscal year.

Article 38. Certificate of Origin

A claim that a good shall be accepted as eligible for preferential tariff treatment shall be supported by a Certificate of Origin (Form D), as set out in Annex 7 issued by a Government authority designated by the exporting Member State and notified to the other Member States in accordance with the Operational Certification Procedures, as set out in Annex 8.

Article 39. Sub-Committee on Rules of Origin

1. For the purposes of the effective and uniform implementation of this Chapter, a Sub-Committee on Rules of Origin shall be established pursuant to Article 90.

2. The functions of the Sub-Committee on Rules of Origin shall include:

(a) monitoring of the implementation and operation of this Chapter;

(b) reviewing, as and when necessary, this Chapter to provide appropriate recommendations with the view to enhancing this Chapter to make it responsive to the dynamic changes in the regional and global production processes so as to facilitate trade and investment among Member States, promote a regional production network, encourage the development of Small and Medium Enterprises (SMEs) and narrowing the development gaps;

(c) reviewing, as and when necessary, the operational procedures of this Chapter with the view to simplifying the procedures and making them transparent, predictable and standardised, taking into account the best practices of other regional and international trade agreements;

(d) considering any other matter as Member States may agree related to this Chapter; and

(e) carrying out other functions as may be delegated by the CCA, SEOM and the AFTA Council.

3. The Sub-Committee on Rules of Origin shall be composed of representatives of the Governments of Member States, and may invite representatives of relevant entities other than the Governments of the Member States with necessary expertise relevant to the issues to be discussed, upon agreement of all Member States.

APPENDIX 3. ATIGA

Chapter 4 Non-Tariff Measures

Article 40. Application of Non-Tariff Measures

1. Each Member State shall not adopt or maintain any non-tariff measure on the importation of any good of any other Member State or on the exportation of any good destined for the territory of any other Member State, except in accordance with its WTO rights and obligations or in accordance with this Agreement.
2. Each Member State shall ensure the transparency of its non-tariff measures permitted in paragraph 1 of this Article in accordance with Article 12 and shall ensure that any such measures are not prepared, adopted or applied with the view to, or with the effect of, creating unnecessary obstacles in trade among the Member States.
3. Any new measure or modification to the existing measure shall be duly notified in accordance with Article 11.
4. The database on non-tariff measures applied in Member States shall be further developed and included in the ASEAN Trade Repository as referred in Article 13.

Article 41. General Elimination of Quantitative Restrictions

Each Member State undertakes not to adopt or maintain any prohibition or quantitative restriction on the importation of any goods of the other Member States or on the exportation of any goods destined for the territory of the other Member States, except in accordance with its WTO rights and obligations or other provisions in this Agreement. To this end, Article XI of GATT 1994, shall be incorporated into and form part of this Agreement, *mutatis mutandis*.

Article 42. Elimination of Other Non-Tariff Barriers

1. Member States shall review the non-tariff measures in the database referred to in paragraph 4 of Article 40 with a view to identifying non-tariff barriers (NTBs) other than quantitative restrictions for elimination. The elimination of the identified NTBs shall be dealt with by the Co-ordinating Committee for the Implementation of the ATIGA (CCA), the ASEAN Consultative Committee on Standards and Quality (ACCSQ), the ASEAN Committee on Sanitary and Phytosanitary (AC-SPS), the working bodies under ASEAN Directors-General of Customs and other relevant ASEAN bodies, as appropriate, in accordance with the provisions of this Agreement, which shall submit their recommendations on the identified non-tariff barriers to the AFTA Council through SEOM.
2. Unless otherwise agreed by the AFTA Council, the identified NTBs shall be eliminated in three (3) tranches as follows:

   (a) Brunei, Indonesia, Malaysia, Singapore and Thailand shall eliminate in three (3) tranches by 1 January of 2008, 2009 and 2010;

   (b) The Philippines shall eliminate in three (3) tranches by 1 January of 2010, 2011 and 2012;

   (c) Cambodia, Lao PDR, Myanmar and Viet Nam shall eliminate in three (3) tranches by 1 January of 2013, 2014 and 2015 with flexibilities up to 2018.

3. The list of identified NTBs to be eliminated in each tranche shall be agreed upon by the AFTA Council meeting in the year before the effective elimination date of such NTBs.
4. Notwithstanding paragraphs 1 to 3 of this Article, the CCA, in consultation with the relevant ASEAN bodies, shall review any non-tariff measure notified or reported by any other Member State or by the private sector with a view to determining whether the measure constitutes as a NTB. If such review results in an identification of a NTB, the NTB shall be eliminated by the Member State applying such NTB in accordance with this Agreement.
5. The CCA shall serve as a focal point for the notification and review referred to in paragraph 4 of this Article.
6. Exceptions to this Article shall be allowed for the reasons provided in Article 8.
7. Nothing in this Agreement shall be construed to prevent a Member State, which is a party to the Basel Convention on the Control of Transboundary Movements of Hazardous Wastes and their Disposal or other relevant international agreements, from adopting or enforcing any measure in relation to hazardous wastes or substances based on its laws and regulations, in accordance with such international agreements.

Article 43. Foreign Exchange Restrictions

Member States shall make exceptions to their foreign exchange restrictions relating to payments for the products under this Agreement, as well as repatriation of such payments without prejudice to their rights under Article XVIII of

GATT 1994 and relevant provisions of the Articles of Agreement of the International Monetary Fund (IMF).

Article 44. Import Licensing Procedures

1. Each Member State shall ensure that all automatic and nonautomatic import licensing procedures are implemented in a transparent and predictable manner, and applied in accordance with the Agreement on Import Licensing Procedures as contained in Annex 1A to the WTO Agreement.
2. Promptly after entry into force of this Agreement, each Member State shall notify the other Member States of any existing import licensing procedures. Thereafter, each Member State shall notify the other Member States of any new import licensing procedure and any modification to its existing import licensing procedures, to the extent possible sixty (60) days before it takes effect, but in any case no later than the effective date of the licensing requirement. A notification provided under this Article shall include the information specified in Article 5 of the Agreement on Import Licensing Procedures as contained in Annex 1A to the WTO Agreement.
3. Each Member State shall answer within sixty (60) days all reasonable enquiries from another Member State with regard to the criteria employed by its respective licensing authorities in granting or denying import licences. The importing Member State shall also consider publication of such criteria.
4. Elements in non-automatic import licensing procedures that are found to be impeding trade shall be identified, with a view to remove such barriers, and to the extent possible work towards automatic import licensing procedures.

APPENDIX 3. ATIGA

Chapter 5 Trade Facilitation

Article 45. Work Programme on Trade Facilitation and its Objectives

1. Member States shall develop and implement a comprehensive ASEAN Trade Facilitation Work Programme, which sets out all concrete actions and measures with clear targets and timelines of implementation necessary for creating a consistent, transparent, and predictable environment for international trade transactions that increases trading opportunities and help businesses, including small and medium sized enterprises (SMEs), to save time and reduce costs.
2. The ASEAN Trade Facilitation Work Programme shall set out actions and measures to be implemented at both ASEAN and national levels.

Article 46. Scope of the ASEAN Trade Facilitation Work Programme

The ASEAN Trade Facilitation Work Programme referred to in Article 45 shall cover the areas of customs procedures, trade regulations and procedures, standards and conformance, sanitary and phytosanitary measures, ASEAN Single Window and other areas as identified by the AFTA Council.

Article 47. Principles on Trade Facilitation

Member States shall be guided by the following principles in relation to trade facilitation measures and initiatives at both ASEAN and national levels:

APPENDIX 3. ATIGA

(a) **Transparency**: Information on policies, laws, regulations, administrative rulings, licensing, certification, qualification and registration requirements, technical regulations, standards, guidelines, procedures and practices relating to trade in goods (hereinafter referred to as "rules and procedures relating to trade") to be made available to all interested parties, consistently and in a timely manner at no cost or a reasonable cost;

(b) **Communications and Consultations**: The authorities shall endeavour to facilitate and promote effective mechanisms for exchanges with the business and trading community, including opportunities for consultation when formulating, implementing and reviewing rules and procedures relating to trade;

(c) **Simplification, practicability and efficiency**: Rules and procedures relating to trade to be simplified to ensure that they are no more burdensome or restrictive than necessary to achieve their legitimate objectives;

(d) **Non-discrimination**: Rules and procedures relating to trade to be applied in a non-discriminatory manner and be based on market principles;

(e) **Consistency and predictability**: Rules and procedures relating to trade to be applied in a consistent, predictable and uniform manner so as to minimise uncertainty to the trade and trade related parties. Rules and procedures relating to trade to provide clear and precise procedural guidance to the appropriate authorities with standard policies and operating procedures and be applied in a non-discretionary manner;

(f) **Harmonisation, standardisation and recognition**: While accepting the need of each Member State to regulate or set rules for legitimate objectives such as protection of health, safety or public morals and conservation of exhaustible natural resources, regulations, rules and procedures affecting the acceptance of goods between Member States to be harmonised as far as possible on the basis of international standards where appropriate. The development of mutual recognition arrangements for standards and conformity assessment results, and continuing co-operation on technical infrastructure development, are encouraged;

(g) **Modernisation and use of new technology**: Rules and procedures relating to trade to be reviewed and updated if necessary, taking into account changed circumstances, including new information and new business practices, and based on the adoption, where appropriate, of modern techniques and new technology. Where new technology is used, relevant authorities shall make best efforts to spread the accompanying benefits to all parties through ensuring the openness of the information on the adopted technologies and extending co-operation to authorities of other economies and the private sector in establishing inter-operability and/or inter-connectivity of the technologies;

(h) **Due process**: Access to adequate legal appeal procedures, adding greater certainty to trade transactions, in accordance with the applicable laws of Member States; and

(i) **Co-operation**: Member States shall strive to work closely with private sector in the introduction of measures conducive to trade facilitation, including by open channels of communication and co-operation between both governments and business. Member States shall continue to work in partnership to focus on opportunities for increased co-operation including integrated technical assistance and capacity-building; exchanges of best practices critical to implementing trade facilitation initiatives and the co-ordination of positions concerning topics of common interest discussed in the framework of regional and international organisations.

Article 48. Progress Monitoring of Trade Facilitation

1. Member States, individually and collectively, shall undertake assessments once in every two (2) years, on implementation of the trade facilitation measures set out in this Agreement and in the ASEAN Trade Facilitation Work Programme to ensure effective implementation of trade facilitation measures. For this purpose, an ASEAN Trade Facilitation Framework shall be agreed by Member States within six (6) months after entry into force of this Agreement, to serve as a guideline to further enhance trade facilitation in ASEAN.
2. The ASEAN Work Programme on Trade Facilitation shall be reviewed based on the results of the regular assessment pursuant to paragraph 1 of this Article. The ASEAN Trade Facilitation Work Programme and the ASEAN Trade Facilitation Framework and any revisions thereto shall be administratively annexed to this Agreement and serve as an integral part of this Agreement.

APPENDIX 3. ATIGA

Article 49. Establishment of the ASEAN Single Window

Member States shall undertake necessary measures to establish and operate their respective National Single Windows and the ASEAN Single Window in accordance with the provisions of the Agreement to Establish and Implement the ASEAN Single Window and the Protocol to Establish and Implement the ASEAN Single Window.

Article 50. Implementation Arrangement

1. The progress in the implementation of the ASEAN Work Programme on Trade Facilitation and the outcomes of its assessment shall be reported to the AFTA Council. The SEOM, assisted by the CCA, shall be the main co-ordinator in monitoring the progress of the implementation of the ASEAN Work Programme on Trade Facilitation, in close co-ordination with the various ASEAN Committees in charge of the implementation of the measures under the Work Programme.
2. Each Member State shall establish a Trade Facilitation Coordinating Committee or relevant focal point at the national level.

Chapter 6 Customs

Article 51. Objectives

The objectives of this Chapter are to:

(a) ensure predictability, consistency and transparency in the application of customs laws of Member States;

(b) promote efficient and economical administration of customs procedures, and expeditious clearance of goods;
(c) simplify and harmonise customs procedures and practices to the extent possible; and
(d) promote cooperation among the customs authorities.

Article 52. Definitions

For the purposes of this Chapter:

(a) **Authorised Economic Operator** means a party involved in the international movement of goods in any function that has been approved by the customs authorities as complying with statutory and/or regulatory requirements of Member States, taking into account international supply chain security standards;
(b) **customs control** means measures applied by the customs authorities to ensure compliance with customs laws of Member States;
(c) **customs procedures** means the treatment applied by the customs authorities of each Member State to goods, which are subject to customs laws;
(d) **Customs Valuation Agreement** means the Agreement on Implementation of Article VII of the General Agreement on Tariffs and Trade 1994, contained in Annex 1A to the WTO Agreement;
(e) **drawback** means the amount of import duties and taxes repaid under the drawback procedure;
(f) **drawback procedure** means customs procedures which, when goods are exported, provide for a repayment (total

or partial) to be made in respect of the import duties and taxes charged on the goods, or on materials contained in them or consumed in their production;
(g) **goods declaration** means a statement made in the manner prescribed by the customs authorities, by which the persons concerned indicate the customs procedure to be applied to the goods and furnish the particulars which the customs authorities require for its application;
(h) **repayment** means the refund, in whole or in part, of duties and taxes paid on goods and the remission, in whole or in part, of duties and taxes where payment has not been made;
(i) **security** means that which ensures to the satisfaction of the customs authorities that an obligation to the customs authorities will be fulfilled; and
(j) **temporary admission** means customs procedures under which certain goods can be brought into a customs territory conditionally relieved totally or partially from payment of import duties and taxes; such goods must be imported for a specific purpose and must be intended for re-exportation within a specified period and without having undergone any change except normal depreciation due to the use made of them.

Article 53. Scope

This Chapter applies, in accordance with the Member States' respective laws, regulations and policies, to customs procedures applied to goods traded among Member States.

Article 54. Customs Procedures and Control

1. Each Member State shall ensure that its customs procedures and practices are predictable, consistent, transparent and trade facilitating, including through the expeditious clearance of goods.
2. Customs procedures of Member States shall, where possible and to the extent permitted by their respective customs law, conform to standards and recommended practices of the World Customs Organisation and other international organisations as relevant to customs.
3. The customs authorities of each Member State shall review its customs procedures with a view to their simplification to facilitate trade.
4. Customs control shall be limited to that which is necessary to ensure compliance with customs laws of Member States.

Article 55. Pre-arrival Documentation

Member States shall endeavour to make provision for the lodging and registering or checking of the goods declaration and its supporting documents prior to the arrival of the goods.

Article 56. Management

Member States shall use risk management to determine control measures with the view to facilitate customs clearance and release of goods.

Article 57. Customs Valuation

1. For the purposes of determining the customs value of goods traded between and among the Member States, provisions

of Part I of Customs Valuation Agreement, shall apply *mutatis mutandis*[7].

2. Member States shall harmonise, to the extent possible, administrative procedures and practices in the assessment of value of goods for customs purposes.

Article 58. Application of Information Technology

Member States, where applicable, shall apply information technology in customs operations based on internationally accepted standards for expeditious customs clearance and release of goods.

Article 59 Authorised Economic Operators

1. Member States shall endeavour to establish the programme of Authorised Economic Operators (AEO) to promote informed compliance and efficiency of customs control.
2. Member States shall endeavour to work towards mutual recognition of AEO.

Article 60. Repayment, Drawback and Security

1. Decisions on claims for repayment shall be reached, and notified in writing to the persons concerned, without undue

---

[7] In the case of Cambodia, the Agreement on Customs Valuation, as implemented in accordance with the provision of the protocol on the Accession of the Kingdom of Cambodia to the WTO, shall apply mutatis mutandis.

delay, and repayment of amounts overcharged shall be made as soon as possible after the verification of claims.
2. Drawback shall be paid as soon as possible after the verification of claims.
3. Where security has been furnished, it shall be discharged as soon as possible after the customs authorities are satisfied that the obligations under which the security was required have been duly fulfilled.

Article 61. Post Clearance Audit

Member States shall establish and operate Post Clearance Audit (PCA) for expeditious customs clearance and enhanced customs control.

Article 62. Advance Rulings

1. Each Member State, through its customs authorities and/or other relevant authorities, shall, to the extent permitted by its respective laws, regulations and administrative determinations, provide in writing advance rulings on the application of a person described in paragraph 2(a) of this Article, in respect of the tariff classification, questions arising from the application of the principles of Customs Valuation Agreement and/or origin of goods.
2. Where available, each Member State shall adopt or maintain procedures for advance rulings, which shall:

    (a) provide that an importer in its territory or an exporter or producer in the territory of another Member State may apply for an advance ruling before the importation of goods in question;

(b) require that an applicant for an advance ruling provide a detailed description of the goods and all relevant information needed to process an application for an advance ruling;

(c) provide that its customs authorities may, at any time during the course of evaluation of an application for an advance ruling, request that the applicant provide additional information within a specified period;

(d) provide that any advance ruling be based on the facts and circumstances presented by the applicant, and any other relevant information in the possession of the decision-maker; and

(e) provide that an advance ruling be issued to the applicant expeditiously, within the period specified in each Member State's respective laws, regulations or administrative determinations.

3. A Member State may reject requests for an advance ruling where the additional information requested in accordance with paragraph 2(c) of this Article is not provided within a specified time.

4. Subject to paragraphs 1 and 5 of this Article and where available, each Member State shall apply an advance ruling to all importations of goods described in that ruling imported into its territory for three (3) years from the date of that ruling, or such other period as specified in that Member State's respective laws, regulations or administrative determinations.

5. A Member State may modify or revoke an advance ruling upon a determination that the ruling was based on an

error of fact or law (including human error), the information provided is false or inaccurate, there is a change in its law consistent with this Agreement, or there is a change in a material fact, or circumstances on which the ruling was based.

6. Where an importer claims that the treatment accorded to an imported good should be governed by an advance ruling, the customs authorities may evaluate whether the facts and circumstances of the importation are consistent with the facts and circumstances upon which an advance ruling was based.

Article 63. Temporary Admission

Member States shall facilitate movement of goods under temporary admission to the greatest extent possible.

Article 64. Customs Co-operation

To the extent permitted by their laws, Member States may, as deemed appropriate, assist each other on customs matters.

Article 65. Transparency

1. Member States will facilitate the timely publication, dissemination of statutory and regulatory information, decisions and rulings on customs matters.
2. Each Member State shall publish on the internet and/or in print form all statutory and regulatory provisions and any customs administrative procedures applicable or enforceable by its customs administration, except law enforcement procedures and internal operational guidelines.

Article 66. Enquiry Points

Each Member State shall designate one (1) or more enquiry points to address enquiries from interested persons concerning customs matters, and shall make available on the internet and/or in print form information concerning procedures for making such enquiries.

Article 67. Consultation

The customs authorities of Member States will encourage consultation with each other regarding customs issues that affect goods traded between and among Member States.

Article 68. Confidentiality

1. Nothing in this Chapter shall be construed to require any Member State to furnish or allow access to confidential information pursuant to this Chapter the disclosure of which it considers would:

   (a) be contrary to the public interest as determined by its laws;
   (b) be contrary to any of its laws, including but not limited, to those protecting personal privacy or the financial affairs and accounts of individual customers of financial institutions;
   (c) impede law enforcement; or
   (d) prejudice legitimate commercial interests, which may include competitive position of particular enterprises, public or private.

2. Where a Member State provides information to another Member State in accordance with this Chapter and designates the information as confidential, the Member State receiving the information shall maintain the confidentiality of the information, use it only for the purposes specified by the Member State providing the information, and not disclose it without the specific written permission of the Member State providing the information.

Article 69. Review and Appeal

1. Each Member State shall ensure that any person, in its territory, being aggrieved by any customs decision pertinent to this Agreement have access to administrative review within the customs authorities that issued the decision subject to review or, where applicable, by the higher authority supervising the administration and/or judicial review of the determination taken at the final level of administrative review, in accordance with the Member State's law.
2. The decision on appeal shall be given to the appellant and the reasons for such decision shall be provided in writing.

Article 70. Implementation and Institutional Arrangements

The ASEAN Directors-General of Customs, supported by customs working bodies, shall be responsible to implement the provisions of this Chapter and any other provisions relevant to customs in this Agreement.

APPENDIX 3. ATIGA

Chapter 7 Standards, Technical Regulations and Conformity Assessment Procedures

Article 71. Objective

The objective of this Chapter is to establish provisions on standards, technical regulations and conformity assessment procedures to ensure that these do not create unnecessary obstacles to trade in establishing ASEAN as a single market and production base, and at the same time ensure that the legitimate objectives of Member States are met.

Article 72. Terms and Definitions

General terms concerning standardisation and conformity assessment used in this Chapter have the meaning given to them in the definitions contained in the appropriate editions of ISO/IEC Guide 2 and ISO/IEC 17000 of the International Organization for Standardization (ISO) and the International Electrotechnical Commission (IEC) as cited in the ASEAN Framework Agreement on Mutual Recognition Arrangements and the relevant ASEAN Sectoral Mutual Recognition Arrangements.

Article 73. General Provisions

1. Member States reaffirm and are committed to abide by the rights and obligations under the Agreement on Technical Barriers to Trade contained in Annex 1A to the WTO Agreement.

2. Member States shall take any of the following possible measures or their combinations to mitigate, if not totally eliminate, unnecessary technical barriers to trade:

   (a) harmonise national standards with relevant international standards and practices;
   (b) promote mutual recognition of conformity assessment results among Member States;
   (c) develop and implement ASEAN Sectoral Mutual Recognition Arrangements and develop ASEAN Harmonised Regulatory Regimes in the regulated areas where applicable; and
   (d) encourage the co-operation among National Accreditation Bodies and National Metrology Institutes (NMIs) including relevant legal metrology authorities in ASEAN to facilitate the implementation of Mutual Recognition Arrangements (MRAs) in regulated and non-regulated sectors.

3. To facilitate the free movement of goods within ASEAN, Member States shall develop and implement a Marking Scheme, where appropriate, for products covered under the ASEAN Harmonised Regulatory Regimes or Directives.

Article 74. Standards

1. Each Member State undertakes that its national standards authorities accept and follow the Code of Good Practice for the Preparation, Adoption and Application of Standards as provided for in Annex 3 of the Agreement on Technical

Barriers to Trade as contained in Annex 1A to the WTO Agreement.

2. In harmonising national standards, Member States shall, as the first and preferred option, adopt the relevant international standards when preparing new national standards or revising existing standards. Where international standards are not available, national standards shall be aligned among Member States.

3. Member States are encouraged to actively participate in the development of international standards, particularly in those sectors that have trade potential for ASEAN.

4. Harmonisation of the existing national standards and adoption of international standards into new national standards should be based on "Adoption of International Standards as Regional or National Standards", as contained in the ISO/IEC Guide 21 or its latest edition.

5. Whenever modifications of contents and structure of the relevant international standards are necessary, Member States shall ensure an easy comparison of the contents and structure of their national standards with the referenced international standards and provide information to explain the reason(s) for such modifications.

6. Member States shall ensure that:

   (a) the modifications of contents of international standards are not prepared and adopted with a view to, or with the effect of, creating unnecessary technical barriers to trade; and

   (b) the modifications of contents shall not be more restrictive than necessary.

Article 75. Technical Regulations

1. In adopting technical regulations, Member States shall ensure that:

    (a) these are not adopted with a view, to or with the effect of, creating technical barriers to trade;
    (b) these are based on international or national standards that are harmonised to international standards, except where legitimate reasons for deviations exist;
    (c) alternative means that are least trade restrictive to achieve the desired objectives are considered before a decision is taken on the adoption of technical regulations;
    (d) the adoption of prescriptive standards is avoided to ensure that unnecessary obstacles to trade are not introduced, to enhance fair competition in the market or that it does not lead to a reduction of business flexibility; and
    (e) treatment accorded to products imported from Member States is no less favourable than that accorded to like products of national origin and to like products originating from any other Member State.

2. Member States shall ensure that only those parts of a standard that represent minimum requirements to fulfil the desired objectives are referred to in the technical regulations.
3. Member States shall also ensure that, wherever applicable, the preparation, adoption and application of technical regulations are to facilitate the implementation of the respective ASEAN Sectoral Mutual Recognition Arrangements.
4. Whenever the need for technical regulations is urgent for overcoming problems that arise or threaten to arise within

the territory of a Member State and the available time does not allow such Member State to harmonise the relevant national standards, that Member State shall consider using the appropriate international standards or the relevant parts of them as the first alternative.

5. Member States shall comply with the notification procedures as stipulated in Article 11. However, in the case of technical regulations under this Article, other Member States shall present their comments, if any, within sixty (60) days of the notification. Member States shall, upon request, provide to other Member States the draft of the technical regulation and other information regarding the deviations from the relevant international standards and the applicable pre-market conformity assessment procedure.

6. Except in urgent circumstances, Member States shall allow at least six (6) months between the publication of technical regulations and their entry into force in order to provide sufficient time for producers in exporting Member States to adapt their products or methods of production to the requirements of importing Member States.

Article 76. Conformity Assessment Procedures

1. Member States shall ensure that conformity assessment procedures are not prepared, adopted or applied with a view to, or with the effect of, creating unnecessary technical barriers to trade and that conformity assessment procedures that have to be complied with by suppliers of products originating in the territories of other Member States are not

more stringent than those accorded to suppliers of like products of national origin.
2. Member States shall adopt conformity assessment procedures that are consistent with international standards and practices and wherever such procedures cannot be achieved because of differences in legitimate objectives, the differences of conformity assessment procedures shall be minimised as far as possible.
3. Member States shall develop and implement ASEAN Sectoral Mutual Recognition Arrangement in the regulated areas, where appropriate, in accordance with the provisions of the ASEAN Framework Agreement on Mutual Recognition Arrangements.
4. Member States shall accept the results of conformity assessment produced by conformity assessment bodies designated by other Member States in accordance with the provisions of the ASEAN Framework Agreement on Mutual Recognition Arrangements and the provisions of the respective ASEAN Sectoral Mutual Recognition Arrangements in all regulated areas.
5. Member States shall establish co-operation among National Accreditation Bodies and National Metrology Institutes (NMIs), including legal metrology in ASEAN to facilitate the implementation of MRAs in regulated and non-regulated sectors.

Article 77. Post Market Surveillance

1. Member States shall establish post market surveillance systems to complement the implementation of the ASEAN

APPENDIX 3. ATIGA

Sectoral Mutual Recognition Arrangements and ASEAN Harmonised Regulatory Regimes and/or Directives.

2. The relevant authority that undertakes the post market surveillance system of the Member States shall take the necessary actions to ensure compliance of products placed in the market with the applicable ASEAN Sectoral Mutual Recognition Arrangements and ASEAN Harmonised Regulatory Regimes and/or Directives.
3. Member States should ensure that the necessary laws and technical infrastructure are in place to support post market surveillance systems.
4. The effectiveness of the post market surveillance systems shall be further enhanced through the establishment of Alert Systems among Member States.

Article 78. Implementation

1. Member States shall take all necessary measures to ensure implementation of all the ASEAN Sectoral Mutual Recognition Arrangements, ASEAN Harmonised Regulatory Regimes and the relevant provisions of this Agreement within the time frame stipulated in the aforesaid agreements and to ensure compliance with aforesaid harmonised requirements.
2. The following instruments, and any future instruments agreed by Member States to implement the provisions of this Agreement, shall form an integral part of this Agreement:

   (a) ASEAN Framework Agreement on Mutual Recognition Arrangements;

(b) ASEAN Sectoral Mutual Recognition Arrangement for Electrical and Electronic Equipment;
(c) Agreement on the ASEAN Harmonized Electrical and Electronic Equipment (EEE) Regulatory Regime; and
(d) Agreement on the ASEAN Harmonized Cosmetic Regulatory Scheme.

3. The ASEAN Consultative Committee for Standards and Quality (ACCSQ) shall be responsible for:

   (a) identifying and initiating sectoral MRAs;
   (b) monitoring the effective implementation of the relevant provisions of this Agreement in respect of standards, technical regulations and conformity assessment procedures;
   (c) providing support to the respective Joint Sectoral Committees when required; and
   (d) collaborating with the ASEAN Secretariat to provide regular feedback on the implementation of this Agreement.

4. The ACCSQ shall provide support and co-operation under the relevant ASEAN Free Trade Agreements (FTAs) with Dialogue Partners, including capacity building and institutional strengthening programmes for Standards, Technical Regulations and Conformity Assessment Procedures Chapters in such ASEAN FTAs.

5. The ACCSQ shall take the necessary actions to ensure effective implementation of the ASEAN Sectoral Mutual Recognition Arrangements and ASEAN Harmonised Regulatory Regimes.

APPENDIX 3. ATIGA

Chapter 8 Sanitary and Phytosanitary Measures

Article 79. Objectives

The objectives of this Chapter are to:

(a) facilitate trade between and among Member States while protecting human, animal or plant life or health in each Member State;
(b) provide a framework and guidelines on requirements in the application of sanitary and phytosanitary measures among Member States, particularly to achieve commitments set forth in the ASEAN Economic Community Blueprint;
(c) strengthen co-operation among Member States in protecting human, animal or plant life or health; and
(d) facilitate and strengthen implementation of this Chapter in accordance with the principles and disciplines in the Agreement on the Application of Sanitary and Phytosanitary Measures contained in Annex 1A to the WTO Agreement and this Agreement.

Article 80. Definitions

For the purposes of this Chapter:

(a) **international standards, guidelines and recommendations** shall have the same meaning as in Annex A of paragraph 3 to the SPS Agreement;

(b) **sanitary or phytosanitary measures** shall have the same meaning as in Annex A of paragraph 1 to the SPS Agreement; and
(c) **SPS Agreement** means the Agreement on the Application of Sanitary and Phytosanitary Measures contained in Annex 1A to the WTO Agreement.

Article 81. General Provisions and Obligations

1. The provisions of this Chapter apply to all sanitary and phytosanitary measures of a Member State that may, directly or indirectly, affect trade between and among Member States.
2. Member States affirm their rights and obligations with respect to each other under the SPS Agreement.
3. Each Member State commits to apply the principles of the SPS Agreement in the development, application or recognition of any sanitary or phytosanitary measures with the intent to facilitate trade between and among Member States while protecting human, animal or plant life or health in each Member State.
4. In the implementation of their sanitary or phytosanitary measures, Member States agree to be guided, where applicable, by relevant international standards, guidelines and recommendations developed by international organisations such as, the Codex Alimentarius Commission (Codex), the World Organisation for Animal Health (OIE), the International Plant Protection Convention (IPPC) and ASEAN.
5. Member States hereby agree that the laws, regulations, and procedures for application of SPS measures in their respective territories shall be listed in Annex 9, which form an integral part of this Agreement. Member States hereby

agree to ensure that their respective national sanitary and phytosanitary laws, regulations and procedures as listed in Annex 9 are readily available and accessible to any interested Member States.
6. Any change to national sanitary and phytosanitary laws, regulations and procedures shall be subject to Article 11.

Article 82. Implementation and Institutional Arrangements

1. For effective implementation of this Chapter, an ASEAN Committee on Sanitary and Phytosanitary Measures (AC-SPS) shall be established to conduct committee meetings at least once a year among Member States.
2. The functions of the AC-SPS shall be to:
   (a) facilitate exchange of information on such matters as occurrences of sanitary or phytosanitary incidents in the Member States and non-Member States, and change or introduction of sanitary and phytosanitary-related regulations and standards of the Member States, which may, directly or indirectly, affect trade between and among Member States;
   (b) facilitate co-operation in the area of sanitary or phytosanitary measures including capacity building, technical assistance and exchange of experts, subject to the availability of appropriated funds and the applicable laws and regulations of each Member State;
   (c) endeavour to resolve sanitary and phytosanitary matters with a view to facilitate trade between and among Member States. The AC-SPS may establish ad hoc task force to undertake science-based consultations to identify

and address specific issues that may arise from the application of sanitary or phytosanitary measures; and
(d) submit regular reports of developments and recommendations in the implementation of this Chapter to the AFTA Council, through SEOM for further action.

3. Each Member State shall establish a contact point for effective communication and co-operation. The list of respective designated contact points appears in Annex 10.
4. Each Member State shall ensure the information in Annex 10 is updated.

Article 83. Notification under Emergency Situation

1. Each Member State acknowledges the value of exchanging information, particularly in an emergency situation on food safety crisis, interception, control of pests and/or disease outbreaks and its sanitary or phytosanitary measures.
2. Member States shall immediately notify all contact points and the ASEAN Secretariat should the following situations occur:

    (a) in case of food safety crisis, pest or disease outbreaks; and
    (b) provisional sanitary or phytosanitary measures against or affecting the exports of the other Member States are considered necessary to protect the human, animal or plant life or health of the importing Member State.

3. The exporting Member State should, to the extent possible, endeavour to provide information to the importing Member State if the exporting Member State identifies that

an export consignment which may be associated with a significant sanitary or phytosanitary risk has been exported.

Article 84. Equivalence

1. Each Member State shall initiate and further strengthen cooperation on equivalence in accordance with the SPS Agreement and relevant international standards, guidelines and recommendations, in order to facilitate trade between and among the Member States.
2. To facilitate trade, Member States may develop equivalence arrangements and recommend equivalence decisions, in particular in accordance with Article 4 of the SPS Agreement and with the guidance provided by the relevant international and regional standard setting bodies namely Codex, OIE, IPPC and ASEAN and by the Committee on Sanitary and Phytosanitary Measures established in accordance with Article 12 of the SPS Agreement.
3. Each Member State shall, upon request, enter into consultations with the aim of achieving bilateral and/or regional recognition arrangements of the equivalence of specified sanitary or phytosanitary measures.

Article 85. Co-operation

1. Each Member State shall explore opportunities for further cooperation, technical assistance, collaboration and information exchange with other Member States on sanitary and phytosanitary matters of mutual interest consistent with the objectives of this Chapter and the commitments set forth in the ASEAN Economic Community Blueprint.

2. Member States shall further strengthen co-operation for the control and eradication of pests and disease outbreaks, and other emergency cases related to sanitary or phytosanitary measures as well as to assist other Member States to comply with SPS requirements.
3. In implementing the provisions of paragraph 1 of this Article, Member States shall co-ordinate their undertakings with the activities conducted in the regional and multilateral context, with the objectives of avoiding unnecessary duplication and maximising efficiency of efforts of the Member States in this field.
4. Any two (2) Member States may, by mutual agreement, cooperate on adaptation to regional conditions including the concept of pests and disease free areas and areas of low pests or disease prevalence, in accordance with the SPS Agreement and relevant international standards, guidelines and recommendations, in order to facilitate trade between the Member States.

Chapter 9 Trade Remedy Measures

Article 86. Safeguard Measures

Each Member State which is a WTO member retains its rights and obligations under Article XIX of GATT 1994, and the Agreement on Safeguards or Article 5 of the Agreement on Agriculture.

Article 87. Anti-dumping and Countervailing Duties

1. Member States affirm their rights and obligations with respect to each other relating to the application of anti-dumping

under Article VI of GATT 1994 and the Agreement on Implementation of Article VI of General Agreement on Tariffs and Trade 1994 as contained in Annex 1A to the WTO Agreement.

2. Member States affirm their rights and obligations with respect to each other relating to subsidies and countervailing measures under Article XVI of GATT 1994 and the Agreement on Subsidies and Countervailing Measures as contained in Annex 1A to the WTO Agreement.

Chapter 10 Institutional Provisions

Article 88. Advisory and Consultative Mechanism

The ASEAN Consultations to Solve Trade and Investment Issues (ACT) and the ASEAN Compliance Monitoring Body (ACB) as contained in the Declaration on ASEAN Concord II (Bali Concord II) may be invoked to settle disputes that may arise from this Agreement. Any Member State who does not wish to avail of the ACT/ACB may resort to the mechanism provided in the ASEAN Protocol on Enhanced Dispute Settlement Mechanism.

Article 89. Dispute Settlement

The ASEAN Protocol on Enhanced Dispute Settlement Mechanism, signed on 29 November 2004 in Vientiane, Lao PDR and amendments thereto, shall apply in relation to any dispute arising from, or any difference between Member

APPENDIX 3. ATIGA

States concerning the interpretation or application of this Agreement.

Article 90. Institutional Arrangements

1. The ASEAN Economic Ministers (AEM) shall, for the purposes of this Agreement, establish an ASEAN Free Trade Area (AFTA) Council comprising one (1) ministerial-level nominee from each Member State and the Secretary-General of ASEAN. In the performance of its functions, the AFTA Council shall also be supported by the Senior Economic Officials' Meeting (SEOM). In the fulfilment of its functions, the SEOM may establish bodies, as appropriate, to assist them such as the Coordinating Committee on the implementation of ATIGA (CCA). The SEOM, assisted by the CCA, shall ensure the effective implementation of this Agreement and, shall coordinate and be supported by technical bodies and committees under this Agreement.
2. Each Member State shall establish a National AFTA Unit, which shall serve a national focal point for the coordination of the implementation of this Agreement.
3. The ASEAN Secretariat shall:

   (a) provide support to the AEM and AFTA Council in supervising, co-ordinating and reviewing the implementation of this Agreement as well as assistance in all related matters; and

   (b) monitor and regularly report to the AFTA Council on the progress in the implementation of this Agreement.

APPENDIX 3. ATIGA

Chapter 11 Final Provisions

Article 91. Relation to Other Agreements

1. Subject to paragraph 2 of this Article, all ASEAN economic agreements that exist before the entry into force of ATIGA shall continue to be valid.
2. Member States shall agree on the list of agreements to be superseded within six (6) months from the date of entry into force and such list shall be administratively annexed to this Agreement and serve as an integral part of this Agreement.
3. In case of inconsistency between this Agreement and any ASEAN economic agreements that are not superseded under paragraph 2 of this Article, this Agreement shall prevail.

Article 92. Amended or Successor International Agreements

If any international agreement or a provision therein referred to, or incorporated into, this Agreement, and such agreement or provision is amended, the Member States shall consult on whether it is necessary to amend this Agreement, unless this Agreement provides otherwise.

Article 93. Annexes, Attachments and Future Instruments

1. The Annexes and Attachments to this Agreement shall form an integral part of this Agreement.
2. Member States may adopt legal instruments in the future pursuant to the provisions of this Agreement. Upon their

respective entry into force, such instruments shall form part of this Agreement.

Article 94. Amendments

1. The provisions of this Agreement may be modified through amendments mutually agreed upon in writing by the Member States.
2. Notwithstanding paragraph 1 of this Article, the Annexes and Attachments to this Agreement may be modified through amendments endorsed by the AFTA Council. The said amendments shall be administratively annexed to this Agreement and serve as an integral part of this Agreement.

Article 95. Review

The AFTA Council or their designated representatives shall meet within one (1) year of the date of entry into force of this Agreement and then every two (2) years or otherwise as appropriate to review this Agreement for the purpose of fulfilling the objective of this Agreement.

Article 96. Entry into Force

1. This Agreement shall be signed by the ASEAN Economic Ministers.
2. This Agreement shall enter into force, after all Member States have notified or, where necessary, deposited instruments of ratifications with the Secretary-General of ASEAN upon completion of their internal procedures, which shall not take more than one hundred and eighty (180) days after the signing of this Agreement.

3. The Secretary-General of ASEAN shall promptly notify all Member States of the notifications or deposit of each instrument of ratification referred to in paragraph 2 of this Article.

Article 97. Reservations

No reservations shall be made with respect to any of the provisions of this Agreement.

Article 98. Depositary

This Agreement shall be deposited with the Secretary-General of ASEAN who shall promptly furnish a certified copy thereof to each Member State.

IN WITNESS WHEREOF, the undersigned, being duly authorised thereto by their respective Governments, have signed the ASEAN Trade in Goods Agreement.

DONE at Cha-am, Thailand, this Twenty-Sixth Day of February in the Year Two Thousand and Nine, in a single original copy in the English language.

For Brunei Darussalam: **LIM JOCK SENG**, Second Minister of Foreign Affairs and Trade
For the Kingdom of Cambodia: **CHAM PRASIDH**, Senior Minister and Minister of Commerce
For the Republic of Indonesia: **MARI ELKA PANGESTU**, Minister of Trade
For the Lao People's Democratic Republic: **NAM VIYAKETH**, Minister of Industry and Commerce
For Malaysia: **MUHYIDDIN BIN MOHAMMAD YASSIN**, Minister of International Trade and Industry

APPENDIX 3. ATIGA

For the Union of Myanmar: **U SOE THA**, Minister for National Planning and Economic Development

For the Republic of the Philippines: **PETER B. FAVILA**, Secretary of Trade and Industry

For the Republic of Singapore: **LIM HNG KIANG**, Minister for Trade and Industry

For the Kingdom of Thailand: **PORNTIVA NAKASAI**, Minister of Commerce

For the Socialist Republic of Viet Nam: **VU HUY HOANG**, Minister of Industry and Trade

Appendix 4

ATIGA Annex 3, Attachment 1 Substantial Transformation Criterion for Textiles and Textile Products

A. Fibres and Yarns

Working or Processing Carried Out on Non-Originating Materials that Confers Originating Status:

- Manufacture through process of fibre-making (polymerisation, polycondensation and extrusion) spinning, twisting, texturizing or braiding from a blend or any of following:
  - Silk
  - Wool, fine/coarse animal hair
  - Cotton fibres
  - Vegetable textile fibres
  - Synthetic or artificial filaments/man-made filaments
  - Synthetic or artificial staple fibres/man-made staple fibres

B. Fabric/Carpets and Other Textile Floor Coverings; Special Yarns, Twine, Cordage and Ropes and Cables and Articles thereof

Working or Processing Carried Out on Non-Originating Materials that Confers Originating Status:

- Manufacture from:
  - Polymer (non-woven)
  - Fibres (non-woven)

- Yarns (fabrics)
- Raw or Unbleached Fabrics (finished fabrics)
- through substantial transformation process of either:
  - needle punching / spin bonding / chemical bonding
  - weaving or knitting;
  - crocheting or wadding or tufting; or
  - dyeing or printing and finishing; or impregnation, coating, covering or lamination.

C. Article of Apparel and Clothing Accessories and Other Made Up Textile Articles

Working or Processing Carried Out on Non-Originating Materials that Confers Originating Status:

- Manufacture through the processes of cutting and assembly of parts into a complete article (for apparel and tents) and incorporating embroidery or embellishment or printing (for made-up articles) from:
  - raw or unbleached fabric
  - finished fabric

Appendix 5

ATIGA Annex 5 Principles and Guidelines for Calculating Regional Value Content on the ATIGA

A. Principles to Determine Cost for Regional Value Content

i. Materiality – all cost material to the evaluation, assessment and determination of origin;
ii. Consistency – costing allocation method should be consistent unless justified by commercial reality;
iii. Reliability – costing information must be reliable and supported by appropriate information;
iv. Relevance – costs must be allocated based on objective and quantifiable data;
v. Accuracy – costing methodology should provide an accurate representation of the cost element in question;
vi. Application of GAAP of the exporting country – costing information must be prepared in accordance with the generally accepted accounting principles and this includes the avoidance of double-counting of cost items;
vii. Currency – updated costing information from existing accounting and costing records of companies should be used to calculate origin.

B. Guidelines for Costing Methodologies

i. Actual Costs – basis for actual costs should be defined by the company. Actual costs should include all direct and indirect costs incurred in producing the product;

ii. Projected and Budgeted Costs – projected costs may be used if it is justified. Companies should provide variance analysis and proof during the period origin is claimed to indicate accuracy of projections;

iii. Standards Costs – the basis for standards costs should be indicated. Companies should provide evidence that the costs are used for accounting purposes;

iv. Average/Moving Average Costs – average costs may be used if justified; the basis for calculating average costs, including time period, etc. should be highlighted. Companies should provide variance analysis and proof during the period origin is claimed to indicate accuracy of average costs;

v. Fixed Costs – fixed costs should be apportioned according to sound cost accounting principles. They should be a representative reflection of unit costs for the company in the particular period in question. The method for apportionment should be indicated.

Appendix 6

ATIGA Annex 6 Implementing Guidelines for Partial Cumulation under Article 30(2) on ASEAN Cumulative Rules of Origin

For the purposes of implementing paragraph 2 of Article 30 of this Agreement:

(a) a good shall be deemed to be eligible for partial cumulation, if at least twenty percent (20%) of the Regional Value Content (RVC) of the good is originating in the Member State where working or processing of the good has taken place;

(b) RVC of the good specified in paragraph (a) shall be calculated in accordance with the formula provided in Article 29 of this Agreement;

(c) a good exported under this arrangement shall not be eligible for tariff preference accorded by the importing Member State under this Agreement;

(d) a good exported under this arrangement shall be accompanied by a valid Certificate of Origin (Form D) duly and prominently marked "Partial Cumulation";

(e) the relevant sections of the Annex 8 (Operational Certification Procedures), including Rule 18 (retroactive check) and 19 (verification visit), shall be applicable to Certificate(s) of Origin (Form D) issued for partial cumulation purposes.

Appendix 7

ATIGA Form D

ATIGA Annex 7 Original (Duplicate/ Triplicate)

1. Goods consigned from (Exporter's business name, address, country)	Reference No.
2. Goods consigned to (Consignee's name, address, country)	ASEAN TRADE IN GOODS AGREEMENT/ ASEAN INDUSTRIAL COOPERATION SCHEME CERTIFICATE OF ORIGIN (Combined Declaration and Certificate) Issued in = $\dfrac{\text{FORM D}}{\text{(Country)}}$ See Overleaf Notes
3. Means of transport and route (as far as known) Departure date Vessel's name/Aircraft etc. Port of Discharge	4. For Official Use Preferential Treatment Given Under ASEAN Trade in Goods Agreement Preferential Treatment Given Under ASEAN Industrial Cooperation Scheme Preferential Treatment Not Given (Please state reason/s) ……………………………………..…. Signature of Authorised Signatory of the Importing Country

5. Item number	6. Marks and numbers on packages	7. Number and type of packages, description of goods (including quantity where appropriate and HS number of the importing country)	8. Origin criterion (see Overleaf Notes)	9. Gross weight or other quantity and value (FOB)	10. Number and date of invoices

11. Declaration by the exporter The undersigned hereby declares that the above details and statement are correct; that all the goods were produced in …………………………………..… (Country) and that they comply with the origin requirements specified for these goods in the ASEAN Trade in Goods Agreement for the goods exported to …………………………………..… (Importing Country) …………………………………. Place and date, signature of authorised signatory	12. Certification It is hereby certified, on the basis of control carried out, that the declaration by the exporter is correct. ……………………………………………………. Place and date, signature and stamp of certifying authority
13 ☐ Third Country Invoicing ☐ Exhibition ☐ Accumulation ☐ De Minimis ☐ Back-to-Back CO ☐ Issued Retroactively ☐ Partial Cumulation	

APPENDIX 7. FORM D

Overleaf Notes

1. Member States which accept this form for the purpose of preferential treatment under the ASEAN Trade in Goods Agreement (ATIGA) or the ASEAN Industrial Cooperation (AICO) Scheme:

BRUNEI DARRUSSALAM	CAMBODIA	INDONESIA
LAOPDR	MALAYSIA	MYANMAR
PHILIPPINES	SINGAPORE	THAILAND
VIETNAM		

2. CONDITIONS: The main conditions for admission to the preferential treatment under the ATIGA or the AICO Scheme are that goods sent to any Member States listed above must:
   (i) fall within a description of products eligible for concessions in the country of destination;
   (ii) comply with the consignment conditions in accordance with Article 32 (Direct Consignment) of Chapter 3 of the ATIGA; and
   (iii) comply with the origin criteria set out in Chapter 3 of the ATIGA.
3. ORIGIN CRITERIA: For goods that meet the origin criteria, the exporter and/or producer must indicate in Box 8 of this Form, the origin criteria met, in the manner shown in the following table:

APPENDIX 7. FORM D

Circumstances of production or manufacture in the first country named in Box 11 of this form	Insert in Box 8
(a) Goods wholly obtained or produced in the exporting Member State satisfying Article 27 (Wholly Obtained) of the ATIGA	"WO"
(b) Goods satisfying Article 28 (Non-wholly obtained) of the ATIGA • Regional Value Content • Change in Tariff Classification • Specific Processes • Combination Criteria	Percentage of Regional Value Content, example "40%" The actual CTC rule, example "CC" or "CTH" or "CTSH" "SP" The actual combination criterion, example "CTSH + 35%"
(c) Goods satisfying paragraph 2 of Article 30 (Partial Cumulation) of the ATIGA	"PC x%", where x would be the percentage of Regional Value Content of less than 40%, example "PC 25%"

4. EACH ARTICLE MUST QUALIFY: It should be noted that all the goods in a consignment must qualify separately in their own right. This is of particular relevance when similar articles of different sizes or spare parts are sent.
5. DESCRIPTION OF PRODUCTS: The description of products must be sufficiently detailed to enable the products to be identified by the Customs Officers examining them. Name of manufacturer and any trade mark shall also be specified.
6. HARMONISED SYSTEM NUMBER: The Harmonised System number shall be that of in ASEAN Harmonised

APPENDIX 7. FORM D

Tariff Nomenclature (AHTN) Code of the importing Member State.
7. EXPORTER: The term "Exporter" in Box 11 may include the manufacturer or the producer.
8. FOR OFFICIAL USE: The Customs Authority of the importing Member State must indicate (√) in the relevant boxes in column 4 whether or not preferential treatment is accorded.
9. MULTIPLE ITEMS: For multiple items declared in the same Form D, if preferential treatment is not granted to any of the items, this is also to be indicated accordingly in box 4 and the item number circled or marked appropriately in box 5.
10. THIRD COUNTRY INVOICING: In cases where invoices are issued by a third country, "the Third Country Invoicing" box should be ticked (√) and such information as name and country of the company issuing the invoice shall be indicated in box 7.
11. BACK-TO-BACK CERTIFICATE OF ORIGIN: In cases of Back-to-Back CO, in accordance with Rule 11 (Back-to-back CO) of Annex 8 of the ATIGA, the "Back-to-Back CO" box should be ticked (√).
12. EXHIBITIONS: In cases where goods are sent from the exporting Member State for exhibition in another country and sold during or after the exhibition for importation into a Member State, in accordance with Rule 22 of Annex 8 of the ATIGA, the "Exhibitions" box should be ticked (√) and the name and address of the exhibition indicated in box 2.
13. ISSUED RETROACTIVELY: In exceptional cases, due to involuntary errors or omissions or other valid causes, the

APPENDIX 7. FORM D

Certificate of Origin (Form D) may be issued retroactively, in accordance with paragraph 2 of Rule 10 of Annex 8 of the ATIGA, the "Issued Retroactively" box should be ticked (√).

14. ACCUMULATION: In cases where goods originating in a Member State are used in another Member State as materials for finished goods, in accordance with paragraph 1 of Article 30 of the ATIGA, the "Accumulation" box should be ticked (√).

15. PARTIAL CUMULATION (PC): If the Regional Value Content of the material is less than forty percent (40%), the Certificate of Origin (Form D) may be issued for cumulation purposes, in accordance with paragraph 2 of Article 30 of the ATIGA, the "Partial Cumulation" box should be ticked (√).

16. DE MINIMIS: If a good that does not undergo the required change in tariff classification does not exceed ten percent (10%) of the FOB value, in accordance with Article 33 of the ATIGA, the "De Minimis" box should be ticked (√).

Appendix 8

ATIGA Annex 8 Operational Certification Procedure for the Rules of Origin under Chapter 3

For the purposes of implementing the Rules of Origin set out in Chapter 3 (hereinafter referred to as "ASEAN ROO"), the following operational procedures on the issuance and verification of the Certificate of Origin (Form D) and other related administrative matters shall be observed.

Rule 1 Definitions

For the purposes of this Annex:

(a) **back-to-back Certificate of Origin** means a Certificate of Origin issued by an intermediate exporting Member State based on the Certificate of Origin issued by the first exporting Member State;

(b) **exporter** means a natural or juridical person located in the territory of a Member State where a good is exported from by such a person;

(c) **importer** means a natural or juridical person located in the territory of a Member State where a good is imported into by such a person;

(d) **issuing authority** means the Government authority of the exporting Member State designated to issue a

Certificate of Origin (Form D) and notified to all the other Member States in accordance with this Annex; and
(e) **producer** means a natural or juridical person who carries out production as set out in Article 25 of this Agreement in the territory of a Member State.

Rule 2 Specimen Signatures and Official Seals of the Issuing Authorities

1. Each Member State shall provide a list of the names, addresses, specimen signatures and specimen of official seals of its issuing authorities, in hard copy and soft copy format, through the ASEAN Secretariat for dissemination to other Member States in soft copy format. Any change in the said list shall be promptly provided in the same manner.
2. The specimen signatures and official seals of the issuing authorities, compiled by the ASEAN Secretariat, shall be updated annually. Any Certificate of Origin (Form D) issued by an official not included in the list referred to in paragraph 1 shall not be honoured by the receiving Member State.

Rule 3 Supporting Documents

For the purposes of determining originating status, the issuing authorities shall have the right to request for supporting documentary evidence or to carry out check(s) considered appropriate in accordance with respective laws and regulations of a Member State.

Rule 4 Pre-exportation Verification

1. The producer and/or exporter of the good, or its authorised representative, shall apply to the issuing authority, in accordance with the Member State's laws and regulations, requesting pre-exportation examination of the origin of the good. The result of the examination, subject to review periodically or whenever appropriate, shall be accepted as the supporting evidence in determining the origin of the said good to be exported thereafter. The pre-exportation examination may not apply to the good of which, by its nature, origin can be easily determined.
2. For locally-procured materials, self-declaration by the final manufacturer exporting under this Agreement shall be used as a basis when applying for the issuance of the Certificate of Origin (Form D).

Rule 5 Application for Certificate of Origin

At the time of carrying out the formalities for exporting the products under preferential treatment, the exporter or his authorised representative shall submit a written application for the Certificate of Origin (Form D) together with appropriate supporting documents proving that the products to be exported qualify for the issuance of a Certificate of Origin (Form D).

Rule 6 Examination of Application for a Certificate of Origin

The issuing authority shall, to the best of its competence and ability, carry out proper examination, in accordance with the

APPENDIX 8. ATIGA OCP

laws and regulations of the Member State, upon each application for a Certification of Origin (Form D) to ensure that:

(a) The application and the Certificate of Origin (Form D) are duly completed and signed by the authorised signatory;
(b) The origin of the product is in conformity with the provisions of Chapter 3 of this Agreement;
(c) The other statements of the Certificate of Origin (Form D) correspond to supporting documentary evidence submitted;
(d) Description, quantity and weight of goods, marks and number of packages, number and kinds of packages, as specified, conform to the products to be exported;
(e) Multiple items declared on the same Certificate of Origin (Form D) shall be allowed provided that each item qualifies separately in its own right.

Rule 7 Certificate of Origin (Form D)

1. The Certificate of Origin (Form D) must be on ISO A4 size white paper in conformity to the specimen shown in Annex 7 of this Agreement. It shall be made in the English language.
2. The Certificate of Origin (Form D) shall comprise one (1) original and two (2) carbon copies (Duplicate and Triplicate).
3. Each Certificate of Origin (Form D) shall bear a reference number separately given by each place or office of issuance.
4. Each Certificate of Origin (Form D) shall bear the manually executed signature and seal of the authorised issuing authority.

5. The original copy shall be forwarded by the exporter to the importer for submission to the customs authority at the port or place of importation. The duplicate shall be retained by the issuing authority in the exporting Member State. The triplicate shall be retained by the exporter.

Rule 8 Declaration of Origin Criterion

To implement the provisions of Article 26 of this Agreement, the Certificate of Origin (Form D) issued by the final exporting Member State shall indicate the relevant applicable origin criterion in Box 8.

Rule 9 Treatment of Erroneous Declaration in the Certificate of Origin

Neither erasures nor superimpositions shall be allowed on the Certificate of Origin (Form D). Any alteration shall be made by:

(a) striking out the erroneous materials and making any addition required. Such alterations shall be approved by an official authorised to sign the Certificate of Origin (Form D) and certified by the issuing authorities. Unused spaces shall be crossed out to prevent any subsequent addition; or
(b) issuing a new Certificate of Origin (Form D) to replace the erroneous one.

Rule 10 Issuance of the certificate of origin

1. The Certificate of Origin (Form D) shall be issued by the issuing authorities of the exporting Member State at the

time of exportation or soon thereafter whenever the products to be exported can be considered originating in that Member State within the meaning of Chapter 3 of this Agreement.

2. In exceptional cases where a Certificate of Origin (Form D) has not been issued at the time of exportation or no later than three (3) days from the declared shipment date, due to involuntary errors or omissions or other valid causes, the Certificate of Origin (Form D) may be issued retroactively but no longer than one (1) year from the date of shipment and shall be duly and prominently marked "Issued Retroactively".

Rule 11 Back-to-Back Certificate of Origin

The issuing authority of the intermediate Member State may issue a back-to-back Certificate of Origin in an application is made by the exporter, provided that:

(a) a valid original Certificate of Origin (Form D) is presented. In the case where no original Certificate of Origin (Form D) is presented, its certified true copy shall be presented;

(b) the back-to-back Certificate of Origin issued should contain some of the same information as the original Certificate of Origin (Form D). In particular, every column in the back-to-back Certificate of Origin should be completed. FOB price of the intermediate Member State in Box 9 should also be reflected in the back-to-back Certificate of Origin;

(c) For partial export shipments, the partial export value shall be shown instead of the full value of the original Certificate of Origin (Form D). The intermediate Member State will ensure that the total quantity re-exported under the partial shipment does not exceed the total quantity of the Certificate of Origin (Form D) from the first Member State when approving the back-to-back Certificate of Origin to the exporters;

(d) In the event that the information is not complete and/or circumvention is suspected, the final importing Member State(s) could request that the original Certificate of Origin (Form D) be submitted to their respective customs authority;

(e) Verification procedures as set out in Rules 18 and 19 are also applied to Member State issuing the back-to-back Certificate of Origin.

Rule 12 Loss of the Certificate of Origin

In the event of theft, loss or destruction of a Certificate of Origin (Form D), the exporter may apply in writing to the issuing authorities for a certified true copy of the original and the triplicate to be made out on the basis of the export documents in their possession bearing the endorsement of the words "CERTIFIED TRUE COPY" in Box 12. This copy shall bear the date of issuance of the original Certificate of Origin. The certified true copy of a Certificate of Origin (Form D) shall be issued no longer than one (1) year from the date of issuance of the original Certificate of Origin (Form D).

APPENDIX 8. ATIGA OCP

Rule 13 Presentation of the Certificate of Origin

1. For the purposes of claiming preferential tariff treatment, the importer shall submit to the customs authority of the importing Member State at the time of import, a declaration, a Certificate of Origin (Form D) including supporting documents (i.e. invoices and, when required, the through Bill of Lading issued in the territory of the exporting Member State) and other documents as required in accordance with the laws and regulations of the importing Member State.
2. In cases when a Certificate of Origin (Form D) is rejected by the customs authority of the importing Member State, the subject Certificate of Origin (Form D) shall be marked accordingly in Box 4 and the original Certificate of Origin (Form D) shall be returned to the issuing authority within a reasonable period not exceeding sixty (60) days. The issuing authority shall be duly notified of the grounds for the denial of tariff preference.
3. In the case where Certificates of Origin (Form D) are not accepted, as stated in the preceding paragraph, the importing Member State should accept and consider the clarifications made by the issuing authorities and assess again whether or not the Form D application can be accepted for the granting of the preferential treatment. The clarifications should be detailed and exhaustive in addressing the grounds of denial of preference raised by the importing Member State.

APPENDIX 8. ATIGA OCP

Rule 14 Validity Period of the Certificate of Origin

The following time limit for the presentation of the Certificate of Origin (Form D) shall be observed:

(a) The Certificate of Origin (Form D) shall be valid for a period of twelve (12) months from the date of issuance and must be submitted to the customs authorities of the importing Member State within that period.
(b) Where the Certificate of Origin (Form D) is submitted to the customs authorities of the importing Member State after the expiration of the time limit for its submission, such Certificate of Origin (Form D) is still to be accepted when failure to observe the time limit results from force majeure or other valid causes beyond the control of the exporter; and
(c) In all cases, the customs authorities in the importing Member State may accept such Certificate of Origin (Form D) provided that the goods have been imported before the expiration of the time limit of the said Certificate of Origin (Form D).

Rule 15 Waiver of Certificate of Origin

In the case of consignments of goods originating in the exporting Member State and not exceeding US$ 200.00 FOB, the production of Certificate of Origin (Form D) shall be waived and the use of simplified declaration by the exporter that the goods in question have originated in the exporting Member State will be accepted. Goods sent through the post not exceeding US$ 200.00 FOB shall also be similarly treated.

Rule 16 Treatment of Minor Discrepancies

1. Where the ASEAN origin of the goods is not in doubt, the discovery of minor discrepancies, such as typographical error in the statements made in the Certificate of Origin (Form D) and those made in the documents submitted to the customs authorities of the importing Member State for the purpose of carrying out the formalities for importing the goods shall not ipso facto invalidate the Certificate of Origin (Form D), if it does in fact correspond to the goods submitted.
2. In cases where the exporting Member State and importing Member State have different tariff classifications for a good subject to preferential tariffs, the goods shall be released at the MFN rates or at the higher preferential rate, subject to the compliance of the applicable ROO, and no penalty or other charges shall be imposed in accordance with relevant laws and regulations of the importing Member State. Once the classification differences have been resolved, the correct rate shall be applied and any overpaid duty shall be refunded if applicable, in accordance with relevant laws and regulations of the importing Member State, as soon as the issues have been resolved.
3. For multiple items declared under the same Certificate of Origin (Form D), a problem encountered with one of the items listed shall not affect or delay the granting of preferential treatment and customs clearance of the remaining

items listed in the Certificate of Origin (Form D). Rule 18 (c) may be applied to the problematic items.

Rule 17 Record Keeping Requirement

1. For the purposes of the verification process pursuant to Rules 18 and 19, the producer and/or exporter applying for the issuance of a Certificate of Origin (Form D) shall, subject to the laws and regulations of the exporting Member State, keep its supporting records for application for not less than three (3) years from the date of issuance of the Certificate of Origin (Form D).
2. The application for Certificates of Origin (Form D) and all documents related to such application shall be retained by the issuing authorities for not less than three (3) years from the date of issuance.
3. Information relating to the validity of the Certificate of Origin (Form D) shall be furnished upon request of the importing Member State by an official authorised to sign the Certificate of Origin (Form D) and certified by the appropriate Government authorities.
4. Any information communicated between the Member States concerned shall be treated as confidential and shall be used for the validation of Certificates of Origin (Form D) purposes only.

Rule 18 Retroactive Check

The importing Member State may request the issuing authority of the exporting Member State to conduct a retroactive check at random and/or when it has reasonable doubt as to the authenticity of the document or as to the accuracy of the information regarding the true origin of the goods in question or of certain parts thereof. Upon such request, the issuing authority of the exporting Member State shall conduct a retroactive check on a producer/exporter's cost statement based on the current cost and prices, within a six-month timeframe, specified at the date of exportation subject to the following conditions:

(a) The request for retroactive check shall be accompanied with the Certificate of Origin (Form D) concerned and shall specify the reasons and any additional information suggesting that the particulars given on the said Certificate of Origin (Form D) may be inaccurate, unless the retroactive check is requested on a random basis;
(b) The issuing authority receiving a request for retroactive check shall respond to the request promptly and reply within ninety (90) days after the receipt of the request;
(c) The customs authorities of the importing Member State may suspend the provisions on preferential treatment while awaiting the result of verification. However, it may release the goods to the importer subject to any administrative measures deemed necessary, provided that they are not held to be subject to import prohibition or restriction and there is no suspicion of fraud;
(d) The issuing authority shall promptly transmit the results of the verification process to the importing Member State which shall then determine whether or not the subject good is originating. The entire process of retroactive

APPENDIX 8. ATIGA OCP

check including the process of notifying the issuing authority of the exporting Member State the result of determination whether or not the good is originating shall be completed within one hundred and eighty (180) days. While awaiting the results of the retroactive check, paragraph (c) shall be applied.

Rule 19 Verification Visit

If the importing Member State is not satisfied with the outcome of the retroactive check, it may, under exceptional cases, request for verification visits to the exporting Member State.

(a) Prior to the conduct of a verification visit, an importing Member State, shall:
  (i) Deliver a written notification of its intention to conduct the verification visit to:
    (1) the exporter/ producer whose premises are to be visited;
    (2) the issuing authority of the Member State in whose territory the verification visit is to occur;
    (3) the customs authorities of the Member State in whose territory the verification visit is to occur; and
    (4) the importer of the goods subject of the verification visit.
  (ii) The written notification mentioned in paragraph (a) (i) shall be as comprehensive as possible including, among others:

APPENDIX 8. ATIGA OCP

   (1) the name of the customs authorities issuing the notification;
   (2) the name of the exporter/producer whose premises are to be visited;
   (3) the proposed date for the verification visit;
   (4) the coverage of the proposed verification visit, including reference to the goods subject of the verification; and
   (5) the names and designation of the officials performing the verification visit.
  (iii) Obtain the written consent of the exporter/producer whose premises are to be visited.
(b) When a written consent from the exporter/producer is not obtained within thirty (30) days upon receipt of the notification pursuant to paragraph (a) (i), the notifying Member State, may deny preferential treatment to the goods that would have been subject of the verification visit.
(c) The issuing authority receiving the notification may postpone the proposed verification visit and notify the importing Member State of such intention. Notwithstanding any postponement, any verification visit shall be carried out within sixty (60) days from the date of such receipt, or for a longer period as the concerned Member States may agree.
(d) The Member State conducting the verification visit shall provide the exporter/producer whose goods are the subject of the verification and the relevant issuing authority with a written determination of whether or not the subject goods qualify as originating goods.

(e) Any suspended preferential treatment shall be reinstated upon the written determination referred to in paragraph (d) that the goods qualify as originating goods.

(f) The exporter/producer will be allowed thirty (30) days, from receipt of the written determination, to provide in writing comments or additional information regarding the eligibility of the goods. If the goods are still found to be non-originating, the final written determination will be communicated to the issuing authority within thirty (30) days from receipt of the comments/additional information from the exporter/producer.

(g) The verification visit process, including the actual visit and determination of whether the subject goods are originating or not, shall be carried out and its results communicated to the issuing authority within a maximum of one hundred and eighty (180) days. While awaiting the results of the verification visit, Rule 18(c) on the suspension of preferential treatment shall be applied.

Rule 20 Confidentiality

Member States shall maintain, in accordance with their laws, the confidentiality of classified business information collected in the process of verification pursuant to Rules 18 and 19 and shall protect that information from disclosure that could prejudice the competitive position of the person who provided the information. The classified business information may only be disclosed to those authorities responsible for the administration and enforcement of origin determination.

APPENDIX 8. ATIGA OCP

Rule 21 Documentation for Implementing Article 32(2) (b) (Direct Consignment)

For the purposes of implementing Article 32(2) (b) of this Agreement, where transportation is effected through the territory of one or more non-Member State, the following shall be produced to the Government authorities of the importing Member State:

(a) A through Bill of Lading issued in the exporting Member State;
(b) A Certificate of Origin (Form D) issued by the relevant Government authorities of the exporting Member State;
(c) A copy of the original commercial invoice in respect of the goods; and
(d) Supporting documents in evidence that the requirements of Article 32(2) (b) paragraphs (i), (ii) and (iii) of this Agreement are being complied with.

Rule 22 Exhibition Goods

1. Goods sent from an exporting Member State for exhibition in another Member State and sold during or after the exhibition for importation into a Member State shall be granted preferential treatment accorded under this Agreement on the condition that the goods meet the requirements as set out in Chapter 3 of this Agreement, provided that it is shown to the satisfaction of the relevant Government authorities of the importing Member State that:

   (a) An exporter has dispatched those goods from the territory of the exporting Member State to the Member

State where the exhibition is held and has exhibited them there;
(b) The exporter has sold the goods or transferred them to a consignee in the importing Member State;
(c) The goods have been consigned during the exhibition or immediately thereafter to the importing Member State in the state in which they were sent for the exhibition.

2. For the purposes of implementing paragraph 1, the Certificate of Origin (Form D) shall be provided to the relevant Government authorities of the importing Member State. The name and address of the exhibition must be indicated. The relevant Government authorities of the Member State where the exhibition took place may provide evidence together with supporting documents prescribed in Rule 21 (d) for the identification of the products and the conditions under which they were exhibited.
3. Paragraph 1 shall apply to any trade, agricultural or crafts exhibition, fair or similar show or display in shops or business premises with the view to the sale of foreign goods and where the goods remain under customs control during the exhibition.

Rule 23 Third Country Invoicing

1. Relevant Government authorities in the importing Member State shall accept Certificates of Origin (Form D) in cases where the sales invoice is issued either by a company located in a third country or by an ASEAN exporter for the account of the said company, provided

that the goods meet the requirements of Chapter 3 of this Agreement.
2. The exporter shall indicate "third country invoicing" and such information as name and country of the company issuing the invoice in the Certificate of Origin (Form D).

Rule 24 Action against Fraudulent Acts

1. When it is suspected that fraudulent acts in connection with the Certificate of Origin (Form D) have been committed, the Government authorities concerned shall cooperate in the action to be taken in the respective Member State against the persons involved.
2. Each Member State shall provide legal sanctions for fraudulent acts related to the Certificate of Origin (Form D).

Appendix 9

Rules of Origin, ASEAN–Australia–New Zealand Free Trade Agreement

Chapter 3 Rules of Origin

Article 1 Definitions

For the purposes of this Chapter:

(a) **aquaculture** means the farming of aquatic organisms including fish, molluscs, crustaceans, other aquatic invertebrates and aquatic plants, from seedstock such as eggs, fry, fingerlings and larvae, by intervention in the rearing or growth processes to enhance production such as regular stocking, feeding, or protection from predators;

(b) **back-to-back Certificate of Origin** means a Certificate of Origin issued by an intermediate exporting Party's Issuing Authority/Body based on the Certificate of Origin issued by the first exporting Party;

(c) **CIF** means the value of the good imported and includes the cost of freight and insurance up to the port or place of entry into the country of importation. The valuation shall be made in accordance with Article VII of GATT 1994 and the Agreement on Customs Valuation;

(d) **FOB** means the free-on-board value of the good, inclusive of the cost of transport to the port or site of final shipment abroad. The valuation shall be made in accordance with Article VII of GATT 1994 and the Agreement on Customs Valuation;

(e) **generally accepted accounting principles** means the recognised consensus or substantial authoritative support in a Party, with respect to the recording of revenues, expenses, costs, assets and liabilities; the disclosure of information; and the preparation of financial statements. These standards may encompass broad guidelines of general application as well as detailed standards, practices and procedures;

(f) **good** means any merchandise, product, article or material;

(g) **identical and interchangeable materials** means materials that are fungible as a result of being of the same kind and commercial quality, possessing the same technical and physical characteristics, and which once they are incorporated into the finished product cannot be distinguished from one another for origin purposes by virtue of any markings or mere visual examination;

(h) **indirect material** means a good used in the production, testing, or inspection of a good but not physically incorporated into the good, or a good used in the maintenance of buildings or the operation of equipment associated with the production of a good, including:

  (i) fuel and energy;
  (ii) tools, dies and moulds;
  (iii) spare parts and materials used in the maintenance of equipment and buildings;
  (iv) lubricants, greases, compounding materials and other materials used in production or used to operate equipment and buildings;

APPENDIX 9. AANZ

    (v) gloves, glasses, footwear, clothing, safety equipment and supplies;
    (vi) equipment, devices and supplies used for testing or inspecting goods;
    (vii) catalysts and solvents; and
    (viii) any other goods that are not incorporated into the good but whose use in the production of the good can reasonably be demonstrated to be a part of that production;

(i) **material** means any matter or substance used or consumed in the production of goods or physically incorporated into a good or subjected to a process in the production of another good;

(j) **non-originating good** or **non-originating material** means a good or material that does not qualify as originating under this Chapter;

(k) **originating material** means a material that qualifies as originating under this Chapter;

(l) **producer** means a person who grows, mines, raises, harvests, fishes, traps, hunts, farms, captures, gathers, collects, breeds, extracts, manufactures, processes or assembles a good;

(m) **production** means methods of obtaining goods including growing, mining, harvesting, farming, raising, breeding, extracting, gathering, collecting, capturing, fishing, trapping, hunting, manufacturing, producing, processing or assembling a good;

(n) **Product Specific Rules** are rules in Annex 2 (Product Specific Rules) that specify that the materials used to produce a good have undergone a change in tariff classification or a specific manufacturing or processing operation, or satisfy a regional value content criterion or a combination of any of these criteria; and

(o) **packing materials and containers for transportation** means goods used to protect a good during its transportation, different from those containers or materials used for its retail sale.

Article 2 Originating Goods

1. For the purposes of this Chapter, a good shall be treated as an originating good if it is either:

    (a) wholly produced or obtained in a Party as provided in Article 3 (Goods Wholly Produced or Obtained);
    (b) not wholly produced or obtained in a Party provided that the good has satisfied the requirements of Article 4 (Goods Not Wholly Produced or Obtained); or
    (c) produced in a Party exclusively from originating materials from one or more of the Parties, and meets all other applicable requirements of this Chapter.

2. A good which complies with the origin requirements of Paragraph 1 will retain its eligibility for preferential tariff treatment if exported to a Party and subsequently re-exported to another Party.

Article 3 Goods Wholly Produced or Obtained

For the purposes of Article 2.1(a) (Originating Goods), the following goods shall be considered as wholly produced or obtained:

APPENDIX 9. AANZ

(a) plants and plant goods, including fruit, flowers, vegetables, trees, seaweed, fungi and live plants, grown, harvested, picked, or gathered in a Party[1];
(b) live animals born and raised in a Party;
(c) goods obtained from live animals in a Party;
(d) goods obtained from hunting, trapping, fishing, farming, aquaculture, gathering, or capturing in a Party;
(e) minerals and other naturally occurring substances extracted or taken from the soil, waters, seabed or beneath the seabed in a Party;
(f) goods of sea-fishing and other marine goods taken from the high seas, in accordance with international law[2], by any vessel registered or recorded with a Party and entitled to fly the flag of that Party;
(g) goods produced on board any factory ship registered or recorded with a Party and entitled to fly the flag of that Party from the goods referred to in Subparagraph (f);
(h) goods taken by a Party, or a person of a Party, from the seabed or beneath the seabed beyond the Exclusive Economic Zone and adjacent Continental Shelf of that Party and beyond areas over which third parties exercise

---

[1] For the purposes of this Article, "in a Party" means the land, territorial sea, Exclusive Economic Zone, Continental Shelf over which a Party exercises sovereignty, sovereign rights or jurisdiction, as the case may be, in accordance with international law.

For the avoidance of doubt, nothing contained in the above definition shall be construed as conferring recognition or acceptance by one Party of the outstanding maritime and territorial claims made by any other Party, nor shall be taken as pre-judging the determination of such claims.

[2] "International law" refers to generally accepted international law such as the United Nations Convention on the Law of the Sea.

jurisdiction under exploitation rights granted in accordance with international law[3];
(i) goods which are:
  (i) waste and scrap derived from production and consumption in a Party provided that such goods are fit only for the recovery of raw materials; or
  (ii) used goods collected in a Party provided that such goods are fit only for the recovery of raw materials; and
(j) goods produced or obtained in a Party solely from products referred to in Subparagraphs (a) to (i) or from their derivatives.

Article 4 Goods Not Wholly Produced or Obtained

1. For the purposes of Article 2.1(b) (Originating Goods), except for those goods covered under Paragraph 2, a good shall be treated as an originating good if:

   (a) the good has a regional value content of not less than 40 per cent of FOB calculated using the formulae as described in Article 5 (Calculation of Regional Value Content), and the final process of production is performed within a Party; or
   (b) all non-originating materials used in the production of the good have undergone a change in tariff classification at the four-digit level (i.e. a change in tariff heading) of the HS Code in a Party.

---

[3] "International law" refers to generally accepted international law such as the United Nations Convention on the Law of the Sea.

2. In accordance with Paragraph 1, a good subject to Product Specific Rules shall be treated as an originating good if it meets those Product Specific Rules.
3. For a good not specified in Annex 2 (Product Specific Rules), a Party shall permit the producer or exporter of the good to decide whether to use Paragraph 1(a) or (b) when determining if the good is originating.
4. If a good is specified in Annex 2 (Product Specific Rules) and the relevant provisions of that Annex provide a choice of rule between a regional value content based rule of origin, a change in tariff classification based rule of origin, a specific process of production, or a combination of any of these, a Party shall permit the producer or exporter of the good to decide which rule to use in determining if the good is originating.

Article 5 Calculation of Regional Value Content

For the purposes of Article 4 (Goods Not Wholly Produced or Obtained), the formula for calculating the regional value content will be either:

(a) Direct Formula

$$\frac{\text{AANZFTA Material Cost} + \text{Labour Cost} + \text{Overhead Cost} + \text{Profit} + \text{Other Costs}}{\text{FOB}} \times 100\%$$

or

(b) Indirect/Build-Down Formula

$$\frac{\text{FOB} - \text{Value of Non-Originating Materials}}{\text{FOB}} \times 100\%$$

APPENDIX 9. AANZ

where:

(a) AANZFTA Material Cost is the value of originating materials, parts or produce that are acquired or self-produced by the producer in the production of the good;
(b) Labour Cost includes wages, remuneration and other employee benefits;
(c) Overhead Cost is the total overhead expense;
(d) Other Costs are the costs incurred in placing the good in the ship or other means of transport for export including, but not limited to, domestic transport costs, storage and warehousing, port handling, brokerage fees and service charges;
(e) FOB is the free-on-board value of the goods as defined in Article 1 (Definitions); and
(f) Value of Non-Originating Materials is the CIF value at the time of importation or the earliest ascertained price paid for all non-originating materials, parts or produce that are acquired by the producer in the production of the good. Non-originating materials include materials of undetermined origin but do not include a material that is self-produced.

2. The value of goods under this Chapter shall be determined in accordance with Article VII of GATT 1994 and the Agreement on Customs Valuation.

Article 6 Cumulative Rules of Origin

For the purposes of Article 2 (Originating Goods), a good which complies with the origin requirements provided therein and which is used in another Party as a material in the production of another good shall be considered to originate in the Party where working or processing of the finished good has taken place.

Article 7 Minimal Operations and Processes

Where a claim for origin is based solely on a regional value content, the operations or processes listed below, undertaken by themselves or in combination with each other, are considered to be minimal and shall not be taken into account in determining whether or not a good is originating:

(a) ensuring preservation of goods in good condition for the purposes of transport or storage;
(b) facilitating shipment or transportation;
(c) packaging[4] or presenting goods for transportation or sale;
(d) simple processes, consisting of sifting, classifying, washing, cutting, slitting, bending, coiling and uncoiling and other similar operations;
(e) affixing of marks, labels or other like distinguishing signs on products or their packaging; and
(f) mere dilution with water or another substance that does not materially alter the characteristics of the goods.

Article 8 De Minimis

1. A good that does not satisfy a change in tariff classification requirement pursuant to Article 4 (Goods Not

---

[4] This excludes encapsulation which is termed "packaging" by the electronics industry.

Wholly Produced or Obtained) will nonetheless be an originating good if:

(a) (i) for a good, other than that provided for in Chapters 50 to 63 of the HS Code, the value of all non-originating materials used in the production of the good that did not undergo the required change in tariff classification does not exceed 10 per cent of the FOB value of the good;

(ii) for a good provided for in Chapters 50 to 63 of the HS Code, the weight of all non-originating materials used in its production that did not undergo the required change in tariff classification does not exceed 10 per cent of the total weight of the good, or the value of all non-originating materials used in the production of the good that did not undergo the required change in tariff classification does not exceed 10 per cent of the FOB value of the good; and

(b) the good meets all other applicable criteria of this Chapter.

2. The value of such materials shall, however, be included in the value of non-originating materials for any applicable regional value content requirement.

Article 9 Accessories, Spare Parts and Tools

1. For the purposes of determining the origin of a good, accessories, spare parts, tools and instructional or other information materials presented with the good shall be considered part of that good and shall be disregarded in

determining whether all the non-originating materials used in the production of the originating good have undergone the applicable change in tariff classification, provided that:

(a) the accessories, spare parts, tools and instructional or other information materials presented with the good are not invoiced separately from the originating good; and

(b) the quantities and value of the accessories, spare parts, tools and instructional or other information materials presented with the good are customary for that good.

2. Notwithstanding Paragraph 1, if the good is subject to a regional value content requirement, the value of the accessories, spare parts, tools and instructional or other information materials presented with the good shall be taken into account as originating or non-originating materials, as the case may be, in calculating the regional value content of the good.

3. Paragraphs 1 and 2 do not apply where accessories, spare parts, tools and instructional or other information materials presented with the good have been added solely for the purpose of artificially raising the regional value content of that good, provided it is proven subsequently by the importing Party that they are not sold therewith.

Article 10 Identical and Interchangeable Materials

The determination of whether identical and interchangeable materials are originating materials shall be made either by physical segregation of each of the materials or by the use of generally accepted accounting principles of stock control applicable, or inventory management practice, in the exporting Party.

Article 11 Treatment of Packing Materials and Containers

1. Packing materials and containers for transportation and shipment of a good shall not be taken into account in determining the origin of any good.
2. Packing materials and containers in which a good is packaged for retail sale, when classified together with that good, shall not be taken into account in determining whether all of the non-originating materials used in the production of the good have met the applicable change in tariff classification requirements for the good.
3. If a good is subject to a regional value content requirement, the value of the packing materials and containers in which the good is packaged for retail sale shall be taken into account as originating or non-originating materials, as the case may be, in calculating the regional value content of the good.

Article 12 Indirect Materials

An indirect material shall be treated as an originating material without regard to where it is produced and its value shall be the cost registered in the accounting records of the producer of the good.

Article 13 Recording of Costs

For the purposes of this Chapter, all costs shall be recorded and maintained in accordance with the generally accepted accounting principles applicable in the Party in which the goods are produced.

Article 14 Direct Consignment

A good will retain its originating status as determined under Article 2 (Originating Goods) if the following conditions have been met:

(a) the good has been transported to the importing Party without passing through any non-Party; or
(b) the good has transited through a non-Party, provided that:
  (i) the good has not undergone subsequent production or any other operation outside the territories of the Parties other than operations necessary to preserve them in good condition or to transport them to the importing Party;
  (ii) the good has not entered the commerce of a non-Party; and
  (iii) the transit entry is justified for geographical, economic or logistical reasons.

Article 15 Certificate of Origin

A claim that goods are eligible for preferential tariff treatment shall be supported by a Certificate of Origin issued by an

Issuing Authority/Body notified to the other Parties as set out in this Chapter's Annex on Operational Certification Procedures.

Article 16 Denial of Preferential Tariff Treatment

The Customs Authority of the importing Party may deny a claim for preferential tariff treatment when:

(a) the good does not qualify as an originating good; or
(b) the importer, exporter or producer fails to comply with any of the relevant requirements of this Chapter.

Article 17 Review and Appeal

The importing Party shall grant the right of appeal in matters relating to the eligibility for preferential tariff treatment to producers, exporters or importers of goods traded or to be traded between the Parties, in accordance with its domestic laws, regulations and administrative practices.

Article 18 Sub-Committee on Rules of Origin

1. For the purpose of the effective and uniform implementation of this Chapter, the Parties hereby establish a Sub-Committee on Rules of Origin (ROO Sub-Committee). The functions of the ROO Sub-Committee shall include:

APPENDIX 9. AANZ

   (a) monitoring of the implementation and administration of this Chapter;
   (b) discussion of any issue that may have arisen in the course of implementation, including any matters that may have been referred to the ROO Sub-Committee by the Goods Committee established pursuant to Article 11 (Committee on Trade in Goods) of Chapter 2 (Trade in Goods) or the FTA Joint Committee;
   (c) discussion of any proposed modifications of the rules of origin under this Chapter; and
   (d) consultation on issues relating to rules of origin and administrative co-operation.

2. The ROO Sub-Committee shall consist of representatives of the Parties. It shall meet from time to time as mutually determined by the Parties.

3. The ROO Sub-Committee shall commence a review of Article 6 (Cumulative Rules of Origin) no earlier than 12 months, and no later than 18 months following entry into force of this Agreement. This review will consider the extension of the application of cumulation to all value added to a good within AANZFTA. The ROO Sub-Committee shall submit to the Goods Committee established pursuant to Article 11 (Committee on Trade in Goods) of Chapter 2 (Trade in Goods) a final report, including any recommendations, within three years of entry into force of this Agreement.

4. The ROO Sub-Committee shall commence a review of the application of the chemical reaction rule and other chemical process rules to Chapters 28 to 40 of the HS Code and

other Product Specific Rules identified by Parties, no earlier than 12 months and no later than 18 months, following entry into force of this Agreement. The ROO Sub-Committee shall submit to the Goods Committee established pursuant to Article 11 (Committee on Trade in Goods) of Chapter 2 (Trade in Goods) a final report, including any recommendations, within three years of entry into force of this Agreement.

Article 19 Consultations, Review and Modification

1. The Parties shall consult regularly to ensure that this Chapter is administered effectively, uniformly and consistently in order to achieve the spirit and objectives of this Agreement.
2. This Chapter may be reviewed and modified in accordance with Article 6 (Amendments) of Chapter 18 (Final Provisions) as and when necessary, upon request of a Party, and subject to the agreement of the Parties, and may be open to such reviews and modifications as may be agreed upon by the FTA Joint Committee.

Annex On Operational Certification Procedures

For the purpose of implementing Chapter 3 (Rules of Origin), the following operational procedures on the issuance and verification of Certificates of Origin and other related administrative matters shall be observed by each Party.

APPENDIX 9. AANZ

Authorities

Rule 1

The Certificate of Origin shall be issued by an Issuing Authority/Body of the exporting Party. Details of the Issuing Authorities/Bodies shall be notified by each Party, through the ASEAN Secretariat, prior to the entry into force of this Agreement. Any subsequent changes shall be promptly notified by each Party, through the ASEAN Secretariat.

Rule 2

1. The Issuing Authorities/Bodies shall provide the names, addresses, specimen signatures and specimens of the impressions of official seals of their respective Issuing Authorities/Bodies to the other Parties, through the ASEAN Secretariat. The Issuing Authorities/Bodies shall submit electronically to the ASEAN Secretariat the above information and specimens for dissemination to the other Parties. Any subsequent changes shall be promptly notified through the ASEAN Secretariat.
2. Any Certificate of Origin issued by a person not included in the list may not be honoured by the Customs Authority of the importing Party.

Rule 3

For the purpose of determining originating status, the Issuing Authorities/Bodies shall have the right to call for supporting documentary evidence and/or other relevant information to carry out any check considered appropriate in accordance with respective domestic laws, regulations and administrative practices.

Applications

Rule 4

1. The manufacturer, producer, or exporter of the good or its authorised representative shall apply in writing or by electronic means to an Issuing Authority/Body, in accordance with the exporting Party's domestic laws, regulations and the Issuing Authority's/Body's procedures, requesting a pre-exportation examination of the origin of the good to be exported.
2. The result of the examination, subject to review periodically or whenever appropriate, shall be accepted as the supporting evidence in issuing a Certificate of Origin for the good to be exported thereafter.
3. Pre-exportation examination need not apply to a good for which, by its nature, origin can be easily determined.

Rule 5

The manufacturer, producer, or exporter of the good or its authorised representative shall apply for the Certificate of Origin by providing appropriate supporting documents and other relevant information, proving that the good to be exported qualifies as originating.

APPENDIX 9. AANZ

Pre-exportation Examination

Rule 6

The Issuing Authority/Body shall, to the best of its competence and ability, carry out proper examination, in accordance with the domestic laws and regulations of the exporting Party or the procedures of the Issuing Authority/Body, upon each application for the Certificate of Origin to ensure that:

(i) the application and the Certificate of Origin are duly completed and signed by the authorised signatory;
(ii) the good is an originating good in accordance with Article 2 (Originating Goods) of Chapter 3 (Rules of Origin);
(iii) other statements in the Certificate of Origin correspond to appropriate supporting documents and other relevant information; and
(iv) information to meet the minimum data requirements listed in this Annex's Appendix 1 (Minimum Data Requirements – Application for a Certificate of Origin) is provided for the goods being exported.

Issuance of Certificate of Origin

Rule 7

1. The format of the Certificate of Origin is to be determined by the Parties and it must contain the minimum data requirements listed in this Annex's Appendix 2 (Minimum Data Requirements – Certificate of Origin).
2. The Certificate of Origin shall comprise one original and two copies.

3. The Certificate of Origin shall:
    (i) be in hardcopy;
    (ii) bear a unique reference number separately given by each place or office of issuance;
    (iii) be in the English language; and
    (iv) bear an authorised signature and official seal of the Issuing Authority/Body. The signature and official seal may be applied electronically.
4. The original Certificate of Origin shall be forwarded by the exporter to the importer for submission to the Customs Authority of the importing Party. Copies shall be retained by the Issuing Authority/Body and the exporter.
5. Multiple goods declared on the same Certificate of Origin shall be allowed, provided that each good is originating in its own right.

Rule 8

To implement Article 2 (Originating Goods) of Chapter 3 (Rules of Origin), the Certificate of Origin issued by the Issuing Authority/Body shall specify the relevant origin conferring criteria.

Rule 9

Neither erasures nor superimpositions shall be allowed on the Certificate of Origin. Any alteration shall be made by striking out the erroneous material and making any addition required. Such alterations shall be approved by a person authorised to sign the Certificate of Origin and certified by the appropriate

Issuing Authority/Body. Unused spaces shall be crossed out to prevent any subsequent addition.

Rule 10

1. The Certificate of Origin shall be issued as near as possible to, but no later than three working days after, the date of exportation.
2. Where a Certificate of Origin has not been issued as provided for in Paragraph 1 due to involuntary errors or omissions or other valid causes, the Certificate of Origin may be issued retroactively, but no longer than 12 months from the date of exportation, bearing the words "ISSUED RETROACTIVELY".
3. An Issuing Authority/Body of an intermediate Party shall issue a back-to-back Certificate of Origin, if an application is made by the exporter while the good is passing through that intermediate Party, provided that:

    (i) a valid original Certificate of Origin or its certified true copy is presented;
    (ii) the period of validity of the back-to-back Certificate of Origin does not exceed the period of validity of the original Certificate of Origin;
    (iii) the consignment which is to be re-exported using the back-to-back Certificate of Origin does not undergo any further processing in the intermediate Party, except for repacking or logistics activities such as unloading, reloading, storing, or any other operations necessary to preserve them in good condition or to transport them to the importing Party;

(iv) the back-to-back Certificate of Origin contains relevant information from the original Certificate of Origin in accordance with the minimum data requirements in this Annex's Appendix 2 (Minimum Data Requirements – Certificate of Origin). The FOB value shall be the FOB value of the goods exported from the intermediate Party; and

(v) the verification procedures in Rule 17 and Rule 18 shall also apply to the back-to-back Certificate of Origin.

Rule 11

In the event of theft, loss or destruction of a Certificate of Origin, the manufacturer, producer, exporter or its authorised representative may apply to the Issuing Authority/Body for a certified true copy of the original Certificate of Origin. The copy shall be made on the basis of the export documents in their possession and bear the words "CERTIFIED TRUE COPY". This copy shall bear the date of issuance of the original Certificate of Origin. The certified true copy of a Certificate of Origin shall be issued no longer than 12 months from the date of issuance of the original Certificate of Origin.

Presentation

Rule 12

1. For the purpose of claiming preferential tariff treatment, the importer shall submit to the Customs Authority at

the time of import declaration the Certificate of Origin and other documents as required, in accordance with the procedures of the Customs Authority or domestic laws and regulations of the importing Party.
2. Notwithstanding Paragraph 1, a Party may elect not to require the submission of the Certificate of Origin.

Rule 13

The following time limits for the presentation of the Certificate of Origin shall be observed:

(i) the Certificate of Origin shall be valid for a period of 12 months from the date of issue and must be submitted to the Customs Authority of the importing Party within that period;

(ii) where the Certificate of Origin is submitted to the Customs Authority of the importing Party after the expiration of the time limit for its submission, such Certificate of Origin shall still be accepted, subject to the importing Party's domestic laws, regulations or administrative practices, when failure to observe the time limit results from force majeure or other valid causes beyond the control of the importer and/or exporter; and

(iii) the Customs Authority of the importing Party may accept such Certificate of Origin, provided that the goods have been imported before the expiration of the time limit of that Certificate of Origin.

Rule 14

The Certificate of Origin shall not be required for:

(i) goods originating in the exporting Party and not exceeding US$200.00 FOB value or such higher amount specified in the importing Party's domestic laws, regulations or administrative practices; or

(ii) goods sent through the post not exceeding US$200.00 FOB value or such higher amount specified in the importing Party's domestic laws, regulations or administrative practices, provided that the importation does not form part of one or more importations that may reasonably be considered to have been undertaken or arranged for the purpose of avoiding the submission of the Certificate of Origin.

Rule 15

1. Where the origin of the good is not in doubt, the discovery of minor transcription errors or discrepancies in documentation shall not ipso facto invalidate the Certificate of Origin, if it does in fact correspond to the goods submitted.
2. For multiple goods declared under the same Certificate of Origin, a problem encountered with one of the goods listed shall not affect or delay the granting of preferential tariff treatment and customs clearance of the remaining goods listed in the Certificate of Origin.

Rule 16

1. Each Party shall require that the Issuing Authority/Body, manufacturer, producer, exporter, importer, and their

authorised representatives maintain for a period of not less than three years after the date of exportation or importation, as the case may be, all records relating to that exportation or importation which are necessary to demonstrate that the good for which a claim for preferential tariff treatment was made qualifies for preferential tariff treatment. Such records may be in electronic form.
2. Information relating to the validity of the Certificate of Origin shall be furnished upon request of the importing Party by an official authorised to sign the Certificate of Origin and certified by the appropriate Issuing Authority/Body.
3. Any information communicated between the Parties concerned shall be treated as confidential and shall be used for the validation of Certificates of Origin purposes only.[5]

Origin Verification

Rule 17

1. The Customs Authority of the importing Party may verify the eligibility of a good for preferential tariff treatment in accordance with its domestic laws, regulations or administrative practices.
2. If the Customs Authority of the importing Party has reasonable doubts as to the authenticity or accuracy of the information included in the Certificate of Origin or other documentary evidence, it may:

---

[5] This Paragraph shall be read with reference to the confidentiality provisions of Article 5 (Confidentiality) of Chapter 18 (Final Provisions).

(i) institute retroactive checking measures to establish the validity of the Certificate of Origin or other documentary evidence of origin;
(ii) request information from the relevant importer of a good for which preferential tariff treatment was claimed; and
(iii) issue written requests to the Issuing Authority/Body of the exporting Party for information from the exporter or producer.

3. A request for information in accordance with Paragraph 2(iii) shall not preclude the use of the verification visit provided for in Rule 18.
4. The recipient of a request for information under Paragraph 2 shall provide the information requested within a period of 90 days from the date the written request is made.
5. The Customs Authority of the importing Party shall provide written advice as to whether the goods are eligible for preferential tariff treatment to all the relevant parties within 60 days from receipt of information necessary to make a decision.

Verification Visit

Rule 18

1. If the Customs Authority of the importing Party wishes to undertake a verification visit, it shall issue a written request to the Issuing Authority/Body of the exporting Party at least 30 days in advance of the proposed verification visit.

APPENDIX 9. AANZ

2. If the Issuing Authority/Body of the exporting Party is not a government agency, the Customs Authority of the importing Party shall notify the Customs Authority of the exporting Party of the written request to undertake the verification visit.
3. The written request referred to in Paragraphs 1 and 2 shall at a minimum include:

    (i) the identity of the Customs Authority issuing the request;
    (ii) the name of the exporter or the producer of the exporting Party whose good is subject to the verification visit;
    (iii) the date the written request is made;
    (iv) the proposed date and place of the visit;
    (v) the objective and scope of the proposed visit, including specific reference to the good subject to the verification; and
    (vi) the names and titles of the officials of the Customs Authority or other relevant authorities of the importing Party who will participate in the visit.

4. The Issuing Authority/Body of the exporting Party shall notify the exporter or producer of the intended verification visit by the Customs Authority or other relevant authorities of the importing Party and request the exporter or producer to:

    (i) permit the Customs Authority or other relevant authorities of the importing Party to visit their premises or factory; and
    (ii) provide information relating to the origin of the good.

APPENDIX 9. AANZ

5. The Issuing Authority/Body shall advise the exporter or producer that, should they fail to respond by a specified date, preferential tariff treatment may be denied.
6. The Issuing Authority/Body of the exporting Party shall advise the Customs Authority of the importing Party within 30 days of the date of the written request from the Customs Authority of the importing Party whether the exporter or producer has agreed to the request for a verification visit.
7. The Customs Authority of the importing Party shall not visit the premises or factory of any exporter or producer in the territory of the exporting Party without written prior consent from the exporter or producer.
8. The Customs Authority of the importing Party shall complete any action to verify eligibility for preferential tariff treatment and make a decision within 150 days of the date of the request to the Issuing Authority/Body under Paragraph 1. The Customs Authority of the importing Party shall provide written advice as to whether goods are eligible for preferential tariff treatment to the relevant parties within ten days of the decision being made.
9. Parties shall maintain the confidentiality of information classified as confidential collected in the process of verification and shall protect that information from disclosure that could prejudice the competitive position of the person who provided the information. The information classified as confidential may only be disclosed to those authorities responsible for the administration and enforcement of origin determination.[6]

---

[6] This Paragraph shall be read with reference to the confidentiality provisions of Article 5 (Confidentiality) of Chapter 18 (Final Provisions).

APPENDIX 9. AANZ

Suspension of Preferential Tariff Treatment

Rule 19

1. The Customs Authority of the importing Party may suspend preferential tariff treatment to a good that is the subject of an origin verification action under this Annex for the duration of that action or any part thereof.
2. The importing Party may release the goods to the importer subject to any administrative measures deemed necessary, provided that they are not held to be subject to import prohibition or restriction and there is no suspicion of fraud.
3. In the event that a determination is made by the Customs Authority of the importing Party that the good qualifies as an originating good of the exporting Party, any suspended preferential tariff treatment shall be reinstated.

Rule 20

When the destination of any goods exported to a specified Party is changed after their export from the exporting Party, but before clearance by the importing Party, the exporter, manufacturer, producer or its authorised representative shall apply in writing to the Issuing Authority/Body for a new Certificate of Origin for the goods changing destination. The application shall include the original Certificate of Origin relating to the goods.

Rule 21

For the purpose of implementing Article 14 (Direct Consignment) of Chapter 3 (Rules of Origin) where transportation is effected through the territory of any non-Party, the following shall be provided to the Customs Authority of the importing Party:

(i) a through Bill of Lading issued in the exporting Party;
(ii) a Certificate of Origin issued by the relevant Issuing Authority/Body of the exporting Party, unless not required pursuant to Rule 12.2 or Rule 14;
(iii) a copy of the original commercial invoice in respect of the good; and
(iv) supporting documents in evidence that the requirements of Article 14 (Direct Consignment) of Chapter 3 (Rules of Origin) have been complied with.

Rule 22

1. The Customs Authority of the importing Party may accept Certificates of Origin in cases where the sales invoice is issued either by a company located in a third country or by an exporter for the account of that company, provided that the goods meet the requirements of Chapter 3 (Rules of Origin).
2. The words "SUBJECT OF THIRD-PARTY INVOICE (name of company using the invoice)" shall appear on the Certificate of Origin.

Action Against Fraudulent Acts

Rule 23

When it is suspected that fraudulent acts in connection with the Certificate of Origin have been committed, the government authorities concerned shall co-operate in the action to be taken in the respective Party against the persons involved, in accordance with the Party's respective laws and regulations.

Goods in Transport or Storage

Rule 24

Originating goods which are in the process of being transported from the exporting Party to the importing Party, or which are in temporary storage in a bonded area in the importing Party, should be accorded preferential tariff treatment if they are imported into the importing Party on or after the date of entry into force of this Agreement, subject to the submission of a Certificate of Origin issued retroactively to the Customs Authority of the importing Party and subject to domestic laws, regulations or administrative practices of the importing Party.

Settlement of Disputes

Rule 25[7]

1. In the case of a dispute concerning origin determination, classification of goods or other matters, the government authorities concerned in the importing and exporting Parties shall consult each other with a view to resolving the dispute, and the result shall be reported to the other Parties for information.

---

[7] This Rule is without prejudice to a Party's rights under Chapter 17 (Consultations and Dispute Settlement).

APPENDIX 9. AANZ

2. If no settlement can be reached bilaterally, the dispute may be referred to the ROO Sub-Committee established pursuant to Article 18 (Sub-Committee on Rules of Origin) of Chapter 3 (Rules of Origin).

Appendix 1 Minimum Data Requirements – Application for a Certificate of Origin

The minimum data to be included in an application for a Certificate of Origin are:

1. Exporter details	The name, address and contact details of the exporter
2. Shipment details (a separate application must be made for each shipment)	(i) Consignee name and address (ii) Sufficient details to identify the consignment, such as importer's purchase order number, invoice number and date and Air Way Bill or Sea Way Bill or Bill of Lading (iii) Port of Discharge, if known
3. Full description of goods	(i) Detailed description of the goods, including HS Code (6-digit level), and if applicable, product number and brand name (ii) The relevant origin conferring criteria
4. Exporter's declaration	Declaration completed by the exporter or its authorised representative, signed and dated, and annotated with the signatory's name and designation. The declaration shall include a statement that the details provided in the application are true and correct

Appendix 2 Minimum Data Requirements – Certificate of Origin

The minimum data to be included in the Certificate of Origin are:

1. Exporter details	The name and address and contact details of the exporter
2. Shipment details (a Certificate of Origin can only apply to a single shipment of goods)	(i) Consignee name and address (ii) Sufficient details to identify the consignment, such as importer's purchase order number, invoice number and date and Air Way Bill or Sea Way Bill or Bill of Lading (iii) Port of Discharge, if known
3. Full description of goods	(i) Detailed description of the goods, including HS Code (6-digit level), and if applicable, product number and brand name (ii) The relevant origin conferring criteria (iii) FOB Value[8]
4. Certification by Issuing Authority/Body	Certification by the Issuing Authority/Body that, based on the evidence provided, the goods specified in the Certificate of Origin meet all the relevant requirements of Chapter 3 (Rules of Origin)
5. Certificate of Origin number	A unique number assigned to the Certificate of Origin by the Issuing Authority/Body

---

[8] In the case of Australia and New Zealand, a Certificate of Origin or back-to-back Certificate of Origin which does not state the FOB value shall be accompanied by a declaration made by the exporter stating the FOB value of each good described in the Certificate of Origin.

Appendix 10

Rules of Origin, ASEAN–China Free Trade Agreement

Annex 3 Rules of Origin for the ASEAN–China Free Trade Area

In determining the origin of products eligible for the preferential tariff concession pursuant to the Framework Agreement on Comprehensive Economic Co-operation between the Association of Southeast Asian Nations and the People's Republic of China (hereinafter referred to as "the Agreement"), the following Rules shall be applied:

Rule 1: Definitions

For the purpose of this Annex:

(a) "a Party" means the individual parties to the Agreement i.e. Brunei Darussalam, the Kingdom of Cambodia, the Republic of Indonesia, the Lao People's Democratic Republic ("Lao PDR"), Malaysia, the Union of Myanmar, the Republic of the Philippines, the Republic of Singapore, the Kingdom of Thailand, the Socialist Republic of Vietnam and the People's Republic of China ("China").

(b) "materials" shall include ingredients, parts, components, subassembly and/or goods that were physically incorporated into another good or were subject to a process in the production of another good.

(c) "Originating goods" means products that qualify as originating in accordance with the provisions of Rule 2.
(d) "production" means methods of obtaining goods including growing, mining, harvesting, raising, breeding, extracting, gathering, collecting, capturing, fishing, trapping, hunting, manufacturing, producing, processing or assembling a good.
(e) "Product Specific Rules" are rules that specify that the materials have undergone a change in tariff classification or a specific manufacturing or processing operation, or satisfy an ad valorem criterion or a combination of any of these criteria.

Rule 2: Origin Criteria

For the purposes of this Agreement, products imported by a Party shall be deemed to be originating and eligible for preferential concessions if they conform to the origin requirements under any one of the following:

(a) Products which are wholly obtained or produced as set out and defined in Rule 3; or
(b) Products not wholly produced or obtained provided that the said products are eligible under Rule 4, Rule 5 or Rule 6.

Rule 3: Wholly Obtained Products

Within the meaning of Rule 2 (a), the following shall be considered as wholly produced or obtained in a Party:

(a) Plant[1] and plant products harvested, picked or gathered there;
(b) Live animals[2] born and raised there;
(c) Product[3] obtained from live animals referred to in paragraph (b) above;
(d) Products obtained from hunting, trapping, fishing, aquaculture, gathering or capturing conducted there;
(e) Minerals and other naturally occurring substances, not included in paragraphs (a) to (d), extracted or taken from its soil, waters, seabed or beneath their seabed;
(f) Products taken from the waters, seabed or beneath the seabed outside the territorial waters of that Party, provided that that Party has the rights to exploit such waters, seabed and beneath the seabed in accordance with international law;
(g) Products of sea fishing and other marine products taken from the high seas by vessels registered with a Party or entitled to fly the flag of that Party;
(h) Products processed and/or made on board factory ships registered with a Party or entitled to fly the flag of that Party, exclusively from products referred to in paragraph (g) above;

---

[1] Plant here refers to all plant life, including fruit, flowers, vegetables, trees, seaweed, fungi and live plants

[2] Animals referred to in paragraph (b) and (c) covers all animal life, including mammals, birds, fish, crustaceans, molluscs, reptiles, bacteria and viruses.

[3] Products refer to those obtained from live animals without further processing, including milk, eggs, natural honey, hair, wool, semen and dung.

APPENDIX 10. ACFTA

(i) Articles collected there which can no longer perform their original purpose nor are capable of being restored or repaired and are fit only for disposal or recovery of parts of raw materials, or for recycling purposes[4]; and

(j) Goods obtained or produced in a Party solely from products referred to in paragraphs (a) to (i) above.

Rule 4: Not Wholly Produced or Obtained

(a) For the purposes of Rule 2(b), a product shall be deemed to be originating if:

   (i) Not less than 40% of its content originates from any Party; or

   (ii) If the total value of the materials, part or produce originating from outside of the territory of a Party (i.e. non-ACFTA) does not exceed 60% of the FOB value of the product so produced or obtained provided that the final process of the manufacture is performed within the territory of the Party.

(b) For the purposes of this Annex, the originating criteria set out in Rule 4(a)(ii) shall be referred to as the "ACFTA

---

[4] This would cover all scrap and waste including scrap and waste resulting from manufacturing or processing operations or consumption in the same country, scrap machinery, discarded packaging and all products that can no longer perform the purpose for which they were produced and are fit only for discarding or for the recovery of raw materials. Such manufacturing or processing operations shall include all types of processing, not only industrial or chemical but also mining, agriculture, construction, refining, incineration and sewage treatment operations.

content". The formula for the 40% ACFTA content is calculated as follows:

$$\frac{\text{Value of Non-ACFTA materials} + \text{Value of materials of Undetermined origin}}{\text{FOB Price}} \times 100\% < 60\%$$

Therefore, the ACFTA content: 100%−non-ACFTA material = at least 40%

(c) The value of the non-originating materials shall be:

(i) the CIF value at the time of importation of the materials; or

(ii) the earliest ascertained price paid for the materials of undetermined origin in the territory of the Party where the working or processing takes place.

(d) For the purpose of this Rule, "originating material" shall be deemed to be a material whose country of origin, as determined under these rules, is the same country as the country in which the material is used in production.

Rule 5: Cumulative Rule of Origin

Unless otherwise provided for, products which comply with origin requirements provided for in Rule 2 and which are used in the territory of a Party as materials for a finished product eligible for preferential treatment under the Agreement shall be considered as products originating in the territory of the Party where working or processing of the finished product has taken place provided that the aggregate ACFTA content (i.e. full cumulation, applicable among all Parties) on the final product is not less than 40%.

APPENDIX 10. ACFTA

Rule 6: Product Specific Criteria

Products which have undergone sufficient transformation in a Party shall be treated as originating goods of that Party. Products which satisfy the Product Specific Rules provided for in Attachment B shall be considered as goods to which sufficient transformation has been carried out in a Party.

Rule 7: Minimal Operations and Processes

Operations or processes undertaken, by themselves or in combination with each other for the purposes listed below, are considered to be minimal and shall not be taken into account in determining whether a good has been wholly obtained in one country:

(a) ensuring preservation of goods in good condition for the purposes of transport or storage;
(b) facilitating shipment or transportation;
(c) packaging[5] or presenting goods for sale.

Rule 8: Direct Consignment

The following shall be considered as consigned directly from the exporting Party to the importing Party:

(a) If the products are transported passing through the territory of any other ACFTA member states;

---

[5] This excludes encapsulation which is termed "packaging" by the electronics industry.

(b) If the products are transported without passing through the territory of any non-ACFTA member states;
(c) The products whose transport involves transit through one or more intermediate non-ACFTA member states with or without transshipment or temporary storage in such countries, provided that:
  (i) the transit entry is justified for geographical reason or by consideration related exclusively to transport requirements;
  (ii) the products have not entered into trade or consumption there; and
  (iii) the products have not undergone any operation there other than unloading and reloading or any operation required to keep them in good condition.

Rule 9: Treatment of Packing

(a) Where for purposes of assessing customs duties, a Party treats products separately from their packing, it may also, in respect of its imports consigned from another Party, determine separately the origin of such packing.
(b) Where paragraph (a) above is not applied, packing shall be considered as forming a whole with the products and no part of any packing required for their transport or storage shall be considered as having been imported from outside the ACFTA when determining the origin of the products as a whole.

Rule 10: Accessories, Spare Parts and Tools

The origin of accessories, spare parts, tools and instructional or other information materials presented with the goods therewith shall be neglected in determining the origin of the goods, provided that such accessories, spare parts, tools and information materials are classified and collected customs duties with the goods by the importing member state.

Rule 11: Neutral Elements

Unless otherwise provided, for the purpose of determining the origin of goods, the origin of power and fuel, plant and equipment, or machines and tools used to obtain the goods, or the materials used in its manufacture which do not remain in the goods or form part of the goods, shall not be taken into account.

Rule 12: Certificate of Origin

A claim that products shall be accepted as eligible for preferential concession shall be supported by a Certificate of Origin issued by a government authority designated by the exporting Party and notified to the other Parties to the Agreement in accordance with the Operational Certification Procedures, as set out in Attachment A.

Rule 13: Review and Modification

These rules may be reviewed and modified as and when necessary upon request of a Member State and may be open to such reviews and modifications as may be agreed upon by the AEM-MOFCOM.

Attachment A Operational Certification Procedures for the Rules of Origin of the ASEAN-China Free Trade Area

For the purpose of implementing the rules of origin for the ASEAN-China Free Trade Area, the following operational procedures on the issuance and verification of the Certificate of Origin (Form E) and the other related administrative matters shall be followed:

Authorities

Rule 1

The Certificate of Origin shall be issued by the Government authorities of the exporting Party.

Rule 2

(a) The Party shall inform all the other Parties of the names and addresses of their respective Government authorities issuing the Certificate of Origin and shall provide specimen signatures and specimen of official seals used by their said Government authorities.

(b) The above information and specimens shall be provided to every Party to the Agreement and a copy furnished to the ASEAN Secretariat. Any change in names, addresses, or official seals shall be promptly informed in the same manner.

Rule 3

For the purpose of verifying the conditions for preferential treatment, the Government authorities designated to issue the Certificate of Origin shall have the right to call for any supporting documentary evidence or to carry out any check considered appropriate. If such right cannot be obtained through the existing national laws and regulations, it shall be inserted as a clause in the application form referred to in the following Rules 4 and 5.

Applications

Rule 4

The exporter and/or the manufacturer of the products qualified for preferential treatment shall apply in writing to the Government authorities requesting for the pre-exportation verification of the origin of the products. The result of the verification, subject to review periodically or whenever appropriate, shall be accepted as the supporting evidence in verifying the origin of the said products to be exported thereafter. The pre-verification may not apply to the products of which, by their nature, origin can be easily verified.

Rule 5

At the time of carrying out the formalities for exporting the products under preferential treatment, the exporter or his authorised representative shall submit a written application for the Certificate of Origin together with appropriate supporting documents proving that the products to be exported qualify for the issuance of a Certificate of Origin.

Pre-exportation Examination

Rule 6

The Government authorities designated to issue the Certificate of Origin shall, to the best of their competence and ability, carry out proper examination upon each application for the Certificate of Origin to ensure that:

(a) The application and the Certificate of Origin are duly completed and signed by the authorised signatory;
(b) The origin of the product is in conformity with the ASEAN-China Rules of Origin;
(c) The other statements of the Certificate of Origin correspond to supporting documentary evidence submitted;
(d) Description, quantity and weight of goods, marks and number of packages, number and kinds of packages, as specified, conform to the products to be exported.

Issuance of Certificate of Origin

Rule 7

(a) The Certificate of Origin must be in ISO A4 size paper in conformity to the specimen as shown in Attachment C. It shall be made in English.

APPENDIX 10. ACFTA

Original   - Beige (Pantone color code: 727c)
Duplicate   - Light Green (Pantone color code: 622c)
Triplicate   - Light Green (Pantone color code: 622c)
Quadruplicate   - Light Green (Pantone color code: 622c)

(b) The Certificate of Origin shall comprise one original and three (3) carbon copies of the following colours:
(c) Each Certificate of Origin shall bear a reference number separately given by each place of office of issuance.
(d) The original copy shall be forwarded, together with the triplicate, by the exporter to the importer for submission to the Customs Authority at the port or place of importation. The duplicate shall be retained by the issuing authority in the exporting Party. The quadruplicate shall be retained by the exporter. After the importation of the products, the triplicate shall be marked accordingly in Box 4 and returned to the issuing authority within a reasonable period of time.

Rule 8

To implement the provisions of Rules 4 and 5 of the ASEAN-China Rules of Origin, the Certificate of Origin issued by the final exporting Party shall indicate the relevant rules and applicable percentage of ACFTA content in Box 8.

Rule 9

Neither erasures nor superimposition shall be allowed on the Certificate of Origin. Any alteration shall be made by striking out the erroneous materials and making any addition required. Such alterations shall be approved by the person who made them and certified by the appropriate Government authorities. Unused spaces shall be crossed out to prevent any subsequent addition.

Rule 10

(a) The Certificate of Origin shall be issued by the relevant Government authorities of the exporting Party at the time of exportation or soon thereafter whenever the products to be exported can be considered originating in that Party within the meaning of the ASEAN-China Rules of Origin.
(b) In exceptional cases where a Certificate of Origin has not been issued at the time of exportation or soon thereafter due to involuntary errors or omissions or other valid causes, the Certificate of Origin may be issued retroactively but no longer than one year from the date of shipment, bearing the words "ISSUED RETROACTIVELY".

Rule 11

In the event of theft, loss or destruction of a Certificate of Origin, the exporter may apply in writing to the Government authorities which issued it for the certified true copy of the original and the triplicate to be made on the basis of the export documents in their possession bearing the endorsement of the words "CERTIFIED TRUE COPY" in Box 12. This copy shall bear the date of the original Certificate of Origin. The certified true copy of a Certificate of Origin shall be issued not longer than one year from the date of issuance of the original Certificate of Origin and on condition that the exporter provides to the relevant issuing authority the fourth copy.

Presentation

Rule 12

The original Certificate of Origin shall be submitted together with the triplicate to the Customs Authorities at the time of lodging the import entry for the products concerned.

Rule 13

The following time limit for the presentation of the Certificate of Origin shall be observed:

(a) Certificate of Origin shall be submitted to the Customs Authorities of the importing Party within four (4) months from the date of endorsement by the relevant Government authorities of the exporting Party;

(b) Where the products pass through the territory of one or more non-parties in accordance with the provisions of Rule 8 (c) of the ASEAN-China Rules of Origin, the time limit laid down in paragraph (a) above for the submission of the Certificate of Origin is extended to six (6) months;

(c) Where the Certificate of Origin is submitted to the relevant Government authorities of the importing Party after the expiration of the time limit for its submission, such Certificate is still to be accepted when failure to observe the time limit results from force majeure or other valid causes beyond the control of the exporter; and

(d) In all cases, the relevant Government authorities in the importing Party may accept such Certificate of Origin provided that the products have been imported before the expiration of the time limit of the said Certificate of Origin.

Rule 14

In the case of consignments of products originating in the exporting Party and not exceeding US$200.00 FOB, the production of a Certificate of Origin shall be waived and the use of simplified declaration by the exporter that the products in question have originated in the exporting Party will be accepted. Products sent through the post not exceeding US $200.00 FOB shall also be similarly treated.

Rule 15

The discovery of minor discrepancies between the statements made in the Certificate of Origin and those made in the documents submitted to the Customs Authorities of the importing Party for the purpose of carrying out the formalities for importing the products shall not ipso-facto invalidate the Certificate of Origin, if it does in fact correspond to the products submitted.

Rule 16

(a) The importing Party may request a retroactive check at random and/or when it has reasonable doubt as to the authenticity of the document or as to the accuracy of the information regarding the true origin of the products in question or of certain parts thereof.

(b) The request shall be accompanied with the Certificate of Origin concerned and shall specify the reasons and any additional information suggesting that the particulars given on the said Certificate of Origin may be inaccurate, unless the retroactive check is requested on a random basis.

(c) The Customs Authorities of the importing Party may suspend the provisions on preferential treatment while awaiting the result of verification. However, it may release the products to the importer subject to any administrative measures deemed necessary, provided that they are not held to be subject to import prohibition or restriction and there is no suspicion of fraud.

(d) The issuing Government authorities receiving a request for retroactive check shall respond to the request promptly and reply not later than six (6) months after the receipt of the request.

Rule 17

(a) The application for Certificates of Origin and all documents related to such application shall be retained by the issuing authorities for not less than two (2) years from the date of issuance.

(b) Information relating to the validity of the Certificate of Origin shall be furnished upon request of the importing Party.

(c) Any information communicated between the Parties concerned shall be treated as confidential and shall be used for the validation of Certificates of Origin purposes only.

APPENDIX 10. ACFTA

Special Cases

Rule 18

When destination of all or parts of the products exported to a specified Party is changed, before or after their arrival in the Party, the following rules shall be observed:

(a) If the products have already been submitted to the Customs Authorities in the specified importing Party, the Certificate of Origin shall, by a written application of the importer be endorsed to this effect for all or parts of products by the said authorities and the original returned to the importer. The triplicate shall be returned to the issuing authorities.

(b) If the changing of destination occurs during transportation to the importing Party as specified in the Certificate of Origin, the exporter shall apply in writing, accompanied with the issued Certificate of Origin, for the new issuance for all or parts of products.

Rule 19

For the purpose of implementing Rule 8(c) of the ASEAN-China Rules of Origin, where transportation is effected through the territory of one or more non-ACFTA member states, the following shall be produced to the Government authorities of the importing Member State:

(a) A through Bill of Lading issued in the exporting Member State;
(b) A Certificate of Origin issued by the relevant Government authorities of the exporting Member State;

APPENDIX 10. ACFTA

(c) A copy of the original commercial invoice in respect of the product; and
(d) Supporting documents in evidence that the requirements of Rule 8(c) sub-paragraphs (i), (ii) and (iii) of the ASEAN-China Rules of Origin are being complied with.

Rule 20

(a) Products sent from an exporting Party for exhibition in another Party and sold during or after the exhibition into a Party shall benefit from the ASEAN-China preferential tariff treatment on the condition that the products meet the requirements of the ASEAN-China Rules of Origin provided it is shown to the satisfaction of the relevant Government authorities of the importing Party that:

   (i) an exporter has dispatched those products from the territory of the exporting Party to the country where the exhibition is held and has exhibited them there;
   (ii) the exporter has sold the goods or transferred them to a consignee in the importing Party; and
   (iii) the products have been consigned during the exhibition or immediately thereafter to the importing Party in the state in which they were sent for exhibition.

(b) For purposes of implementing the above provisions, the Certificate of Origin must be produced to the relevant Government authorities of the importing Party. The name and address of the exhibition must be indicated, a certificate issued by the relevant Government authorities of the Party where the exhibition took place together with supporting documents prescribed in Rule 19(d) may be required.

(c) Paragraph (a) shall apply to any trade, agricultural or crafts exhibition, fair or similar show or display in shops or business premises with the view to the sale of foreign products and where the products remain under Customs control during the exhibition.

Action Against Fraudulent Acts

Rule 21

(a) When it is suspected that fraudulent acts in connection with the Certificate of Origin have been committed, the Government authorities concerned shall co-operate in the action to be taken in the territory of the respective Party against the persons involved.

(b) Each Party shall be responsible for providing legal sanctions for fraudulent acts related to the Certificate of Origin.

Rule 22

In the case of a dispute concerning origin determination, classification or products or other matters, the Government authorities concerned in the importing and exporting Member States shall consult each other with a view to resolving the dispute, and the result shall be reported to the other Member States for information.

APPENDIX 10. ACFTA

Attachment B Product Specific Rules

A. Exclusive Rule/Criterion

The following product specific criteria shall be the sole criteria for determining the originating status of the following products. When applying for a Certificate of Origin Form E for these products, the exporter concerned can only use the product specific criteria as set out below:

Serial No.	HS Code		Origin Criteria
1	5103.20	Waste of wool or of fine animal hair, not garneted stock	Obtained from sheep, lambs or other animals raised in ACFTA
2	5103.30	Waste of coarse animal hair	Obtained from sheep, lambs or other animals raised in ACFTA
3	5104.00	Garneted stock of wool or of fine or coarse animal hair	Obtained from sheep, lambs or other animals raised in ACFTA
4	5105.31	Fine animal hair of Kashmir (cashmere) goats, carded or combed	Obtained from sheep, lambs or other animals raised in ACFTA
5	5105.39	Other fine animal hair, carded or combed	Obtained from sheep, lambs or other animals raised in ACFTA
6	5105.40	Coarse animal hair, carded or combed	Obtained from sheep, lambs or other animals raised in ACFTA

APPENDIX 10. ACFTA

B. Alternative Rules

The following criteria shall be applied as alternative rule to the general rule prescribed in Rule 4 of the ASEAN-China FTA Rules of Origin. When applying for a Certificate of Origin Form E, the exporter can use either the general rule prescribed in Rule 4 of the ASEAN-China FTA Rules of Origin or the Rules set out in this Attachment.

1. *Change in Tariff Classification*

Serial No	HS Code	Product Description	Origin Criteria
1	1604.11	– Salmon, whole or in pieces, but not minced	Change to subheading 160411 from any other chapter (CC)
2	1604.12	– Herrings, whole or in pieces, but not minced	Change to subheading 160412 from any other chapter (CC)
3	4201.00	Saddlery and harness for any animal (including traces, leads, knees pads, muzzles, saddle cloths, saddle bags, dog coats and the like), of any material	Change to heading 4201 from any other heading
4	4202.11	Trunks, suitcases, vanity-cases, executive-cases, brief-cases, school satchels	Change to heading 4202 from any other heading

APPENDIX 10. ACFTA

(cont.)

Serial No	HS Code	Product Description	Origin Criteria
		and similar containers, with outer surface of leather, of composition leather or of patent leather	
5	4202.12	Other vanity-cases, executive-cases, brief-cases, school satchels and similar containers, with outer surface of plastics or of textile materials	Change to heading 4202 from any other heading
6	4202.19	Other trunks, suitcases, vanity-cases, executive-cases, brief-cases, school satchels and similar containers (for example, with outer surface of vulcanized fibre or of paperboard)	Change to heading 4202 from any other heading
7	4202.21	Handbags, whether or not with shoulder strap, including those without handle, with outer surface of leather of composition leather or of patent leather	Change to heading 4202 from any other heading
8	4202.22	Handbags, whether or not with shoulder strap, including those	Change to heading 4202 from any other heading

APPENDIX 10. ACFTA

(cont.)

Serial No	HS Code	Product Description	Origin Criteria
		without handle, with outer surface of plastic sheeting or of textile materials	
9	4202.29	Other handbags, whether or not with shoulder strap, including those without handle, nes (for example, with outer surface of vulcanized fibre or of paperboard)	Change to heading 4202 from any other heading
10	4202.31	Articles of a kind normally carried in the pocket or handbag, with outer surface of leather, of composition leather or of patent leather	Change to heading 4202 from any other heading
11	4202.32	Articles of a kind normally carried in the pocket or handbag, with outer surface of plastic sheeting or of textile materials	Change to heading 4202 from any other heading
12	4202.39	Other articles of a kind normally carried in the pocket or handbag (for example, with	Change to heading 4202 from any other heading

APPENDIX 10. ACFTA

(cont.)

Serial No	HS Code	Product Description	Origin Criteria
		outer surface of vulcanized fibre or of paperboard)	
13	4202.91	Tool bags, cutlery cases and containers nes, with outer surface of leather, of composition leather or of patent leather	Change to heading 4202 from any other heading
14	4202.92	Tool bags, cutlery cases and containers nes, with outer surface of plastic sheeting or of textile materials	Change to heading 4202 from any other heading
15	4202.99	Other tool bags, cutlery cases and containers (for example, with outer surface of vulcanized fibre or of paperboard)	Change to heading 4202 from any other heading
16	4203.10	Articles of apparel, of leather or of composition leather	Change to heading 4203 from any other heading
17	4203.21	Gloves, mittens and mitts, specially designed for use in sports, of leather or of composition leather	Change to heading 4203 from any other heading
18	4203.29	Other gloves, mittens and mitts of leather or of composition leather	Change to heading 4203 from any other heading

APPENDIX 10. ACFTA

(cont.)

Serial No	HS Code	Product Description	Origin Criteria
19	4203.30	Belts and bandoliers, of leather or of composition leather	Change to heading 4203 from any other heading
20	4203.40	Other clothing accessories, of leather or of composition leather	Change to heading 4203 from any other heading
21	4204.00	Articles of leather or of composition leather, of a kind used in machinery or mechanical appliances or for other technical uses	Change to heading 4204 from any other heading
22	4205.00	Other articles of leather or of composition leather	Change to heading 4205 from any other heading
23	4206.10	Catgut	Change to heading 4206 from any other heading
24	4206.90	Other articles of gut (other than silk-worm gut), of goldbeater's skin, of bladders or of tendons	Change to heading 4206 from any other heading
25	4301.10	Raw furskins of mink, whole, with or without head, tail or paws	Change to heading 4301 from any other heading
26	4301.30	Raw furskins of lamb, the following: Astrakhan, Broadtail,	Change to heading 4301 from any other heading

APPENDIX 10. ACFTA

(cont.)

Serial No	HS Code	Product Description	Origin Criteria
		Caracul, Persian and similar lamb, Indian, Chinese, Mongolian or Tibetan lamb, whole, with or without head, tail or paws	
27	4301.60	Raw furskins of fox, whole, with or without head, tail or paws	Change to heading 4301 from any other heading
28	4301.70	Raw furskins of seal, whole, with or without head, tail or paws	Change to heading 4301 from any other heading
29	4301.80	Other furskins, whole, with or without head, tail or paws	Change to heading 4301 from any other heading
30	4301.90	Heads, tails, paws and other pieces or cuttings, suitable for furriers' use	Change to heading 4301 from any other heading
31	4302.11	Tanned or dressed whole skins of mink, with or without head, tail or paws, not assembled	Change to heading 4302 from any other heading
32	4302.13	Tanned or dressed whole skins of lamb, the following:	Change to heading 4302 from any other heading

APPENDIX 10. ACFTA

(cont.)

Serial No	HS Code	Product Description	Origin Criteria
		Astrakhan, Broadtail, Caracul, Persian and similar lamb, Indian, Chinese, Mongolian or Tibetan lamb, with or without head, tail or paws, not assembled	
33	4302.19	Other tanned or dressed whole skins, with or without head, tail or paws, not assembled	Change to heading 4302 from any other heading
34	4302.20	Tanned or dressed heads, tails, paws and other pieces or cuttings, not assembled	Change to heading 4302 from any other heading
35	4302.30	Tanned or dressed whole skins and pieces or cutting thereof, assembled	Change to heading 4302 from any other heading
36	4303.10	Articles of apparel and clothing accessories of furskin	Change to heading 4303 from any other heading
37	4303.90	Other articles of furskin	Change to heading 4303 from any other heading
38	4304.00	Artificial fur and articles thereof	Change to heading 4304 from any other heading

APPENDIX 10. ACFTA

(cont.)

Serial No	HS Code	Product Description	Origin Criteria
39	6406.10	Uppers and parts thereof, other than stiffeners	Change to heading 6406 from any other heading
40	6406.20	Outer soles and heels, of rubber or plastics	Change to heading 6406 from any other heading
41	6406.91	Wood parts of footwear (excluding uppers, outer soles and heels)	Change to heading 6406 from any other heading
42	6406.99	Non-wood parts of footwear (excluding uppers, outer soles and heels)	Change to heading 6406 from any other heading

2. *Process Criterion for Textile and Textile Products – Working or Processing Carried Out on Non-Originating Materials that Confers Originating Status*[6]

(a) Fibres and Yarns

Manufacture through process of fibre-making (polymerisation, polycondensation and extrusion) spinning, twisting, texturizing or braiding from a blend or any of following:-

---

[6] Products shall be considered as originating if they result exclusively from the processes and/or operations set out in this Attachment.

APPENDIX 10. ACFTA

- Silk
- Wool, fine/coarse animal hair
- Cotton fibres
- Vegetable textile fibres
- Synthetic or artificial filaments/man-made filaments
- Synthetic or artificial staple fibres/man-made staple fibres

Serial No	HS Code	Description
	Ch.52 Cotton	
43	5204.11	Cotton sewing thread >/= 85% by weight of cotton, not put up for retail sale
44	5204.19	Cotton sewing thread, <85% by weight of cotton, not put up for retail sale
45	5204.20	Cotton sewing thread, put up for retail sale
46	5205.11	Cotton yarn, >/=85%, single, uncombed, >/=714.29 dtex, not put up
47	5205.12	Cotton yarn, >/=85%, single, uncombed, 714.29 >/= 232.56, not put up
48	5205.13	Cotton yarn, >/=85%, single, uncombed, 232.56 > dtex >/= 192.31, not put up
49	5205.14	Cotton yarn, >/=85%, single, uncombed, 192.31 > dtex >/=125, not put up
50	5205.15	Cotton yarn, >/==85%, single, uncombed, < 125 dtex, not put up for retail sale
51	5205.21	Cotton yarn, >/=85%, single, combed, >/= 714.29, not put up
52	5202.22	Cotton yarn, >/=85%, single, combed, 714.29 > dtex. >/= 232.56, not put up
53	5205.23	Cotton yarn, >/=85%, single, combed. 232.56 > dtex >/= 192.31, not put up

APPENDIX 10. ACFTA

(cont.)

Serial No	HS Code	Description
54	5205.24	Cotton yarn, >/=85%, single, combed, 192.31 > dtex >/= 125, not put up
55	5205.26	Cotton yarn, >/=85%, single, combed, 106.38 <= dtex < 125, not put up for retail sale
56	5205.27	Cotton yarn, >/=85%, single, combed, 83.33 <= dtex < 106.38, not put up for retail sale
57	5205.28	Cotton yarn, >/=85%, single, combed, < 83.33 dtex (>120 metrix number), not put up for retail sale
58	5205.31	Cotton yarn, >/=85%, multi, uncombed, >/= 714.29 dtex, not put up, nes
59	5205.32	Cotton yarn, >/=85%, multi, uncombed, 714.29 >dtex >/= 232.56, not put up, nes
60	5205.33	Cotton yarn, >/=85%, multi, uncombed, 232.56 > dtex >/= 192.31, not put up, nes
61	5205.34	Cotton yarn, >/=85%, multi, uncombed, 192.31 > dtex >/= 125, not put up, nes
62	5205.35	Cotton yarn, >/=85%, multi, uncombed, < 125 dtex, not put up, nes
63	5205.41	Cotton yarn, >/=85%, multiple, combed, >/= 714.29 dtex, not put up, nes
64	5205.42	Cotton yarn, >/=85%, multi, combed, 714.29 > dtex >/= 232.56, not put up. nes
65	5205.43	Cotton yarn; >/=85%, multi, combed, 232.56 > dtex >/= 192.31, not put up. nes
66	5205.44	Cotton yarn, >/=85%, multiple, combed, 192.31 > dtex >/= 125, not put up, nes
67	5205.46	Cotton yarn, >/=85%, multiple, combed, 106.38 <= dtex < 125, not put up, nes
68	5205.47	Cotton yarn, >/=85%, multiple, combed, 83.33 <= dtex < 106.38, not put up, nes

APPENDIX 10. ACFTA

(cont.)

Serial No	HS Code	Description
69	5205.48	Cotton yarn, >/=85%, multiple, combed, < 83.33 dtex, not put up, nes
70	5206.11	Cotton yarn, <85%, single, uncombed, >/= 714.29, not put up
71	5206.12	Cotton yarn, <85%, single, uncombed, 714.29 > dtex >/= 232.56, not put up
72	5206.13	Cotton yarn, <85%, single, uncombed, 232.56 > dtex >/= 192.31, not put up
73	5206.14	Cotton yarn, <85%, single, uncombed, 192.31 > dtex >/= 125, not put up
74	5206.15	Cotton yarn, <85%, single, uncombed, < 125 dtex, not put up for retail sale
75	5206.21	Cotton yarn, <85%, single, combed, >/= 714.29 dtex, not put up
76	5206.22	Cotton yarn, <85%, single, combed, 714.29 > dtex >/= 232.56, not put up -
77	5206.23	Cotton yarn, <85%, single, combed. 232.56 > dtex >/= 192.31, not put up
78	5206.24	Cotton yarn, <85%, single, combed, 192.31 > dtex >/=125, not put up
79	5206.25	Cotton yarn, <85%, single, combed, < 125 dtex, not put up for retail sale
80	5206.31	Cotton yarn, <85%, multiple, uncombed, >/= 714.29, not put up, nes
81	5206.32	Cotton yarn, <85%, multiple, uncombed, 714.29 > dtex >/= 232.56, not put
82	5206.33	Cotton yarn, <85%, multiple, uncombed, 232.56 > dtex >/= 192.31, not put up, nes
83	5206.34	Cotton yarn, <85%, multiple, uncombed, 192.31 > dtex >/= 125, not put up. nes

APPENDIX 10. ACFTA

(cont.)

Serial No	HS Code	Description
84	5206.35	Cotton yarn, <85%, multiple, uncombed, < 125 dtex, not put up, nes
85	5206.41	Cotton yarn, <85%, multiple, combed, >/= 714.29, not put up, nes
86	5206.42	Cotton yarn, <85%, multiple, combed, 714.29 > dtex >/= 232.56, not put up, nes
87	5206.43	Cotton yarn, <85%, multiple, combed, 232.56 >dtex >/= 192.31, not put up, nes
88	5206.44	Cotton yarn, <85%, multiple, combed, 192.31>dtex >/= 125, not put up, nes
89	5206.45	Cotton yarn, <85%. multiple, combed. < 125 dtex. not put up, nes
90	5207.10	Cotton yarn (other than sewing thread) >/= 85% by weight of cotton put up
91	5207.90	Cotton yarn (other than sewg thread) < 85% by-wt of cotton. put up for retail sale

(b) Fabric/Carpets And Other Textile Floor Coverings; Special Yarns, twine, cordage and ropes and cables and articles thereof.

Manufacture from:

- Polymer (non-woven)
- Fibres (non-woven)
- Yarns (fabrics)
- Raw or Unbleached Fabrics (finished fabrics)

APPENDIX 10. ACFTA

through substantial transformation process of either:
- needle punching / spin bonding / chemical bonding
- weaving or knitting;
- crochetting or wadding or tufting; or
- dyeing or printing and finishing; or impregnation, coating, covering or lamination.

Serial No	HS Code	Description
	Ch.52 Cotton	
92	5208.11	Plain weave cotton fabric. >/= 85%, not more than 100 g/m2; unbleached
93	5208.12	Plain weave cotton fabric, >/= 85%, > 100 g/m2 to 200 g/m2, unbleached
94	5208.13	Twill weave cotton fabric, >/= 85%, not more than 200g/m2, bleached
95	5208.19	Woven fabrics of cotton, >/= 85%, not more than 200 g/m2, unbleached, nes
96	5208.21	Plain weave cotton fabrics, >/= 85%, not more than 100g/m2, bleached
97	5208.22	Plain weave cotton fabric, >/ = 85%, > 100 g/m2 to 200 g/m2. bleached
98	5208.23	Twill weave cotton fabric, >/= 85%, not more than 200g/m2, bleached
99	5208.29	Woven fabrics of cotton, >/= 85%, nt more than 200 g/m2, bleached, nes
100	5208.41	Plain weave cotton fabric, >/= 85%, not more than 100 g/m2, yarns of other colors
101	5208.42	Plain weave cotton fabrics, >/= 85%, > 100 g/m2 to 200 g/m2, yarns of other colors
102	5208.43	Twill weave cotton fabric, >/= 85%, not more than 200 g/m2, yarns of other colors
103	5208.49	Woven fabrics of cotton, >/= 85%, nt more than 200 g/m2, yarns of other colors, nes

APPENDIX 10. ACFTA

(cont.)

Serial No	HS Code	Description
104	5209.11	Plain weave cotton fabric, >/= 85%, more than 200 g/m2, unbleached
105	5209.12	Twill weave cotton fabric, >/= 85%, more than 200 g/m2, unbleached
106	5209.19	Woven fabrics of cotton, >/= 85%, more than 200 g/m2, unbleached, nes
107	5209.21	Plain weave cotton fabric, >/= 85%, more than 200 g/m2, bleached
108	5209.22	Twill weave cotton fabrics, >/= 85%, more than 200:g/m2, bleached
109	5209.29	Woven fabrics of cotton, >/= 85%, more than 200 g/m2, bleached, nes
110	5209.41	Plain weave cotton fabrics, >/= 85%, more than 200 g/m2, yarns of other colors
111	5209.42	Denim fabrics of cotton, >/= 85%, more than 200 g/m2
112	5209.43	Twill weave cotton fab, other than denim, >/= 85%, more than 200 g/m2, yarn dyec
113	5209.49	Woven fabrics of cotton, >/= 85%, more than 200 g/m2, yarns of other colors, nes
114	5210.11	Plain weave cotton fab, < 85% mixd w m-m fib, not more than 200 g/m2, unbl
115	5210.12	Twill weave cotton fab, < 85% mixd w m-m fib, not more than 200 g/m2, unbl
116	5210.19	Woven fab of cotton, < 85% mixd with m-m fib, </= 200 g/m2, unbl, nes
117	5210.21	Plain weave cotton fab, < 85% mixd w m-m fib, not more than 200 g/m2, bl
118	5210.22	Twill weave cotton fab, < 85% mixd w m-m fib, not more than 200 g/m2, bl
119	5210.29	Woven fabrics of cotton, < 85% mixd with m-m fib, </= 200 g/m2, bl, nes
120	5210.41	Plain weave cotton tab. < 85% mixd w m-m fib. nt mor inn 200g/m2 yarns of other colors

APPENDIX 10. ACFTA

(cont.)

Serial No	HS Code	Description
121	5210.42	Twill weave cotton fab, <85% mixd w m-m fib. nt mor thn 200 g/m2. yarns of other colors
122	5210.49	Woven fabrics of cotton. <85% mixd with m-m fib, </= 200 g/m2. yarns of other colors. Nes
123	5211.11	Plain weave cotton fab. <85% mixd w m-m fib, more thn 200 g/m2. unbleached
124	5211.12	Twill weave cotton fab. <85% mixed w m-m fib. more than 200 g/m2. unbl
125	5211.19	Woven fabrics of cotton, <85% mixd with m-m fib, more thn 200 g/m2. unbl. nes
126	5211.21	Plain weave cotton fab, <85% mixd w m-m fib, more than 200 g/m2. bleached
127	5211.22	Twill weave cotton fab. <85% mixd w m-m fib. more than 200 g/m2, bleached
128	5211.29	Woven fabrics of cotton. < 85% mixd with m-m fib, more than 200 g/m2, bl, nes
129	5211.41	Plain weave cotton fab. <85% mixd w m-m fib, more than 200 g/m2, yarns of other colors
130	5211.42	Denim fabrics of cotton. < 85% mixed with m-m fib, more than 200 g/m2
131	5211.43	Twill weave cotton fab, other than denim, <85% mixd w m-m fib, > 200 g/m2, yarn dye
132	5211.49	Woven fabrics of cotton, <85% mixd with m-m fib, > 200 g/m2. yarns of other colors. nes
133	5212.11	Woven fabrics of cotton, weighing not more than 200 g/m2, unbleached, nes
134	5212.12	Woven fabrics of cotton, weighing not more than 200 g/m2, bleached, nes
135	5212.14	Woven fabrics of cotton. </=200 g/m2. of yarns of different colours, nes
136	5212.21	Woven fabrics of cotton, weighing more than 200 g/m2, unbleached, nes

APPENDIX 10. ACFTA

(cont.)

Serial No	HS Code	Description
137	5212.22	Woven fabrics of cotton, weighing more than 200 g/m2. bleached, nes
138	5212.24	Woven fabrics of cotton, >200 g/m2, of yarns of different colours, nes
	Ch. 60	Knitted or crocheted fabrics
139	6001.10	Long pile knitted or crocheted textile fabrics
140	6001.21	Looped pile knitted or crocheted fabrics, of cotton
141	6001.22	Looped pile knitted or crocheted fabrics, of man-made fibres
142	6001.29	Looped pile knitted or crocheted fabrics, of other textile materials
143	6002.40	Knitted or crocheted tex fab, w </= 30 cm, >/= 5% of elastomeric, not containing rubber thread
144	6002.90	Knitted or crocheted tex fab, w </= 30 cm, >/= 5% of elastomeric, containing rubber thread
145	6003.10	Knitted or crocheted fabrics, w </=30 cm, of wool or fine animal hair
146	6003.20	Knitted or crocheted fabrics, w </=30 cm, of cotton
147	6003.30	Knitted or crocheted fabrics, w </=30 cm, of synthetic fibres
148	6003.40	Knitted or crocheted fabrics, w </=30 cm, of artificial fibres
149	6003.90	Knitted or crocheted fabrics, w </=30 cm, of nes
150	6004.10	Knitted or crocheted tex fab, w > 30 cm, >/= 5% of elastomeric, not containing rubber thread
151	6004.90	Knitted or crocheted tex fab, w > 30 cm, >/= 5% of elastomeric, containing rubber thread
152	6005.10	Warp knitted fabrics, of wool or fine animal hair, nes
153	6005.21	Warp knitted fabrics, of unbleached or bleached cotton, nes
154	6005.22	Warp knitted fabrics, of dyed cotton, nes
155	6005.23	Warp knitted fabrics, of yarn of different colours cotton, nes

APPENDIX 10. ACFTA

(cont.)

Serial No	HS Code	Description
156	6005.24	Warp knitted fabrics, of printed cotton, nes
157	6005.31	Warp knitted fabrics, of unbleached or bleached synthetic fibres, nes
158	6005.32	Warp knitted fabrics, of dyed synthetic fibres, nes
159	6005.33	Warp knitted fabrics, of yarn of different colours synthetic fibres, nes
160	6005.41	Warp knitted fabrics, of unbleached or bleached artificial fibres, nes
161	6005.42	Warp knitted fabrics, of dyed artificial fibres, nes
162	6005.43	Warp knitted fabrics, of yarn of different colours artificial fibres, nes
163	6005.44	Warp knitted fabrics, of printed artificial fibres, nes
164	6005.90	Warp knitted fabrics, of other materials, nes
165	6006.10	Knitted or crocheted fabrics, of wool or of fine animal hair, nes
166	6006.31	Knitted or crocheted fabrics, of unbleached or bleached synthetic fibres, nes
167	6006.32	Knitted or crocheted fabrics, of dyed synthetic fibres, nes
168	6006.33	Knitted or crocheted fabrics, of yarn of different colours of synthetic fibres, nes
169	6006.34	Knitted or crocheted fabrics, of printed synthetic fibres, nes
170	6006.41	Knitted or crocheted fabrics, of unbleached or bleached artificial fibres, nes
171	6006.42	Knitted or crocheted fabrics, of dyed artificial fibres, nes
172	6006.43	Knitted or crocheted fabrics, of yarn of different colours of artificial fibres, nes
173	6006.44	Knitted or crocheted fabrics, of printed artificial fibres, nes
174	6006.90	Knitted or crocheted fabrics, of other materials, nes

(c) Article of Apparel and Clothing Accessories and Other Made Up Textile Articles

Manufacture through the processes of cutting and assembly of parts into a complete article (for apparel and tents) and incorporating embroidery or embellishment or printing (for made-up articles) from:

- raw or unbleached fabric
- finished fabric

Serial No		Description
	Ch.61	Art of apparel & clothing access, knitted or crocheted
175	6101.10	Mens/boys overcoats, anoraks etc, of wool or fine animal hair, knitted
176	6101.20	Mens/boys overcoats, anoraks, etc of cotton, knitted.
177	6101.30	Mens/boys overcoats, anoraks etc, of man-made fibres, knitted
178	6101.90	Mens/boys overcoats, anoraks etc, of other textile materials, knitted
179	6102.10	Womens/girls overcoats, anoraks etc, of wool or fine animal hair, knitted
180	6102.20	Womens/girls overcoats, anoraks etc, of cotton, knitted
181	6102.30	Womens/girls overcoats, anoraks etc, of man-made fibres, knitted
182	6102.90	Womens/girls overcoats, anoraks etc, of other textile materials, knitted
183	6103.11	Mens/boys suits, of wool or fine animal hair, knitted
184	6103.12	Mens/boys suits, of synthetic fibres, knitted
185	6103.19	Mens/boys suits, of other textile.materials, knitted
186	6103.21	Mens/boys ensembles, of wool or fine animal hair, knitted
187	6103.22	Mens/boys ensembles, of cotton, knitted
188	6103.23	Mens/boys ensembles, of synthetic fibres, knitted
189	6103.29	Mens/boys ensembles, of other textile materials, knitted

(cont.)

Serial No		Description
190	6103.31	Mens/boys jackets and blazers, of wool or fine animal hair, knitted
191	6103.32	Mens/boys jackets and blazers, of cotton, knitted
192	6103.33	Mens/boys jackets and blazers, of synthetic fibres, knitted
193	6103.39	Mens/boys jackets and blazers, of other textile materials, knitted
194	6103.41	Mens/boys trousers and shorts, of wool or fine animal hair, knitted
195	6103.42	Mens/boys trousers and shorts, of cotton, knitted
196	6103.43	Mens/boys trousers and shorts, of synthetic fibres, knitted
197	6103.49	Mens/boys trousers and shorts, of other textile materials, knitted
198	6104.11	Womens/girls suits, of wool or fine animal hair; knitted
199	6104.12	Womens/girls suits, of cotton, knitted
200	6104.13	Womens/girls suits, of synthetic fibres, knitted
201	6104.19	Womens/girls suits, of other textile materials, knitted
202	6104.21	Womens/girls ensembles, of wool or fine animal hair, knitted
203	6104.22	Womens/girls ensembles, of cotton, knitted
204	6104.23	Womens/girls ensembles, of synthetic fibres, knitted
205	6104.29	Womens/girls ensembles, of other textile materials, knitted
206	6104.31	Womens/girls jackets, of wool or fine animal hair, knitted
207	6104.32	Womens/girls jackets, of cotton, knitted
208	6104.33	Womens/girls jackets, of synthetic fibres, knitted
209	6104.39	Womens/girls jackets, of other textile materials, knitted
210	6104.41	Womens/girls dresses, of wool or fine animal hair, knitted
211	6104.42	Womens/girls dresses, of cotton, knitted
212	6104.43	Womens/girls dresses, of synthetic fibres, knitted
213	6104.44	Womens/girls dresses, of artificial fibres, knitted
214	6104.49	Womens/girls dresses, of other textile materials, knitted
215	6104.51	Womens/girls skirts, of wool or fine animal hair, knitted
216	6104.52	Womens/girls skirts, of cotton, knitted

APPENDIX 10. ACFTA

(cont.)

Serial No		Description
217	6104.53	Womens/girls skirts, of synthetic fibres, knitted
218	6104.59	Womens/girls skirts, of other textile materials, knitted
219	6104.61	Womens/girls trousers and shorts, of wool or fine animal hair, knitted
220	6104.62	Womens/girls trousers and shorts, of cotton, knitted.
221	6104.63	Womens/girls trousers and shorts, of synthetic fibres, knitted
222	6104.69	Womens/girls trousers and shorts, of other textile materials, knitted
223	6105.10	Mens/boys shirts, of cotton, knitted
224	6105.20	Mens/boys shirts, of man-made fibres, knitted
225	6105.90	Mens/boys shirts, of other textile materials, knitted
226	6106.10	Womens/girls blouses and shirts, of cotton, knitted
227	6106.20	Womens/girls blouses and shirts, of man-made fibres, knitted
228	6106.90	Womens/girls blouses and shirts, of other materials, knitted
229	6107.11	Mens/boys underpants and briefs, of cotton, knitted
230	6107.12	Mens/boys underpants and briefs, of man-made fibres, knitted
231	6107.19	Mens/boys underpants and briefs, of other textile materials, knitted
232	6107.21	Mens/boys nightshirts and pyjamas,.of cotton, knitted
233	6107.22	Mens/boys nightshirts and pyjamas, of man-made fibres, knitted
234	6107.29	Mens/boys nightshirts and pyjamas, of other textile materials, knitted
235	6107.91	Mens/boys bathrobes, dressing gowns etc of cotton, knitted
236	6107.92	Mens/boys bathrobes, dressing gowns etc of man-made fibres, knitted
237	6107.99	Mens/boys bathrobes, dressing gowns etc of oth textile materials, knitted

APPENDIX 10. ACFTA

(cont.)

Serial No		Description
238	6108.11	Womens/girls slips and petticoats, of man-made fibres, knitted
239	6108.19	Womens/girls slips and petticoats, of other textile materials, knitted
240	6108.21	Womens/girls briefs and panties, of cotton, knitted
241	6108.22	Womens/girls briefs and panties, of man-made fibres, knitted
242	6108.29	Womens/girls briefs and panties, of other textile materials, knitted
243	6108.31	Womens/girls nightdresses and pyjamas, of cotton, knitted
244	6108.32	Womens/girls nightdresses and pyjamas, of man-made fibres, knitted
245	6108.39	Womens/girls nightdresses and pyjamas, of oth textile materials, knitted
246	6108.91	Womens/girls bathrobes, dressing gowns, etc, of cotton, knitted
247	6108.92	Womens/girls bathrobes, dressing gowns, etc, of man-made fibres, knitted
248	6108.99	Womens/girls bathrobes, dressg gowns.etc.of oth textile materials, knittd
249	6109.10	T-shirts, singlets and other vests, of cotton, knitted
250	6109.90	T-shirts, singlets and other vests, of other textile materials, knitted
251	6110.11	Pullovers.cardigans&similiar article of wool or fine animal hair, knittd: of wool
252	6110.12	Pullovers.cardigans&similiar article of wool or fine animal hair, knittd: of kashmir goats
253	6110.19	Pullovers.cardigans&similiar article of wool or fine animal hair, knittd: of other animal hair.
254	6110.20	Pullovers, cardigans & similiar articles of cotton, knitted
255	6110.30	Pullovers,cardigans & similiar articles of man-made fibres, knitted

APPENDIX 10. ACFTA

(cont.)

Serial No		Description
256	6110.90	Pullovers,cardigans&similiar articles of oth textile materials, knitted
257	6111.10	Babies garments&clothg accessories of wool or fine animal hair, knitted
258	6111.20	Babies garments & clothing accessories of cotton, knitted
259	6111.30	Babies garments & clothing accessories of synthetic fibres, knitted
260	6111.90	Babies garments&clothg accessories of other textile materials, knitted
261	6112.11	Track suits, of cotton, knitted
262	6112.12	Track suits, of synthetic fibres, knitted
263	6112.19	Track suits, of other textile materials, knitted
264	6112.20	Ski suits, of textile materials, knitted
265	6112.31	Mens/boys swimwear, of synthetic fibres, knitted
266	6112.39	Mens/boys swimwear, of other textile materials, knitted
267	6112.41	Womens/girls swimwear, of synthetic fibres, kniited
268	6112.49	Womens/girls swimwear, of other textile materials, knitted
269	6113.00	Garments made up of impreg, coatd, coverd or laminatd textile knittd fab
270	6114.10	Garments nes, of wool or fine animal hair, knittd
271	6114.20	Garments nes, of cotton, knitted
272	6114.30	Garments nes, of man-made fibres, knitted
273	6114.90	Garments nes, of other textile materials knitted
274	6115.11	Panty hose&tights, of synthetic fibre yarns <67 dtex/single yarn knittd
275	6115.12	Panty hose&tights, of synthetic fibre yarns >/=67 dtex/single yarn knittd
276	6115.19	Panty hose & tights, of other textile materials, knitted
277	6115.20	Women mll-l/knee-1 hosiery, of textile yarn < 67 dtex/single yarn knittd
278	6115.91	Hosiery nes, of wool or fine animal hair, knitted
279	6115.92	Hosiery nes, of cotton, knitted

APPENDIX 10. ACFTA

(cont.)

Serial No		Description
280	6115.93	Hosiery nes, of synthetic fibres, knitted
281	6115.99	Hosiery nes, of other textile materials, knitted
282	6116.10	Gloves impregnated, coated or covered with plastics or ubber, knitted
283	6116.91	Gloves, mittens and mitts, nes, of wool or fine animal hair, knitted
284	6116.92	Gloves, mittens and mitts, nes, of cotton, knitted
285	6116.93	Gloves, mittens and mitts, nes, of synthetic fibres, knitted
286	6116.99	Gloves, mittens and mitts, nes, of other textile materials, knitted
287	6117.10	Shawls, scarves, veils and the like, of textile materials, knitted
288	6117.20	Ties, bow ties and cravats, of textile materials, knitted
289	6117.80	Clothing accessories nes, of textile materials, knitted
290	6117.90	Parts of garments/of clothg accessories, of textile materials, knittd
	Ch.62	Art of apparel & clothing access, not knitted/crocheted
291	6201.11	Mens/boys overcoats&similar articles of wool/fine animal hair,nt knit
292	6201.12	Mens/boys overcoats & similar articles of cotton, not knitted
293	6201.13	Mens/boys overcoats & similar articles of man-made fibres, not knitted
294	6201.19	Mens/boys overcoats & similar articles of oth tex materials, nt knitted
295	6201.91	Mens/boys anoraks&similar articles of wool/fine animal hair, not knitted
296	6201.92	Mens/boys anoraks & similar articles of cotton, not knitted
297	6201.93	Mens/boys anoraks & similar articles of man-made fibres, not knitted
298	6201.99	Mens/boys anoraks & similar articles of oth tex materials, not knitted

APPENDIX 10. ACFTA

(cont.)

Serial No		Description
299	6202.11	Womens/girls o/coats&similar articles of wool/fine animal hair, not knit
300	6202.12	Womens/girls overcoats & similar articles of cotton, not knitted
301	6202.13	Womens/girls o/coats & similar articles of man-made fibres, not knitted
302	6202.19	Womens/girls o/coats&similar articles of oth textile materials, not knit
303	6202.91	Womens/girls anoraks&similar articles of wool/fine animal hair, not knit
304	6202.92	Womens/girls anoraks & similar articles of cotton, not knitted
305	6202.93	Womens/girls anoraks & similar articles of man-made fibres, not knitted
306	6202.99	Womens/girls anoraks & similar articles of oth tex materials, not knit
307	6203.11	Mens/boys suits, of wool or fine animal hair, not knitted
308	6203.12	Mens/boys suits, of synthetic fibres, not knitted
309	6203.19	Mens/boys suits, of other textile materials, not knitted
310	6203.21	Mens/boys ensembles, of wool or fine animal hair, not knitted
311	6203.22	Mens/boys ensembles, of cotton, not knitted
312	6203.23	Mens/boys ensembles, of synthetic fibres, not knitted
313	6203.29	Mens/boys ensembles, of other textile materials, not knitted
314	6203.31	Mens/boys jackets and blazers, of wool or fine animal hair, not knitted
315	6203.32	Mens/boys jackets and blazers, of cotton, not knitted
316	6203.33	Mens/boys jackets and blazers, of synthetic fibres, not knitted
317	6203.39	Mens/boys jackets and blazers, of other textile materials, not knitted
318	6203.41	Mens/boys trousers and shorts, of wool or fine animal hair, not knitted

APPENDIX 10. ACFTA

(cont.)

Serial No		Description
319	6203.42	Mens/boys trousers and shorts, of cotton, not knitted
320	6203.43	Mens/boys trousers and shorts, of synthetic fibres, not knitted
321	6203.49	Mens/boys trousers and shorts, of other textile materials, not knitted
322	6204.11	Womens/girls suits, of wool or fine animal hair, not knitted
323	6204.12	Womens/girls suits, of cotton, not knitted
324	6204.13	Womens/girls suits, of synthetic fibres, not knitted
325	6204.19	Womens/girls suits, of other textile materials, not knitted
326	6204.21	Womens/girls ensembles, of wool or fine animal hair, not knitted
327	6204.22	Womens/girls ensembles, of cotton, not knitted
328	6204.23	Womens/girls ensembles, of synthetic fibres, not knitted
329	6204.29	Womens/girls ensembles, of other textile materials, not knitted
330	6204.31	Womens/girls jackets, of wool or fine animal hair, not knitted
331	6204.32	Womens/girls jackets, of cotton, not knitted
332	6204.33	Womens/girls jackets, of synthetic fibres, not knitted
333	6204.39	Womens/girls jackets, of other textile materials, not knitted
334	6204.41	Womens/girls dresses, of wool or fine animal hair, not knitted
335	6204.42	Womens/girls dresses, of cotton, not knitted
336	6204.43	Womens/girls dresses, of synthetic fibres, not knitted
337	6204.44	Womens/girls dresses, of artificial fibres, not knitted
338	6204.49	Womens/girls dresses, of other textile materials, not knitted
339	6204.51	Womens/girls skirts, of wool or fine animal hair, not knitted
340	6204.52	Womens/girls skirts, of cotton, not knitted
341	6204.53	Womens/girls skirts, of synthetic fibres, not knitted

APPENDIX 10. ACFTA

(cont.)

Serial No		Description
342	6204.59	Womens/girls skirts, of other textile materials, not knitted
343	6204.61	Womens/girls trousers & shorts, of wool or fine animal hair, not knitted
344	6204.62	Womens/girls trousers and shorts, of cotton, not knitted
345	6204.63	Womens/girls trousers and shorts, of synthetic fibres, not knitted
346	6204.69	Womens/girls trousers & shorts, of other textile materials, not knitted
347	6205.10	Mens/boys shirts, of wool or fine animal hair, not knitted
348	6205.20	Mens/boys shirts, of cotton, not knitted
349	6205.30	Mens/boys shirts, of man-made fibres, not knitted
350	6205.90	Mens/boys shirts, of other textile materials, not knitted
351	6206.10	Womens/girls blouses and shirts, of silk or silk waste, -not knitted
352	6206.20	Womens/girls blouses & shirts, of wool or fine animal hair, not knitted
353	6206.30	Womens/girls blouses and shirts, of cotton, not knitted
354	6206.40	Womens/girls blouses and shirts, of man-made fibres, not knitted
355	6206.90	Womens/girls blouses and shirts, of other textile materials, not knitted
356	6207.11	Mens/boys underpants and briefs, of cotton, not knitted
357	6207.19	Mens/boys underpants and briefs, of other textile materials, not knitted
358	6207.21	Mens/boys nightshirts and pyjamas, of cotton, not knitted
359	6207.22	Mens/boys nightshirts and pyjamas, of man-made fibres, not knitted
360	6207.29	Mens/boys nightshirts & pyjamas, of other textile materials, not knitted
361	6207.91	Mens/boys bathrobes, dressing gowns, etc of cotton, not knitted
362	6207.92	Mens/boys bathrobes, dressing gowns, etc of man-made fibres, not knitted

APPENDIX 10. ACFTA

(cont.)

Serial No		Description
363	6207.99	Mens/boys bathrobes,dressing gowns.etc of oth tex materials, not knit
364	6208.11	Womens/girls slips and petticoats, of man-made fibres, not knitted
365	6208.19	Womens/girls slips & petticoats, of other textile materials, not knitted
366	6208.21	Womens/girls nightdresses and pyjamas, of cotton, not knitted
367	6208.22	Womens/girls nightdresses and pyjamas, of man-made fibres, not knitted
368	6208.29	Womens/girls nightdresses &pyjamas,of oth textile materials, not knitted
369	6208.91	Womens/girls panties, bathrobes, etc, of cotton, not knitted
370	6208.92	Womens/girls panties, bathrobes, etc, of man-made fibres, not knitted
371	6208.99	Womens/girls panties,bathrobes,etc,of oth tex materials, not knitted
372	6209.10	Babies garments &clothg accessories of wool o tine animal hair, not knit
373	6209.20	Babies garments & clothing accessories of cotton, not knitted
374	6209.30	Babies garments & clothing accessories of synthetic fibres, not knitted
375	6209.90	Babies garments &clothg accessories of oth tex materials, not knitted
376	6210.10	Garments made up of textile of felts and of nonwoven textile fabrics
377	6210.20	Mens/boys overcoats & similar articles of impreg.ctd.cov etc.tex wov fab
378	6210.40	Mens/boys garments nes, made up of of impreg, ctd, cov, etc. tex woven fab
378	6210.30	Womens/girls overcoats&sim articles of impreg, ctd, cov etc, tex wov fab

APPENDIX 10. ACFTA

(cont.)

Serial No		Description
380	6210.50	Womens/girls garments nes, of impreg, ctd, cov etc, textile woven fab
381	6211.11	Mens/boys swimwear, of textile materials, not knitted
382	6211.12	Womens/girls swimwear, of textile materials, not knitted
383	6211.20	Ski suits, of textile materials, not knitted
384	6211.31	Mens/boys garments nes, of wool or fine animal hair, not knitted
385	6211.32	Mens/boys garments nes, of cotton, not knitted.
386	6211.33	Mens/boys garments nes, of man-made fibres, not knitted
387	6211.39	Mens/boys garments nes, of other textile materials, not knitted
388	6211.41	Womens/girls garments nes, of wool or fine animal hair, not knitted
389	6211.42	Womens/girls garments nes, of cotton, not knitted
390	6211.43	Womens/girls garments nes, of man-made fibres, not knitted
391	6211.49	Womens/girls garments nes, of other textile materials, not knitted
392	6212.10	Brassieres and part thereof, of textile materials
393	6212.20	Girdles, panty girdles and parts thereof, of textile materials
394	6212.30	Corselettes and parts thereof, of textile materials
395	6212.90	Corsets, braces & similar articles & parts thereof, of textile materials
396	6213.10	Handkerchiefs, of silk or silk waste, not knitted
397	6213.20	Handkerchiefs, of cotton, not knitted
398	6213.90	Handkerchiefs, of other textile materials, not knitted
399	6214.10	Shawls, scarves, veils and the like, of silk or silk waste, not knitted
400	6214.20	Shawls.scarves,veils & the like.ofwool or fine animal hair. not knitted
401	6214.30	Shawls, scarves, veils and the like, of synthetic fibres, not knitted
402	6214.40	Shawls, scarves, veils and the like, of artificial fibres, not knitted

(cont.)

Serial No		Description
403	6214.90	Shawls,scarves,veils & the like.ofoth tex materials fibres, not knitted
404	6215.10	Ties, bow ties and cravats, of silk or silk waste, not knitted
405	6215.20	Ties, bow ties and cravats, of man-made fibres, not knitted
406	6215.90	Ties, bow ties and cravats, of other textile materials, not knitted
407	6216.00	Gloves, mittens and mitts, of textile materials, not knitted
408	6217.10	Clothing accessories nes, of textile materials, not knitted
409	6217.90	Parts of garments or of clothg accessories nes, of tex mat, not knittd
	Ch. 63	Other made up textile articles; sets; worn clothing etc
410	6301.10	Electric blankets, of textile materials
411	6301.20	Blankets (other than electric) & travelg rugs, of wool or fine animal hair
412	6301.30	Blankets (other than electric) and travelling rugs, of cotion
413	6301.40	Blankets (other than electric) and travelling rugs. of synthetic fibres
414	6301.90	Blankets (oth than electric) and travellg rugs. of oth textile materials
415	6302.10	Bed linen, of textile knitted or crocheted materials
416	6302.21	Bed linen, of cotton, printed, not knitted
417	6302.22	Bed linen, of man-made fibres, printed, not knitted
418	6302.29	Bed linen, of other textile materials, printed, not knitted
419	6302.31	Bed linen, of cotton, nes
420	6302.32	Bed linen, of man-made fibres, nes
421	6302.39	Bed linen, of other textile materials, nes
422	6302.40	Table linen, of textile knitted or crocheted materials
423	6302.51	Table linen, of cotton, not knitted
424	6302.52	Table linen, of flax, not knitted
425	6302.53	Table linen, of man-made fibres, not knitted
426	6302.59	Table linen, of other textile materials, not knitted
427	6302.60	Toilet & kitchen linen, of terry towellg or similar terry fab, of cotton

APPENDIX 10. ACFTA

(cont.)

Serial No		Description
428	6302.91	Toilet and kitchen linen, of cotton, nes
429	6302.92	Toilet and kitchen linen, of flax
430	6302.93	Toilet and kitchen linen, of man-made fibres
431	6302.99	Toilet and kitchen linen, of other textile materials
432	6303.11	Curtains.drapes, interior blinds&curtain or bed valances, of cotton, knit
433	6303.12	Curtains, drapes, interior blinds & curtain or bed valances, of synthetic fib, knittd
434	6303.19	Curtains, drapes, interior blinds & curtain or bed valances, of other tex. mat, knit
435	6303.91	Curtains/drapes/interior blinds&curtain/bed valances,of cotton, not knit
436	6303.92	Curtains/drapes/interior blinds&curtain/bed valances,of syn fib, nt knit
437	6303.99	Curtains/drapes/interior blinds&curtain/bed valance,of other tex mat, not knit
438	6304.11	Bedspreads of textile materials, nes, knitted or crocheted
439	6304.19	Bedspreads of textile materials, nes, not knitted or crocheted
440	6304.91	Furnishing articles nes, of textile materials, knitted or crocheted
441	6304.92	Furnishing articles nes, of cotton, not knitted or crocheted
442	6304.93	Furnishing articles nes, of synthetic fibres, not knitted or crocheted
443	6304.99	Furnishing articles nes, of other tex materials, not knitted or crocheted
444	6305.1	Sacks & bags, for packing of goods, of jute or of other textile bast fibres
445	6305.2	Sacks and bags, for packing of goods, of cotton
446	6305.33	Sacks & bags, for packing of goods, of polyethylene or polypropylene strips
447	6305.32	Sacks & bags, for packing of goods, flexible intermediate bulk containers of man-made textile materials

APPENDIX 10. ACFTA

(cont.)

Serial No		Description
448	6305.39	Sacks & bags, for packing of goods, of other man-made textile materials
449	6305.90	Sacks and bags, for packing of goods, of other textile materials
450	6306.11	Tarpaulins, awnings and sunblinds, of cotton
451	6306.12	Tarpaulins, awnings and sunblinds, of synthetic fibres
452	6306.19	Tarpaulins, awnings and sunblinds, of other textile materials
453	6306.21	Tents, of cotton
454	6306.22	Tents, of synthetic fibres
455	6306.29	Tents, of other textile materials
456	6306.31	Sails, of synthetic fibres
457	6306.39	Sails, of other textile materials
458	6306.41	Pneumatic mattresses, of cotton
459	6306.49	Pneumatic mattresses, of other textile materials
460	6306.91	Camping goods nes, of cotton
461	6306.99	Camping goods nes, of other textile materials
462	6307.10	Floor-cloths, dish-cloths, dusters & similar cleaning cloths, of tex mat
463	6307.20	Life jackets and life belts, of textile materials
464	6307.90	Made up articles, of textile materials, nes, including dress patterns
465	6308.00	Sets consisting of woven fab 7 yarn, for making up into rugs, tapestries etc
466	6309.00	Worn clothing and other worn articles

Attachment C

Original (Duplicate/Triplicate/Quadruplicate)

APPENDIX 10. ACFTA

1. Goods consigned from (Exporter's business name, address, country)	Reference No.
2. Goods consigned to (Consignee's name, address, country)	ASEAN-CHINA FREE TRADE AREA PREFERENTIAL TARIFF CERTIFICATE OF ORIGIN (Combined Declaration and Certificate) Issued in $\frac{\text{FORM E}}{\text{(Country)}}$ See Notes Overleaf
3. Means of transport and route (as far as known) Departure date Vessel's name/Aircraft etc. Port of Discharge	4. For Official Use ☐ Preferential Treatment Given Under ASEAN-CHINA Free Trade Area Preferential Tariff ☐ Preferential Treatment Not Given (Please state reason/s) .... Signature of Authorised Signatory of the Importing Country

5. Item number	6. Marks and numbers on packages	7. Number and type of packages, description of goods (including quantity where appropriate and HS number of the importing country)	8. Origin criterion (see Notes overleaf)	9. Gross weight or other quantity and value (FOB)	10. Number and date of invoices

11. Declaration by the exporter	12. Certification
The undersigned hereby declares that the above details and statement are correct; that all the goods were produced in .... (Country) and that they comply with the origin requirements specified for these goods in the ASEAN-CHINA Free Trade Area Preferential Tariff for the goods exported to .... (Importing Country) .... Place and date, signature of authorised signatory	It is hereby certified, on the basis of control carried out, that the declaration by the exporter is correct. .... Place and date, signature and stamp of certifying authority

APPENDIX 10. ACFTA

OVERLEAF NOTES

1. Member States which accept this form for the purpose of preferential treatment under the ASEAN-CHINA Free Trade Area Preferential Tariff:

BRUNEI DARUSSALAM	CAMBODIA	CHINA
INDONESIA	LAOS	MALAYSIA
MYANMAR	PHILIPPINES	SINGAPORE
THAILAND	VIETNAM	

2. CONDITIONS: The main conditions for admission to the preferential treatment under the ACFTA Preferential Tariff are that goods sent to any Member States listed above:
   (i) must fall within a description of products eligible for concessions in the country of destination;
   (ii) must comply with the consignment conditions that the goods must be consigned directly from any ACFTA Member State to the importing Member State but transport that involves passing through one or more intermediate non-ACFTA Member States, is also accepted provided that any intermediate transit, transshipment or temporary storage arises only for geographic reasons or transportation requirements; and
   (iii) must comply with the origin criteria given in the next paragraph.
3. ORIGIN CRITERIA: For exports to the above mentioned countries to be eligible for preferential treatment, the requirement is that either:

APPENDIX 10. ACFTA

(i) The products wholly obtained in the exporting Member State as defined in Rule 3 of the ASEAN-China Rules of Origin;

(ii) Subject to sub-paragraph (i) above, for the purpose of implementing the provisions of Rule 2 (b) of the ASEAN-China Rules of Origin, products worked on and processed as a result of which the total value of the materials, parts or produce originating from non-ACFTA Member States or of undetermined origin used does not exceed 60% of the FOB value of the product produced or obtained and the final process of the manufacture is performed within territory of the exporting Member State;

(iii) Products which comply with origin requirements provided for in Rule 2 of the ASEAN-China Rules of Origin and which are used in a Member State as inputs for a finished product eligible for preferential treatment in another Member State/States shall be considered as a product originating in the Member State where working or processing of the finished product has taken place provided that the aggregate ACFTA content of the final product is not less than 40%; or

(iv) Products which satisfy the Product Specific Rules provided for in Attachment B of the ASEAN-China Rules of Origin shall be considered as goods to which sufficient transformation has been carried out in a Party.

If the goods qualify under the above criteria, the exporter must indicate in Box 8 of this form the origin criteria on the basis of which he claims that his goods qualify for preferential treatment, in the manner shown in the following table:

Circumstances of production or manufacture in the first country named in Box 11 of this form	Insert in Box 8
(a) Products wholly produced in the country of exportation (see paragraph 3 (i) above)	"X"
(b) Products worked upon but not wholly produced in the exporting Member State which were produced in conformity with the provisions of paragraph 3 (ii) above	Percentage of single country content, example 40%
(c) Products worked upon but not wholly produced in the exporting Member State which were produced in conformity with the provisions of paragraph 3 (iii) above	Percentage of ACFTA cumulative content, example 40%
(d) Products satisfied the Products Specific Rules	"Products Specific Rules"

4. EACH ARTICLE MUST QUALIFY: It should be noted that all the products in a consignment must qualify separately in their own right. This is of particular relevance when similar articles of different sizes or spare parts are sent.
5. DESCRIPTION OF PRODUCTS: The description of products must be sufficiently detailed to enable the products to be identified by the Customs Officers examining them.

APPENDIX 10. ACFTA

Name of manufacturer, any trade mark shall also be specified.

6. The Harmonised System number shall be that of the importing Member State.
7. The term "Exporter" in Box 11 may include the manufacturer or the producer.
8. FOR OFFICIAL USE: The Customs Authority of the importing Member State must indicate (√) in the relevant boxes in column 4 whether or not preferential treatment is accorded.

Appendix 11

Rules of Origin, ASEAN–India Free Trade Agreement

Annex 2 Rules of Origin for the ASEAN–India Free Trade Area (AIFTA)

In determining the origin of products eligible for the preferential tariff treatment under ASEAN-India Free Trade Area pursuant to Article 4 of this Agreement, the following Rules shall be applied:

Rule 1

Definitions

For the purposes of this Annex, the term:

(a) **CIF** means the value of the good imported, and includes the cost of freight and insurance up to the port or place of entry into the country of importation;
(b) **FOB** means the free-on-board value as defined in paragraph 1 of Appendix A;
(c) **material** means raw materials, ingredients, parts, components, subassembly and/or goods that are physically incorporated into another good or are subject to a process in the production of another good;
(d) **originating products** means products that qualify as originating in accordance with the provisions of Rule 2;

(e) **production** means methods of obtaining goods including growing, mining, harvesting, raising, breeding, extracting, gathering, collecting, capturing, fishing, trapping, hunting, manufacturing, producing, processing or assembling a good;

(f) **Product Specific Rules** are rules that specify that the materials have undergone a change in tariff classification or a specific manufacturing or processing operation, or satisfy an *ad valorem* criterion or a combination of any of these criteria;

(g) **product** means products which are wholly obtained/produced or being manufactured, even if it is intended for later use in another manufacturing operation;

(h) **identical and interchangeable materials** means materials being of the same kind possessing similar technical and physical characteristics, and which once they are incorporated into the finished product cannot be distinguished from one another for origin purposes.

Rule 2

Origin Criteria

For the purposes of this Annex, products imported by a Party which are consigned directly within the meaning of Rule 8 shall be deemed to be originating and eligible for preferential tariff treatment if they conform to the origin requirements under any one of the following:

(a) Products which are wholly obtained or produced in the exporting Party as set out and defined in Rule 3; or

(b) Products not wholly produced or obtained in the exporting Party provided that the said products are eligible under Rule 4 or 5 or 6.

Rule 3

Wholly Produced or Obtained Products

Within the meaning of Rule 2(a), the following shall be considered as wholly produced or obtained in a Party:

(a) plant[1] and plant products grown and harvested in the Party;
(b) live animals[2] born and raised in the Party;
(c) products[3] obtained from live animals referred to in paragraph (b);
(d) products obtained from hunting, trapping, fishing, aquaculture, gathering or capturing conducted in the Party;
(e) minerals and other naturally occurring substances, not included in paragraphs (a) to (d), extracted or taken from the Party's soil, waters, seabed or beneath the seabed;

---

[1] Plant here refers to all plant life, including forestry products, fruit, flowers, vegetables, trees, seaweed, fungi and live plants.

[2] Animals referred to in paragraphs (b) and (c) covers all animal life, including mammals, birds, fish, crustaceans, molluscs, reptiles, and living organisms.

[3] Products refer to those obtained from live animals without further processing, including milk, eggs, natural honey, hair, wool, semen and dung.

(f) products taken from the waters, seabed or beneath the seabed outside the territorial waters of the Party, provided that that Party has the rights to exploit such waters, seabed and beneath the seabed in accordance with the United Nations Convention on the Law of the Sea, 1982;

(g) products of sea-fishing and other marine products taken from the high seas by vessels registered with the Party and entitled to fly the flag of that Party;

(h) products processed and/or made on board factory ships registered with the Party and entitled to fly the flag of that Party, exclusively from products referred to in paragraph (g);

(i) articles collected in the Party which can no longer perform their original purpose nor are capable of being restored or repaired and are fit only for disposal or recovery of parts of raw materials, or for recycling purposes[4]; and

(j) products obtained or produced in the Party solely from products referred to in paragraphs (a) to (i).

---

[4] This would cover all scrap and waste including scrap and waste resulting from manufacturing or processing operations or consumption in the same country, scrap machinery, discarded packaging and all products that can no longer perform the purpose for which they were produced and are fit only for disposal for the recovery of raw materials. Such manufacturing or processing operations shall include all types of processing, not only industrial or chemical but also mining, agriculture, construction, refining, incineration and sewage treatment operations.

APPENDIX 11. AIFTA

Rule 4

Not Wholly Produced or Obtained Products

(a) For the purposes of Rule 2(b), a product shall be deemed to be originating if:

   (i) the AIFTA content is not less than 35 per cent of the FOB value; and
   (ii) the non-originating materials have undergone at least a change in tariff sub-heading (CTSH) level of the Harmonized System,

   provided that the final process of the manufacture is performed within the territory of the exporting Party.

(b) For the purposes of this Rule, the formula for the 35 per cent AIFTA content is calculated respectively as follows[5]:

   (i) Direct Method

$$\frac{\text{AIFTA Material Cost} + \text{Direct Labour Cost} + \text{Direct Overhead Cost} + \text{Other Cost} + \text{Profit}}{\text{FOB Price}} \times 100\% \geq 35\%$$

   (ii) Indirect Method

$$\frac{\text{Value of Imported Non-AIFTA Materials, Parts or Produce} + \text{Value of Undetermined Origin Materials, Parts or Produce}}{\text{FOB Price}} \times 100\% \leq 65\%$$

---

[5] The Parties shall be given the flexibility to adopt the method of calculating the AIFTA Content, whether it is the direct or indirect method. In order to promote transparency, consistency and certainty, each Party shall adhere to one method. Any change in the method of calculation shall be notified to all the other Parties at least six (6) months prior to the adoption of the new method. It is understood that any verification of the AIFTA content by the importing Party shall be done on the basis of the method used by the exporting Party.

(c) The value of the non-originating materials shall be:

   (i) the CIF value at the time of importation of the materials, parts or produce; or
   (ii) the earliest ascertained price paid for the materials, parts or produce of undetermined origin in the territory of the Party where the working or processing takes place.

(d) The method of calculating the AIFTA content is as set out in Appendix A.

Rule 5

Cumulative Rule of Origin

Unless otherwise provided for, products which comply with origin requirements provided for in Rule 2 and which are used in a Party as materials for a product which is eligible for preferential treatment under the Agreement shall be considered as products originating in that Party where working or processing of the product has taken place.

Rule 6

Product Specific Rules

Notwithstanding the provisions of Rule 4, products which satisfy the Product Specific Rules shall be considered as originating from that Party where working or processing of the product has taken place. The list of Product Specific Rules shall be appended as Appendix B.

APPENDIX 11. AIFTA

Rule 7

Minimal Operations and Processes

(a) Notwithstanding any provisions in this Annex, a product shall not be considered originating in a Party if the following operations are undertaken exclusively by itself or in combination in the territory of that Party:
   (i) operations to ensure the preservation of products in good condition during transport and storage (such as drying, freezing, keeping in brine, ventilation, spreading out, chilling, placing in salt, sulphur dioxide or other aqueous solutions, removal of damaged parts, and like operations);
   (ii) simple operations consisting of removal of dust, sifting or screening, sorting, classifying, matching (including the making-up of sets of articles), washing, painting, cutting;
   (iii) changes of packing and breaking up and assembly of consignments;
   (iv) simple cutting, slicing and repacking or placing in bottles, flasks, bags, boxes, fixing on cards or boards, and all other simple packing operations;
   (v) affixing of marks, labels or other like distinguishing signs on products or their packaging;
   (vi) simple mixing of products whether or not of different kinds, where one or more components of the mixture do not meet the conditions laid down in this Annex to enable them to be considered as originating products;
   (vii) simple assembly of parts of products to constitute a complete product;

(viii) disassembly;
(ix) slaughter which means the mere killing of animals; and
(x) mere dilution with water or another substance that does not materially alter the characteristics of the products.

(b) For textiles and textile products listed in Appendix C, an article or material shall not be considered to be originating in a Party by virtue of merely having undergone any of the following:

(i) simple combining operations, labelling, pressing, cleaning or dry cleaning or packaging operations, or any combination thereof;
(ii) cutting to length or width and hemming, stitching or overlocking fabrics which are readily identifiable as being intended for a particular commercial use;
(iii) trimming and/or joining together by sewing, looping, linking, attaching of accessory articles such as straps, bands, beads, cords, rings and eyelets;
(iv) one or more finishing operations on yarns, fabrics or other textile articles, such as bleaching, waterproofing, decating, shrinking, mercerizing, or similar operations; or
(v) dyeing or printing of fabrics or yarns.

Rule 8

Direct Consignment

The following shall be considered as consigned directly from the exporting Party to the importing Party:

(a) If the products are transported passing through the territory of any other AIFTA Parties;
(b) If the products are transported without passing through the territory of any non-AIFTA Parties;
(c) The products whose transport involves transit through one or more intermediate non-Parties with or without transhipment or temporary storage in such non-Parties provided that:
  (i) the transit entry is justified for geographical reason or by consideration related exclusively to transport requirements;
  (ii) the products have not entered into trade or consumption there; and
  (iii) the products have not undergone any operation there other than unloading and reloading or any operation required to keep them in good condition.

Rule 9

Treatment of Packing

(a) Packages and packing materials for retail sale, when classified together with the packaged product, shall not be taken into account in considering whether all non-originating materials used in the manufacture of a product fulfil the criterion corresponding to a change of tariff classification of the said product.
(b) Where a product is subject to an ad valorem percentage criterion, the value of the packages and packing materials for retail sale shall be taken into account in its origin

assessment, in case the packing is considered as forming a whole with products.

(c) The containers and packing materials exclusively used for the transport of a product shall not be taken into account for determining the origin of any good.

Rule 10

Accessories, Spare Parts, Tools and Instructional or Other Information Material

The origin of accessories, spare parts, tools and instructional or other information materials presented with the products shall not be taken into account in determining the origin of the products, provided that such accessories, spare parts, tools and instructional or other information materials are:

(a) in accordance with standard trade practices in the domestic market of the exporting Party; and
(b) classified with the products at the time of assessment of customs duties by the importing Party.

However, if the products are subject to a qualifying AIFTA content requirement, the value of such accessories, spare parts tools and instructional or other information material shall be taken into account as originating or non-originating materials, as the case may be, in calculating the qualifying AIFTA content.

Rule 11

Indirect Materials

In order to determine whether a product originates in a Party, any indirect material such as power and fuel, plant and equipment, or machines and tools used to obtain such products shall be treated as originating whether such material originates in non-Parties or not, and its value shall be the cost registered in the accounting records of the producer of the export goods.

Rule 12

Identical and Interchangeable Materials

For the purposes of establishing if a product is originating when it is manufactured utilising both originating and non-originating materials, mixed or physically combined, the origin of such materials can be determined by generally accepted accounting principles of stock control applicable/inventory management practised in the exporting Party.

Rule 13

Certificate of Origin

A claim that a product shall be accepted as eligible for preferential tariff treatment shall be supported by a Certificate of Origin issued by a government authority designated by the exporting Party and notified to the other Parties in accordance with the Operational Certification Procedures as set out in Appendix D.

Rule 14

Review and Modification

This Annex and the Operational Certification Procedures may be reviewed and modified, as and when necessary, upon request of a Party and as may be agreed upon by the Joint Committee.

APPENDIX 11. AIFTA

Appendix A Method of Calculation for the AIFTA Content

1. FOB price shall be calculated as follows:

    (a) FOB Price = Ex-Factory Price + Other Costs
    (b) Other Costs in the calculation of the FOB price shall refer to the costs incurred in placing the products in the ship for export, including but not limited to, domestic transport costs, storage and warehousing, port handling, brokerage fees, service charges, etc.

2. Formula for ex-factory price:

    (a) Ex-Factory Price = Production Cost + Profit
    (b) Formula for production cost,
      (i) Production Cost = Cost of Raw Materials + Labour Cost + Overhead Cost
      (ii) Raw Materials shall consist of:
        - Cost of raw materials
        - Freight and insurance
      (iii) Labour Cost shall include:
        - Wages
        - Remuneration
        - Other employee benefits associated with the manufacturing process
      (iv) Overhead Costs, (non-exhaustive list) shall include, but not limited to:
        - real property items associated with the production process (insurance, factory rent and leasing, depreciation on buildings, repair and maintenance, taxes, interests on mortgage)

- leasing of and interest payments for plant and equipment
- factory security
- insurance (plant, equipment and materials used in the manufacture of the goods)
- utilities (energy, electricity, water and other utilities directly attributable to the production of the good)
- research, development, design and engineering
- dies, moulds, tooling and the depreciation, maintenance and repair of plant and equipment
- royalties or licenses (in connection with patented machines or processes used in the manufacture of the good or the right to manufacture the good)
- inspection and testing of materials and the goods
- storage and handling in the factory
- disposal of recyclable wastes
- cost elements in computing the value of raw materials, i.e. port and clearance charges and import duties paid for dutiable component

Appendix B Product Specific Rules

Attachment to the OCP

Original (Duplicate/Triplicate/Quadruplicate)

1. Goods consigned from (Exporter's business name, address, country)	Reference No. ASEAN-INDIA FREE TRADE AREA PREFERENTIAL TARIFF CERTIFICATE OF ORIGIN (Combined Declaration and Certificate)			
2. Goods consigned to (Consignee's name, address, country)	Issued in $\dfrac{\text{FORMAI}}{\text{(Country)}}$ See Notes Overleaf			
3. Means of transport and route (as far as known) Departure date Vessel's name/Aircraft etc. Port of Discharge	4. For Official Use ☐ Preferential Tariff Treatment Given Under ASEAN-India Free Trade Area Preferential Tariff ☐ Preferential Tariff Treatment Not Given (Please state reason/s) …………………………………………… Signature of Authorised Signatory of the Importing Country			
5. Item number	6. Marks and numbers on Packages	7. Number and type of packages, description of goods (including quantity where appropriate and HS number of the importing country)	8. Origin criterion (see Notes overleaf)	9. Gross weight or other quantity and value (FOB)	10. Number and date of Invoices

11. Declaration by the exporter
 	
The undersigned hereby declares that the above details and statement are
  correct; that all the goods were produced in
    ………………………………………..
              (Country)
and that they comply with the origin requirements specified for these
  goods in the ASEAN-INDIA Free Trade Area Preferential Tariff for the
  goods exported to
    ………………………………………..
       (Importing Country)
    ………………………………………..
Place and date, signature of authorised signatory
	12. Certification
	
	It is hereby certified, on the basis of control carried out, that the declaration by the exporter is correct.
	
	……………………………………………………….
	Place and date, signature and stamp of certifying authority			

13. Where appropriate please tick:

☐ Third Country Invoicing   ☐ Exhibition   ☐ Back-to-Back CO   ☐ Cumulation

APPENDIX 11. AIFTA

OVERLEAF NOTES

1. Parties which accept this form for the purpose of preferential tariff treatment under the ASEAN-INDIA Free Trade Agreement (AIFTA):

BRUNEI DARUSSALAM	CAMBODIA	INDONESIA
INDIA	LAOS	MALAYSIA
MYANMAR	PHILIPPINES	SINGAPORE
THAILAND	VIETNAM	

2. CONDITIONS: To enjoy preferential tariff under the AIFTA, goods sent to any Parties listed above:
   (i) must fall within a description of goods eligible for concessions in the Party of destination;
   (ii) must comply with the consignment conditions in accordance with Rule 8 of the AIFTA Rules of Origin; and
   (iii) must comply with the origin criteria in the AIFTA Rules of Origin.

3. ORIGIN CRITERIA: For goods that meet the origin criteria, the exporter and/or producer must indicate in box 8 of this Form, the origin criteria met, in the manner shown in the following table:

Circumstances of production or manufacture in the first country named in Box 11 of this form	Insert in Box 8
(a) Goods wholly obtained or produced in the territory of the exporting Party	"WO"
(b) Goods satisfying Rule 4 (Not Wholly Produced or Obtained Products) of the AIFTA Rules of Origin	"RVC []% + CTSH"
(c) Goods satisfying Rule 6 (Product Specific Rules) of the AIFTA Rules of Origin	Appropriate qualifying criteria

4. EACH ARTICLE MUST QUALIFY: It should be noted that all the goods in a consignment must qualify separately in their own right. This is of particular relevance when similar articles of different sizes or spare parts are sent.
5. DESCRIPTION OF GOODS: The description of goods must be sufficiently detailed to enable the goods to be identified by the Customs Officers examining them. Name of manufacturer, any trade mark shall also be specified.
6. HARMONIZED SYSTEM NUMBER: The Harmonized System number shall be that of the importing Party.
7. EXPORTER: The term "Exporter" in Box 11 may include the manufacturer or the producer.
8. FOR OFFICIAL USE: The Customs Authority of the importing Party must indicate (√) in the relevant boxes in column 4 whether or not preferential tariff is accorded.
9. THIRD COUNTRY INVOICING: In cases where invoices are issued by a third country, "Third Country Invoicing" in Box 13 should be ticked (√) and such information as name and country of the company issuing the invoice shall be indicated in Box 7.
10. EXHIBITIONS: In cases where goods are sent from the territory of the exporting Party for exhibition in another country and sold during or after the exhibition for importation into the territory of a Party, in accordance with Article 21 of the Operational Certification Procedures, "Exhibitions" in Box 13 should be ticked (√) and the name and address of the exhibition indicated in Box 2.

APPENDIX 11. AIFTA

11. BACK-TO-BACK CERTIFICATE OF ORIGIN: In cases of Back-to-Back CO, in accordance with Article 11 of the Operational Certification Procedures, "Back-to-Back CO" in Box 13 should be ticked (√). The name of original exporting Party to be indicated in Box 11 and the date of the issuance of CO and the reference number will be indicated in Box 7.

Appendix 12

Rules of Origin, ASEAN–Japan Comprehensive Economic Partnership Agreement

Article 21

Measures to Safeguard the Balance of Payments

Nothing in this Chapter shall be construed to prevent a Party from taking any measure for balance-of-payments purposes. A Party taking such measure shall do so in accordance with the conditions established under Article XII of GATT 1994 and the Understanding on the Balance-of-Payments Provisions of the General Agreement on Tariffs and Trade 1994 in Annex 1A to the WTO Agreement.

Article 22

Customs Procedures

1. Each Party shall endeavour to apply its customs procedures in a predictable, consistent and transparent manner.
2. Recognising the importance of improving transparency in the area of customs procedures, each Party, subject to its laws and regulations, and available resources, shall endeavour to provide information relating to specific matters raised by interested persons of the Parties pertaining to its customs laws. Each Party shall endeavour to supply not only such information but also other pertinent

information which it considers the interested persons should be made aware of.
3. For prompt customs clearance of goods traded among the Parties, each Party, recognising the significant role of customs authorities and the importance of customs procedures in promoting trade facilitation, shall endeavour to:

   (a) simplify its customs procedures; and
   (b) harmonise its customs procedures, to the extent possible, with relevant international standards and recommended practices such as those made under the auspices of the Customs Co-operation Council.

Chapter 3 Rules of Origin

Article 23

Definitions

For the purposes of this Chapter, the term:

(a) "exporter" means a natural or juridical person located in an exporting Party who exports a good from the exporting Party;
(b) "factory ships of the Party" or "vessels of the Party" respectively means factory ships or vessels:
   (i) which are registered in the Party;
   (ii) which sail under the flag of the Party;
   (iii) which are owned to an extent of at least fifty (50) per cent by nationals of one or more of the Parties, or by a juridical person with its head office

in a Party, of which the representatives, chairman of the board of directors, and the majority of the members of such board are nationals of one or more of the Parties, and of which at least fifty (50) per cent of the equity interest is owned by nationals or juridical persons of one or more of the Parties; and

    (iv) of which at least seventy-five (75) per cent of the total of the master, officers and crew are nationals of one or more of the Parties;

(c) "generally accepted accounting principles" means the recognised consensus or substantial authoritative support in a Party, with respect to the recording of revenues, expenses, costs, assets and liabilities; the disclosure of information; and the preparation of financial statements. These standards may encompass broad guidelines of general application as well as detailed standards, practices and procedures;

(d) "good" means any merchandise, product, article or material;

(e) "identical and interchangeable materials" means materials being of the same kind and commercial quality, possessing the same technical and physical characteristics, and which once they are incorporated into the good cannot be distinguished from one another for origin purposes by virtue of any markings;

(f) "importer" means a natural or juridical person who imports a good into the importing Party;

(g) "materials" means any matter or substance used or consumed in the production of a good, physically incorporated into a good, or used in the production of another good;

(h) "originating good" or "originating material" means a good or material that qualifies as originating in accordance with the provisions of this Chapter;

(i) "packing materials and containers for transportation and shipment" means the goods used to protect a good during its transportation and shipment, different from those containers or materials used for its retail sale;

(j) "preferential tariff treatment" means the rate of customs duties applicable to an originating good of the exporting Party in accordance with paragraph 1 of Article 16; and

(k) "production" means methods of obtaining a good including growing, mining, harvesting, raising, breeding, extracting, gathering, collecting, capturing, fishing, trapping, hunting, manufacturing, processing or assembling.

Article 24

Originating Goods

For the purposes of this Agreement, a good shall qualify as an originating good of a Party if it:

(a) is wholly obtained or produced entirely in the Party as provided for in Article 25;

(b) satisfies the requirements of Article 26 when using non-originating materials; or

(c) is produced entirely in the Party exclusively from originating materials of one or more of the Parties, and meets all other applicable requirements of this Chapter.

APPENDIX 12. AJFTA

Article 25

Goods Wholly Obtained or Produced

For the purposes of paragraph (a) of Article 24, the following shall be considered as wholly obtained or produced entirely in a Party:

(a) plant and plant products grown and harvested, picked or gathered in the Party;
Note: For the purposes of this paragraph, the term "plant" refers to all plant life, including fruit, flowers, vegetables, trees, seaweed, fungi and live plants.

(b) live animals born and raised in the Party; Note: For the purposes of paragraphs (b) and (c), the term "animals" covers all animal life, including mammals, birds, fish, crustaceans, molluscs, reptiles, bacteria and viruses.

(c) goods obtained from live animals in the Party;

(d) goods obtained from hunting, trapping, fishing, gathering or capturing conducted in the Party;

(e) minerals and other naturally occurring substances, not included in paragraphs (a) through (d), extracted or taken from soil, waters, seabed or beneath the seabed of the Party;

(f) goods taken from the waters, seabed or beneath the seabed outside the territorial waters of the Party, provided that the Party has the rights to exploit such waters, seabed and beneath the seabed in accordance with its laws and regulations and international law;
Note: Nothing in this Agreement shall affect the rights and obligations of the Parties under international law,

including those under the United Nations Convention on the Law of the Sea.

(g) goods of sea-fishing and other marine products taken by vessels of the Party from outside the territorial sea of any Party;

(h) goods processed and/or made on board factory ships of the Party exclusively from products referred to in paragraph (g);

(i) articles collected in the Party which can no longer perform their original purpose or be restored or repaired, and are fit only for disposal, for the recovery of parts or raw materials, or for recycling purposes;

(j) scrap and waste derived from manufacturing or processing operations, including mining, agriculture, construction, refining, incineration and sewage treatment operations, or from consumption, in the Party, and fit only for disposal or for the recovery of raw materials;
and

(k) goods obtained or produced in the Party exclusively from goods referred to in paragraphs (a) through (j).

Article 26

Goods Not Wholly Obtained or Produced

1. For the purposes of paragraph (b) of Article 24, a good shall qualify as an originating good of a Party if:

   (a) the good has a regional value content (hereinafter referred to as "RVC"), calculated using the formula

APPENDIX 12. AJFTA

set out in Article 27, of not less than forty (40) per cent, and the final process of production has been performed in the Party; or

(b) all non-originating materials used in the production of the good have undergone in the Party a change in tariff classification (hereinafter referred to as "CTC") at the 4-digit level (i.e. a change in tariff heading) of Harmonized System.

Note: For the purposes of this subparagraph, "Harmonized System" is that on which the product specific rules set out in Annex 2 are based.

Each Party shall permit the exporter of the good to decide whether to use subparagraph (a) or (b) when determining whether the good qualifies as an originating good of the Party.

2. Notwithstanding paragraph 1, a good subject to product specific rules shall qualify as an originating good if it satisfies the applicable product specific rules set out in Annex 2. Where a product specific rule provides a choice of rules from a RVC-based rule of origin, a CTC-based rule of origin, a specific manufacturing or processing operation, or a combination of any of these, each Party shall permit the exporter of the good to decide which rule to use in determining whether the good qualifies as an originating good of the Party.

3. For the purposes of subparagraph 1(a) and the relevant product specific rules set out in Annex 2 which specify a certain RVC, it is required that the RVC of a good, calculated using the formula set out in Article 27, is not less than the percentage specified by the rule for the good.

4. For the purposes of subparagraph 1(b) and the relevant product specific rules set out in Annex 2, the rules requiring that the materials used have undergone CTC, or a specific manufacturing or processing operation, shall apply only to non-originating materials.
5. For the purposes of this Chapter, Annex 3 shall apply.

Article 27

Calculation of Regional Value Content

1. For the purposes of calculating the RVC of a good, the following formula shall be used:

$$\text{RVC} = \frac{\text{FOB} - \text{VNM}}{\text{FOB}} \times 100\%$$

2. For the purposes of this Article:

   (a) "FOB" is, except as provided for in paragraph 3, the free-on-board value of a good, inclusive of the cost of transport from the producer to the port or site of final shipment abroad;

   (b) "RVC" is the RVC of a good, expressed as a percentage; and

   (c) "VNM" is the value of non-originating materials used in the production of a good.

3. FOB referred to in subparagraph 2(a) shall be the value:

   (a) adjusted to the first ascertainable price paid for a good from the buyer to the producer of the good, if there is free-on-board value of the good, but it is unknown and cannot be ascertained; or

APPENDIX 12. AJFTA

(b) determined in accordance with Articles 1 through 8 of the Agreement on Customs Valuation, if there is no free-on-board value of a good.

4. For the purposes of paragraph 1, the value of non-originating materials used in the production of a good in a Party:

    (a) shall be determined in accordance with the Agreement on Customs Valuation and shall include freight, insurance, and where appropriate, packing and all other costs incurred in transporting the material to the importation port in the Party where the producer of the good is located; or

    (b) if such value is unknown and cannot be ascertained, shall be the first ascertainable price paid for the material in the Party, but may exclude all the costs incurred in the Party in transporting the material from the warehouse of the supplier of the material to the place where the producer is located such as freight, insurance and packing as well as any other known and ascertainable cost incurred in the Party.

5. For the purposes of paragraph 1, the VNM of a good shall not include the value of non-originating materials used in the production of originating materials of the Party which are used in the production of the good.

6. For the purposes of subparagraph 3(b) or 4(a), in applying the Agreement on Customs Valuation to determine the value of a good or non-originating material, the Agreement on Customs Valuation shall apply, *mutatis mutandis*, to domestic transactions or to the cases where there is no domestic transaction of the good or non-originating material.

APPENDIX 12. AJFTA

Article 28

De Minimis

1. A good that does not satisfy the requirements of subparagraph 1(b) of Article 26 or an applicable CTC-based rule of origin set out in Annex 2 shall be considered as an originating good of a Party if:

   (a) in the case of a good classified under Chapters 16, 19, 20, 22, 23, 28 through 49, and 64 through 97 of the Harmonized System, the total value of non-originating materials used in the production of the good that have not undergone the required CTC does not exceed ten (10) per cent of the FOB;

   (b) in the case of a particular good classified under Chapters 18 and 21 of the Harmonized System, the total value of non-originating materials used in the production of the good that have not undergone the required CTC does not exceed ten (10) per cent or seven (7) per cent of the FOB, as specified in Annex 2; or

   (c) in the case of a good classified under Chapters 50 through 63 of the Harmonized System, the weight of all non-originating materials used in the production of the good that have not undergone the required CTC does not exceed ten (10) per cent of the total weight of the good, provided that it meets all other applicable criteria set out in this Chapter for qualifying as an originating good.

   Note: For the purposes of this paragraph, subparagraph 2 (a) of Article 27 shall apply.

2. The value of non-originating materials referred to in paragraph 1 shall, however, be included in the value of non-originating materials for any applicable RVC-based rule of origin for the good.

Article 29

Accumulation

Originating materials of a Party used in the production of a good in another Party shall be considered as originating materials of that Party where the working or processing of the good has taken place.

Article 30

Non-qualifying Operations

A good shall not be considered to satisfy the requirements of CTC or specific manufacturing or processing operation merely by reason of:

(a) operations to ensure the preservation of products in good condition during transport and storage (such as drying, freezing, keeping in brine) and other similar operations;
(b) changes of packaging and breaking up and assembly of packages;
(c) disassembly;
(d) placing in bottles, cases, boxes and other simple packaging operations;
(e) collection of parts and components classified as a good pursuant to Rule 2(a) of the General Rules for the Interpretation of the Harmonized System;

(f) mere making-up of sets of articles; or
(g) any combination of operations referred to in subparagraphs (a) through (f).

Article 31

Direct Consignment

1. Preferential tariff treatment shall be accorded to an originating good satisfying the requirements of this Chapter and which is consigned directly from the exporting Party to the importing Party.
2. The following shall be considered as consigned directly from the exporting Party to the importing Party:

    (a) a good transported directly from the exporting Party to the importing Party; or
    (b) a good transported through one or more Parties, other than the exporting Party and the importing Party, or through a non-Party, provided that the good does not undergo operations other than transit or temporary storage in warehouses, unloading, reloading, and any other operation to preserve it in good condition.

Article 32

Packing Materials and Containers

1. Packing materials and containers for transportation and shipment of a good shall not be taken into account in determining the origin of any good.

2. Packing materials and containers in which a good is packaged for retail sale, when classified together with the good, shall not be taken into account in determining whether all of the non-originating materials used in the production of the good have met the applicable CTC-based rule of origin for the good.
3. If a good is subject to a RVC-based rule of origin, the value of the packing materials and containers in which the good is packaged for retail sale shall be taken into account as originating or non-originating materials, as the case may be, in calculating the RVC of the good.

Article 33

Accessories, Spare Parts, Tools and Instructional or Other Information Materials

1. If a good is subject to the requirements of CTC or specific manufacturing or processing operation, the origin of accessories, spare parts, tools and instructional or other information materials presented with the good shall not be taken into account in determining whether the good qualifies as an originating good, provided that:

    (a) the accessories, spare parts, tools and instructional or other information materials are not invoiced separately from the good; and
    (b) the quantities and value of the accessories, spare parts, tools and instructional or other information materials are customary for the good.

2. If a good is subject to a RVC-based rule of origin, the value of the accessories, spare parts, tools and instructional or other information materials shall be taken into account as the value of the originating or non-originating materials, as the case may be, in calculating the RVC of the originating goods.

Article 34

Indirect Materials

1. Indirect materials shall be treated as originating materials regardless of where they are produced.
2. For the purposes of this Article, the term "indirect materials" means goods used in the production, testing, or inspection of a good but not physically incorporated into the good, or goods used in the maintenance of buildings or the operation of equipment associated with the production of a good, including:

   (a) fuel and energy;
   (b) tools, dies and moulds;
   (c) spare parts and materials used in the maintenance of equipment and buildings;
   (d) lubricants, greases, compounding materials and other materials used in production or used to operate equipment and buildings;
   (e) gloves, glasses, footwear, clothing, safety equipment and supplies;
   (f) equipment, devices and supplies used for testing or inspecting the good;

(g) catalysts and solvents; and

(h) any other goods that are not incorporated into the good but whose use in the production of the good can reasonably be demonstrated to be a part of that production.

Article 35

Identical and Interchangeable Materials

The determination of whether identical and interchangeable materials are originating materials shall be made by the use of generally accepted accounting principles of stock control applicable, or those of inventory management practised, in the exporting Party.

Article 36

Operational Certification Procedures

The operational certification procedures, as set out in Annex 4, shall apply with respect to procedures regarding certificate of origin and related matters.

Article 37

Sub-Committee on Rules of Origin

1. For the purposes of the effective implementation and operation of this Chapter, a Sub-Committee on Rules of Origin (hereinafter referred to in this Article as "the Sub-Committee") shall be established pursuant to Article 11.

2. The functions of the Sub-Committee shall be to:

(a) review and make appropriate recommendations, as needed, to the Joint Committee on:
 (i) the implementation and operation of this Chapter;
 (ii) any amendments to Annexes 2 and 3, and Attachment to Annex 4, proposed by any Party; and
 (iii) the Implementing Regulations referred to in Rule 11 of Annex 4;

(b) consider any other matter as the Parties may agree related to this Chapter;

(c) report the findings of the Sub-Committee to the Joint Committee; and

(d) carry out other functions as may be delegated by the Joint Committee pursuant to Article 11.

3. The Sub-Committee shall be composed of representatives of the Governments of the Parties, and may invite representatives of relevant entities other than the Governments of the Parties with necessary expertise relevant to the issues to be discussed, upon agreement of all the Parties.

4. The Sub-Committee shall meet at such venues and times as may be agreed by the Parties.

Annex 4 Operational Certification Procedures

Rule 1

Definitions

For the purposes of this Annex, the term:

(a) "competent governmental authority" means the authority that, according to the laws and regulations of each Party,

is responsible for the issuing of a certificate of origin (hereinafter referred to as "CO") or for the designation of entities or bodies issuing a CO; and
(b) "relevant authority" means the authority of the importing Party, other than the customs authority of that Party, that is responsible for verification and verification visit in the importing Party.

Rule 2

Issuance of Certificate of Origin

1. The competent governmental authority of the exporting Party shall, upon request made in writing by the exporter or its authorised agent, issue a CO or, under the authorisation given in accordance with the applicable laws and regulations of the exporting Party, may designate other entities or bodies (hereinafter referred to as "designees") to issue a CO.
2. Each Party shall provide the other Parties with a list of names and addresses, and a list of specimen signatures and specimen of official seals or impressions of stamps for the issuance of a CO, of its competent governmental authority and, if any, its designees.
3. Any CO bearing a signature not included in the list referred to in paragraph 2 shall not be valid.
4. Where the exporter of a good is not the producer of the good in the exporting Party, the exporter may request a CO on the basis of:
    (a) a declaration provided by the exporter to the competent governmental authority or its designees based on

the information provided by the producer of the good to that exporter; or

(b) a declaration voluntarily provided by the producer of the good directly to the competent governmental authority or its designees by the request of the exporter.

5. A CO shall be issued only after the exporter who requests for its issuance, or the producer of the good in the exporting Party referred to in subparagraph 4(b), proves to the competent governmental authority or its designees that the good to be exported qualifies as an originating good of the exporting Party.

6. If, after the issuance of the CO, the exporter or producer referred to in paragraph 5 knows that such a good does not qualify as an originating good of the exporting Party, they shall notify the competent governmental authority or its designees in writing and without delay, subject to the applicable laws and regulations of the exporting Party.

7. The competent governmental authority of the exporting Party or its designees shall, if they receive notification in accordance with paragraph 6, or if they have knowledge after the issuance of the CO that the good does not qualify as an originating good of the exporting Party, cancel the CO and promptly notify the cancellation to the exporter to whom the CO has been issued, and to the customs authority of the importing Party, except in the case where the exporter has returned the CO to the competent governmental authority of the exporting Party.

8. The format of the CO and its contents shall be in the English language and shall include minimum data specified in the Attachment to this Annex.

APPENDIX 12. AJFTA

Rule 3

Presentation of Certificate of Origin

1. For the purposes of claiming preferential tariff treatment, the following shall be submitted to the customs authority of the importing Party by the importer:

    (a) a valid CO; and
    (b) other documents as required in accordance with the laws and regulations of the importing Party (e.g. invoices, including third country invoices, and a through bill of lading issued in the exporting Party).

2. A CO shall not be required for an importation of a consignment of originating goods of the exporting Party whose aggregate customs value does not exceed two hundred United States dollars (USD200) or its equivalent amount in the Party's currency, or such higher amount as the importing Party may establish.

3. Where an originating good of the exporting Party is imported through one or more of the Parties other than the exporting Party and the importing Party, or non-Parties, the importing Party may require importers who claim preferential tariff treatment for the good to submit:

    (a) a copy of through bill of lading; or
    (b) a certificate or any other information given by the customs authorities of such one or more Parties or non-Parties, or other relevant entities, which proves that the good has not undergone operations other than unloading, reloading and any other operation to preserve it in good condition in those Parties or non-Parties.

4.
- (a) Notwithstanding paragraph 5 of Rule 2, where an originating good, for which a CO (hereinafter referred to in this paragraph as "original CO") was issued by the competent governmental authority or its designees of the exporting Party, is to be exported from the importing Party to another Party, the competent governmental authority or its designees of the importing Party may issue a back-to-back CO as a new CO for the originating good, if a request is made by the exporter in the importing Party or its authorised agent with presentation of the valid original CO.
- (b) Where a back-to-back CO is issued in accordance with subparagraph (a), "an originating good of the exporting Party" referred to in Chapter 3 and this Annex shall be construed as an originating good of the Party whose competent governmental authority or its designees has issued the original CO.

Rule 4

Validity of Certificate of Origin

1. A CO shall be submitted to the customs authority of the importing Party within one (1) year from the date of issuance by the competent governmental authority of the exporting Party or its designees.
2. Where the CO is submitted to the customs authority of the importing Party after the expiration of the period for its submission provided for in paragraph 1, that CO shall be

accepted when the failure to observe such a requirement results from force majeure or other valid causes beyond the control of the exporter or importer.
3. An issued CO shall be applicable to a single importation of an originating good of the exporting Party into the importing Party.

Rule 5

Record Keeping

1. Each Party shall, in accordance with its laws and regulations, ensure that the exporter to whom a CO has been issued or the producer of a good in the exporting Party referred to in subparagraph 4(b) of Rule 2 keeps records relating to the origin of the good. For the purposes of this Agreement, the exporter or producer shall keep these records for three (3) years after the date on which the CO was issued.

2. Each Party shall ensure that its competent governmental authority or its designees shall keep a record of the issued CO for a period of three (3) years after the date on which the CO was issued. Such record includes all supporting documents presented to prove the qualification as an originating good of the exporting Party.

Rule 6

Verification

1. For the purposes of determining whether a good imported from another Party and claimed for preferential tariff

treatment qualifies as an originating good of that Party under this Agreement, the customs authority or the relevant authority of the importing Party may request information relating to the origin of the good, provided that such a request is made to the competent governmental authority of the exporting Party on the basis of the CO.

2. For the purposes of paragraph 1, the competent governmental authority of the exporting Party shall, in accordance with its laws and regulations, provide the information requested in a period not exceeding three (3) months after the date of receipt of the request. If the customs authority or the relevant authority of the importing Party considers necessary, it may request additional information relating to the origin of the good. If additional information is requested by the customs authority or the relevant authority of the importing Party, the competent governmental authority of the exporting Party shall, in accordance with its laws and regulations, provide the information requested in a period not exceeding three (3) months after the date of receipt of the request for additional information.

3. For the purposes of paragraph 2, the competent governmental authority of the exporting Party may request the exporter to whom the CO has been issued, or the producer of the good in the exporting Party referred to in subparagraph 4(b) of Rule 2, to provide the former with the information requested.

4. The request for information in accordance with paragraph 1 shall not preclude the use of a verification visit provided for in Rule 7.

5. During the procedures provided for in this Rule and Rule 7, the customs authority of the importing Party may suspend the preferential tariff treatment while awaiting the result of verification, and shall not wait for the procedures to be completed before it releases the good to the importer unless subject to appropriate administrative measures.
6. Each Party shall provide the other Parties with the names of its relevant authority, if any.

Rule 7

Verification Visit

1. The customs authority or the relevant authority of the importing Party may request the exporting Party:

   (a) to collect and provide information relating to the origin of the good and check, for that purpose, the facilities used in the production of the good, through a visit by the competent governmental authority of the exporting Party along with the customs authority or the relevant authority of the importing Party to the premises of the exporter to whom the CO has been issued, or the producer of the good in the exporting Party referred to in subparagraph 4(b) of Rule 2; and

   (b) during the visit pursuant to subparagraph (a), to provide information relating to the origin of the good in the possession of the competent governmental authority of the exporting Party or its designees.

2. When requesting the exporting Party to conduct a visit pursuant to paragraph 1, the customs authority or the

relevant authority of the importing Party shall deliver a written communication with such request to the exporting Party at least sixty (60) days in advance of the proposed date of the visit, the receipt of which is to be confirmed by the exporting Party. The competent governmental authority of the exporting Party shall request the written consent of the exporter, or the producer of the good in the exporting Party whose premises are to be visited.

3. The communication referred to in paragraph 2 shall include:

   (a) the identity of the customs authority or the relevant authority issuing the communication;
   (b) the name of the exporter, or the producer of the good in the exporting Party whose premises are requested to be visited;
   (c) the proposed date and places of the visit;
   (d) the object and scope of the proposed visit, including specific reference to the good subject of the verification referred to in the CO; and
   (e) the names and titles of the officials of the customs authority or the relevant authority of the importing Party to be present during the visit.

4. The exporting Party shall respond in writing to the importing Party, within thirty (30) days from the receipt of the communication referred to in paragraph 2, whether it accepts or refuses to conduct the visit requested pursuant to paragraph 1.

5. The competent governmental authority of the exporting Party shall, in accordance with the laws and regulations of

the Party, provide within forty-five (45) days or any other mutually agreed period from the last day of the visit, to the customs authority or the relevant authority of the importing Party any additional information obtained pursuant to paragraph 1.

Rule 8

Determination of Origin and Preferential Tariff Treatment

1. The customs authority of the importing Party may deny preferential tariff treatment to a good for which an importer claims preferential tariff treatment where the good does not qualify as an originating good of the exporting Party or where the importer fails to comply with any of the relevant requirements of this Annex.
2. In cases where the verification procedures outlined in Rule 6 or 7 are undertaken, the customs authority of the importing Party may determine that a good does not qualify as an originating good of the exporting Party and may deny preferential tariff treatment, under any of the following conditions:

    (a) the competent governmental authority of the exporting Party fails to respond to the request within the period referred to in paragraph 2 of Rule 6 or paragraph 5 of Rule 7;

    (b) the exporting Party refuses to the conduct of the verification visit as requested by the customs authority or the relevant authority of the importing Party, or that

Party fails to respond to the communication referred to in paragraph 2 of Rule 7 within the period referred to in paragraph 4 of Rule 7; or

(c) the information provided to the customs authority or the relevant authority of the importing Party pursuant to Rule 6 or 7 is not sufficient to prove that the good qualifies as an originating good of the exporting Party.

3. In cases where the verification procedures outlined in Rule 6 or 7 are undertaken, the customs authority of the importing Party shall provide the competent governmental authority of the exporting Party with a written determination of whether or not the good qualifies as an originating good of the exporting Party, including findings of fact and the legal basis for the determination, in a period, unless otherwise agreed upon by the importing Party and the exporting Party, not exceeding thirty (30) days after the date of the receipt of the information last provided by the competent governmental authority of the exporting Party in accordance with Rule 6, or sixty (60) days after the last day of the visit referred to in Rule 7.

4. The competent governmental authority of the exporting Party shall notify the determination by the customs authority of the importing Party referred to in paragraph 3, to the exporter, or the producer of the good in the exporting Party whose premises were subject to the visit referred to in Rule 7. In the event that a determination is made that the good qualifies as an originating good of the exporting Party, any suspended preferential tariff treatment shall be reinstated.

Rule 9

Confidentiality

1. Where a Party provides information to another Party pursuant to this Annex and designates the information as confidential, the Party receiving the information shall maintain the confidentiality of the information, protect that information from disclosure that could prejudice the competitive position of the persons providing the information, use the information only for the purposes specified by the Party providing it, and not disclose the information without the specific written permission of the Party providing it.
2. Information obtained by the customs authority or the relevant authority of the importing Party pursuant to this Annex:

    (a) shall only be used by such authority for the purposes of the verification of a CO under this Annex; and
    (b) shall not be used by the importing Party in any criminal proceedings carried out by a court or a judge, in the absence of a specific written permission of the exporting Party that provided the information.

Rule 10

Appropriate Penalties or Other Measures against Fraudulent Acts

Each Party shall establish or maintain, in accordance with its laws and regulations, appropriate penalties or other measures against its exporters or producers who have committed fraudulent acts in connection with a CO, including submission of false declarations or documents to its competent governmental authority or its designees.

Rule 11

Implementing Regulations

The Joint Committee shall, upon the date of entry into force of this Agreement pursuant to paragraph 1 of Article 79, adopt the Implementing Regulations that provide detailed regulations pursuant to which the customs authorities, competent governmental authorities and other authorities concerned of the Parties shall implement their functions under this Annex.

Attachment to Annex 4

Minimum Data Requirement for Certificate of Origin

1. Exporter's name, address and country
2. Importer's or, if applicable, consignee's name, address and country
3. Certification number
4. Origin of good(s)
5. Invoice number and date
6. Transport details (if known)
7. HS tariff classification number

8. Marks, numbers, number and kind of packages; Description of good(s)
9. Quantity (Unit)
10. Preference criterion (including information on CTC, RVC and accumulation)
11. Declaration by the exporter
12. Certification

Appendix 13

Rules of Origin, ASEAN–Korea Free Trade Agreement

Article 5

Rules of Origin

The Rules of Origin and the Operational Certification Procedures applicable to the goods covered under this Agreement are set out in Annex 3 and its Appendices.

Annex 3 Rules of Origin

In determining the origin of a good eligible for preferential tariff treatment pursuant to Article 5 of this Agreement, the following Rules shall apply:

Rule 1

Definitions

For the purposes of this Annex:

CIF means the value of the good imported, and includes the cost of freight and insurance up to the port or place of entry into the country of importation;

APPENDIX 13. AKFTA

FOB means the free-on-board value of a good, inclusive of the cost of transport from the producer to the port or site of final shipment abroad;

goods shall include materials or products, which can be wholly obtained or produced, even if they are intended for later use as materials in another production process. For the purposes of this Annex, the terms "goods" and "products" can be used interchangeably and the terms "good" and "product" shall be interpreted accordingly;

Harmonized System means the nomenclature of the Harmonized Commodity Description and Coding System defined in the International Convention on the Harmonized Commodity Description and Coding System including all legal notes thereto, as in force and as amended from time to time;

APPENDIX 13. AKFTA

identical and interchangeable materials	means materials being of the same kind and commercial quality, possessing the same technical and physical characteristics, and which once they are incorporated into the finished good cannot be distinguished from one another for origin purposes by virtue of any markings, etc.;
materials	shall include ingredients, raw materials, parts, components, sub-assemblies used in the production process;
non-originating goods	means products or materials that do not qualify as originating under this Annex;
originating goods	means products or materials that qualify as originating under this Annex;
packing materials and containers for transportation	means the goods used to protect a good during its transportation, different from those materials or containers used for its retail sale;
preferential tariff treatment	means tariff concessions granted to originating goods as reflected by the tariff rates applicable under this Agreement;

Product Specific Rules	means the rules that specify that the materials have undergone a change in tariff classification or a specific manufacturing or processing operation, or satisfy a regional value content or a combination of any of these criteria;
production	means methods of obtaining a good including growing, mining, harvesting, raising, breeding, extracting, gathering, collecting, capturing, fishing, trapping, hunting, manufacturing, producing, processing or assembling a good; and
third country	means a non-Party or a Party which is not an importing or exporting Party, and the phrase "third countries" shall be interpreted accordingly.

Rule 2

Origin Criteria

1. For the purposes of this Agreement, a good imported into the territory of a Party shall be deemed to be originating and eligible for preferential tariff treatment if it conforms to the origin requirements under any one of the following:

(a) a good which is wholly obtained or produced entirely in the territory of the exporting Party as set out and defined in Rule 3; or

(b) a good not wholly obtained or produced in the territory of the exporting Party, provided that the said good is eligible under Rule 4 or 5 or 6 or 7.

2. Except as provided for in Rule 7, the conditions for acquiring originating status set out in this Annex must be fulfilled without interruption in the territory of the exporting Party.

Rule 3

Wholly Obtained or Produced Goods

Within the meaning of paragraph 1(a) of Rule 2, the following shall be considered to be wholly obtained or produced in the territory of a Party:

(a) plants and plant products harvested, picked or gathered after being grown there;

(b) live animals born and raised there;

(c) goods obtained from live animals referred to in sub-paragraph (b);

(d) goods obtained from hunting, trapping, fishing, aquaculture, gathering or capturing conducted there;

(e) minerals and other naturally occurring substances, not included in sub-paragraphs (a) through (d), extracted or taken from its soil, waters, seabed or beneath its seabed;

(f) products of sea-fishing taken by vessels registered with the Party and entitled to fly its flag, and other products taken by the Party or a person of that Party, from the waters, seabed or beneath the seabed outside the territorial waters of the Party, provided that the Party has the rights to exploit[1] the natural resources of such waters, seabed and beneath the seabed under international law[2];

(g) products of sea-fishing and other marine products taken from the high seas by vessels registered with the Party and entitled to fly its flag;

(h) goods produced and/or made on board factory ships registered with a Party and entitled to fly its flag, exclusively from products referred to in sub-paragraph (g);

(i) goods taken from outer space provided that they are obtained by the Party or a person of that Party;

(j) articles collected from there which can no longer perform their original purpose nor are capable of being restored or repaired and are fit only for the disposal or recovery of parts of raw materials, or for recycling purposes;

(k) waste and scrap derived from:
   (i) production there; or
   (ii) used goods collected there, provided that such goods are fit only for the recovery of raw materials; and

---

[1] The Parties understand that for the purposes of determining the origin of products of sea-fishing and other products, "rights" in sub-paragraph (f) of Rule 3 include those rights of access to the fisheries resources of a coastal state, as accruing from agreements or other arrangements concluded between a Party and the coastal state at the level of governments or duly authorised private entities.

[2] "International law" in sub-paragraph (f) of Rule 3 refers to generally accepted international law such as the United Nations Convention on the Law of the Sea.

(l) goods obtained or produced in the territory of the Party solely from goods referred to in sub-paragraphs (a) through (k).

Rule 4

Not Wholly Obtained or Produced Goods

1. For the purposes of paragraph 1(b) of Rule 2, a good, except those covered under Rule 5 as provided for in Appendix 2, shall be deemed to be originating if the regional value content (hereinafter referred to as the "RVC") is not less than 40% of the FOB value or if a good has undergone a change in tariff classification at four digit-level (change of tariff heading) of the Harmonized System.
2. The formula for calculating the RVC shall be[3]:

(a) Build-Up Method

$$RVC = \frac{VOM}{FOB} \times 100\%$$

VOM means value of originating materials, which includes the value of originating materials, direct labour cost, direct overhead cost, transportation cost and profit

---

[3] The Parties shall be given the flexibility to adopt the method of calculating the RVC, whether it is the build-up or the build-down method. In order to promote transparency, consistency and certainty, each Party shall adhere to one method. Any change in the method of calculation shall be notified to all the other Parties at least six (6) months prior to the adoption of the new method. It is understood that any verification of the RVC by the importing Party shall be done on the basis of the method used by the exporting Party.

(b) Build-Down Method

$$RVC = \frac{FOB - VNM}{FOB} \times 100\%$$

VNM means value of non-originating materials, which shall be: (i) the CIF value at the time of importation of the materials, parts or goods; or (ii) the earliest ascertained price paid for the materials, parts or goods of undetermined origin in the territory of the Party where the working or processing has taken place.

Rule 5

Product Specific Rules

For the purposes of Rule 2, goods which satisfy the Product Specific Rules provided in Appendix 2 shall be considered to be originating in the territory of the Party where working or processing of the goods has taken place.

Rule 6

Treatment for Certain Goods

Notwithstanding Rules 2, 4 and 5, certain goods shall be considered to be originating even if the production process or operation has been undertaken in an area outside the territories of Korea and ASEAN Member Countries (i.e. industrial zone) on materials exported from a Party and subsequently re-imported to that Party. The application of this Rule, including the list of products and the specific procedures related to this application shall be mutually agreed upon by the Parties.

Rule 7

Accumulation

Unless otherwise provided for in this Annex, a good originating in the territory of a Party, which is used in the territory of another Party as material for a finished good eligible for preferential tariff treatment, shall be considered to be originating in the territory of the latter Party where working or processing of the finished good has taken place.

Rule 8

Non-Qualifying Operations

1. Notwithstanding any provisions in this Annex, a good shall not be considered to be originating in the territory of a Party if the following operations are undertaken exclusively by itself or in combination in the territory of that Party:

   (a) preserving operations to ensure that the good remains in good condition during transport and storage;

   (b) changes of packaging, breaking-up and assembly of packages;

   (c) simple[4] washing, cleaning, removal of dust, oxide, oil, paint or other coverings;

   (d) simple[4] painting and polishing operations;

---

[4] "simple" generally describes an activity which does not need special skills, machines, apparatus or equipment especially produced or installed for carrying out the activity.

(e) husking, partial or total bleaching, polishing and glazing of cereals and rice;
(f) operations to colour sugar or form sugar lumps;
(g) simple[4] peeling, stoning, or un-shelling;
(h) sharpening, simple grinding or simple cutting;
(i) sifting, screening, sorting, classifying, grading, matching;
(j) simple placing in bottles, cans, flasks, bags, cases, boxes, fixing on cards or boards and all other simple packaging operations;
(k) affixing or printing marks, labels, logos and other like distinguishing signs on products or their packaging;
(l) simple mixing[5] of products, whether or not of different kinds;
(m) simple[4] assembly of parts of articles to constitute a complete article or disassembly of products into parts;
(n) simple[4] testing or calibrations; or
(o) slaughtering of animals[6]

2. A good originating in the territory of a Party shall retain its initial originating status, when exported from another

---

[5] "simple mixing" generally describes an activity which does not need special skills, machines, apparatus or equipment especially produced or installed for carrying out the activity. However, simple mixing does not include chemical reaction. Chemical reaction means a process (including a biochemical process) which result in a molecule with a new structure by breaking intramolecular bonds and by forming new intramolecular bonds, or by altering the spatial arrangement of atoms in a molecule.

[6] Slaughtering means the mere killing of animals and subsequent processes such as cutting, chilling, freezing, salting, drying or smoking, for the purpose of preservation for storage and transport.

Party, where operations undertaken have not gone beyond those referred to in paragraph 1.

Rule 9

Direct Consignment

1. Preferential tariff treatment shall be applied to a good satisfying the requirements of this Annex and which is transported directly between the territories of the exporting Party and the importing Party.
2. Notwithstanding paragraph 1, a good of which transport involves transit through one or more intermediate third countries, other than the territories of the exporting Party and the importing Party, shall be considered to be consigned directly, provided that:

   (a) the transit is justified for geographical reason or by consideration related exclusively to transport requirement;
   (b) the good has not entered into trade or consumption there; and
   (c) the good has not undergone any operation other than unloading and reloading or any operation required to keep it in good condition.

Rule 10

De Minimis

1. A good that does not undergo a change in tariff classification shall be considered as originating if:

(a) for a good, other than that provided for in Chapters 50 through 63 of the Harmonized System, the value of all non-originating materials used in its production that do not undergo the required change in tariff classification does not exceed ten (10) percent of the FOB value of the good;

(b) for a good provided for in Chapters 50 through 63 of the Harmonized System, the weight of all non-originating materials used in its production that do not undergo the required change in tariff classification does not exceed ten (10) percent of the total weight of the good; and the good specified in sub-paragraph (a) and (b) meets all other applicable criteria set forth in this Annex for qualifying as an originating good.

2. The value of non-originating materials referred to in paragraph 1 shall, however, be included in the value of non-originating materials for any applicable RVC requirement for the good.

Rule 11

Treatment of Packaging and Packing Materials

1.
    (a) If a good is subject to the RVC criterion as set out in Rule 4, the value of the packaging and packing materials for retail sale shall be taken into account in its determination of origin, where the packaging and packing materials are considered to be forming a whole with the good.

(b) Where sub-paragraph (a) is not applicable, the packaging and packing materials for retail sale, when classified together with the packaged good, shall not be taken into account in considering whether all non-originating materials used in the manufacture of the good fulfil the criterion corresponding to a change in tariff classification of the said good.

2. Packing materials and containers for transportation of a good shall not be taken into account in determining the origin of the good.

Rule 12

Accessories, Spare Parts and Tools

The origin of accessories, spare parts, tools, and instructional or other informational materials presented with a good shall not be taken into account in determining the origin of the good, provided that such accessories, spare parts, tools, and instructional or other informational materials are classified with the good and their customs duties are collected with the good by the importing Party.

Rule 13

Neutral Elements

In order to determine whether a good originates, it shall not be necessary to determine the origin of the following which might be used in its production and not incorporated into the good:

(a) fuel and energy;
(b) tools, dies and moulds;
(c) spare parts and materials used in the maintenance of equipment and buildings;
(d) lubricants, greases, compounding materials and other materials used in production or used to operate equipment and buildings;
(e) gloves, glasses, footwear, clothing, safety equipment and supplies;
(f) equipment, devices and supplies used for testing or inspecting the good; and
(g) any other goods that are not incorporated into the good but of which use in the production of the good can reasonably be demonstrated to be a part of that production.

Rule 14

Identical and Interchangeable Materials

1. For the purposes of establishing the origin of a good, when the good is manufactured utilising originating and non-originating materials, mixed or physically combined, the origin of such materials can be determined by generally accepted accounting principles of inventory management practiced in the territory of the exporting Party.
2. Once a decision has been taken on the inventory management method, that method shall be used throughout the fiscal year.

Rule 15

Certificate of Origin

A claim that a good shall be accepted as eligible for preferential tariff treatment shall be supported by a Certificate of Origin issued by a competent authority designated by the exporting Party and notified to all the other Parties in accordance with the Operational Certification Procedures, as set out in Appendix 1.

Rule 16

Consultations, Review and Modification

1. The Parties shall consult regularly to ensure that the Rules in this Annex are administered effectively, uniformly and consistently in order to achieve the spirit and objectives of this Annex.
2. This Annex may be reviewed and modified as and when necessary upon request of a Party and may be open to such reviews and modifications as may be agreed upon in the Implementing Committee established under Article 5.3 of the Framework Agreement.

Rule 17

Institutional Arrangement

Subject to Article 5.3 of the Framework Agreement, the Korea-ASEAN Rules of Origin Committee shall be established and be responsible for administering and enforcing the general rules of origin and customs procedures as provided for in this Annex and endeavour to resolve any differences arising therefrom.

Rule 18

Settlement of Disputes

1. In the case of differences concerning origin determination, classification of a good or other matters relevant to the implementation of this Annex, the government authorities concerned of the importing Party and the exporting Party shall consult each other with a view to resolving the differences, and the result shall be notified to all the other Parties for information.
2. Where no mutually satisfactory solution to the differences has been reached through the consultations mentioned in paragraph 1, the Party concerned may invoke the dispute settlement procedures as set out in the Agreement on Dispute Settlement Mechanism under the Framework Agreement.

Appendix 1 Operational Certification Procedures for the Rules of Origin

For the purposes of implementing Annex 3, the following operational procedures on the issuance of a Certificate of Origin, verification of origin and other related administrative matters shall be observed:

APPENDIX 13. AKFTA

Definitions

Rule 1

For the purposes of this Appendix:

back-to-back Certificate of Origin	means a Certificate of Origin issued by an intermediate exporting Party based on the Certificate of Origin issued by the first exporting Party;
customs authority	means the competent authority that is responsible under the law of a Party for the administration of customs laws and regulations[7];
exporter	means a natural or juridical person located in the territory of a Party from where a good is exported by such a person;
importer	means a natural or juridical person located in the territory of a Party into where a good is imported by such a person; and
issuing authority	means the competent authority designated by the government of the exporting Party to issue a Certificate of Origin and notified to

---

[7] Such laws and regulations administered and enforced by the customs authority of each Party concerning the importation, exportation and transit of goods as they relate to customs duties, charges and other taxes or prohibitions, restrictions and controls with respect to the movement of controlled items across the boundary of the customs authority of each Party.

	all the other Parties in accordance with this Appendix.
producer	means a natural or juridical person who carries out production as set out in Rule 1 of Annex 3 in the territory of a Party.

Issuing Authorities

Rule 2

1. Each Party shall provide the names, addresses, specimen signatures and specimen of official seals of its issuing authorities to all the other Parties, through the ASEAN Secretariat. Any change in the said list shall be promptly provided in the same manner.
2. Any Certificate of Origin issued by an official not included in the said list shall not be honoured by the customs authority.

Rule 3

For the purposes of determining originating status, the issuing authorities shall have the right to request for supporting documentary evidence or to carry out the check considered appropriate in accordance with a Party's respective domestic laws and regulations.

Issuance of a Certificate of Origin

Rule 4

1. The producer and/or exporter of the good, or its authorised representative, shall apply to the issuing authority, in

APPENDIX 13. AKFTA

accordance with the Party's domestic laws and regulations, requesting for pre-exportation examination of the origin of the good. The result of the examination, subject to review periodically or whenever appropriate, shall be accepted as the supporting evidence in determining the origin of the said good to be exported thereafter. The pre-exportation examination may not apply to the good of which, by its nature, origin can be easily determined.

2. The producer and/or exporter or its authorised representative shall apply for a Certificate of Origin together with appropriate supporting documents proving that the good to be exported qualifies for the issuance of a Certificate of Origin, consistent with the domestic laws and regulations of the Party.

3. The issuing authority shall, to the best of its competence and ability, carry out proper examination, in accordance with the domestic laws and regulations of the Party, upon each application for a Certification of Origin to ensure that:

   (a) the Certificate of Origin is duly completed and signed by the authorised signatory;
   (b) the origin of the good is in conformity with Annex 3;
   (c) other statements in the Certificate of Origin correspond to supporting documentary evidence submitted; and
   (d) the description, quantity and weight of the good, marks and number of packages, number and kinds of packages, as specified, conform to the good to be exported.

4. Multiple items declared on the same Certificate of Origin, shall be allowed, provided that each item must qualify separately in its own right.

Rule 5

1. A Certificate of Origin shall be on A4 size paper and shall be in the form attached and referred to as Form AK. It shall be in the English language.
2. A Certificate of Origin shall comprise one original and two (2) copies. The colors of the original and the copies of a Certificate of Origin shall be mutually agreed upon by the Parties.
3. A Certificate of Origin shall bear a reference number separately given by each place or office of issuance.
4. The original copy shall be forwarded by the producer and/or exporter to the importer for submission to the customs authority of the importing Party. The duplicate shall be retained by the issuing authority of the exporting Party. The triplicate shall be retained by the producer and/or exporter.
5. The issuing authority shall endeavour to periodically provide records of issuance of Certificates of Origin, including issuing number and date, producer and/or exporter and description of goods, to the customs authority of the importing Party.
6. In cases where a Certificate of Origin is rejected by the customs authority of the importing Party, the subject Certificate of Origin shall be marked accordingly in box 4 and the original Certificate of Origin shall be returned to the issuing authority within a reasonable period but not exceeding two (2) months. The issuing authority shall be duly notified of the grounds for the denial of preferential tariff treatment.

7. In cases where a Certificate of Origin is not accepted, as stated in paragraph 6, the customs authority of the importing Party, as it deems fit, should accept the clarifications made by the issuing authority to accept the Certificate of Origin and reinstate the preferential tariff treatment. The clarifications should be detailed and exhaustive in addressing the grounds for denial of preferential tariff treatment raised by the importing Party.

Rule 6

Neither erasures nor superimpositions shall be allowed on a Certificate of Origin. Any alteration shall be made by striking out the erroneous materials and making any addition required. Such alterations shall be approved by an official authorised to sign a Certificate of Origin and certified by the issuing authority. Unused spaces shall be crossed out to prevent any subsequent addition.

Rule 7

1. A Certificate of Origin shall be issued at the time of exportation or soon thereafter whenever the good to be exported can be considered to be originating in the territory of the exporting Party within the meaning of Annex 3.
2. The issuing authority of the intermediate Party may issue a back-to-back Certificate of Origin, if an application is made by the exporter while the good is passing through its territory, provided that:

APPENDIX 13. AKFTA

    (a) a valid original Certificate of Origin is presented;
    (b) the importer of the intermediate Party and the exporter who applies for the back-to-back Certificate of Origin in the intermediate Party are the same; and
    (c) verification procedures as set out in Rule 14 is [sic] applied.

3. Upon request of a Party, the Parties shall review the provisions of this Rule and the implementation thereof, and revise it as may be mutually agreed upon by the Parties.
4. In exceptional cases where a Certificate of Origin has not been issued at the time of exportation or soon thereafter due to involuntary errors, omissions or other valid causes, a Certificate of Origin may be issued retroactively but no later than one year from the date of shipment, bearing the words "ISSUED RETROACTIVELY".

Rule 8

In the event of theft, loss or destruction of a Certificate of Origin, the producer and/or exporter may apply to the issuing authority for a certified true copy of the original to be made out on the basis of the export documents in its possession bearing the endorsement of the words "CERTIFIED TRUE COPY" in box 12 of a Certificate of Origin. This copy shall bear the date of issuance of the original Certificate of Origin. The certified true copy of a Certificate of Origin shall be issued no later than one year from the date of issuance of the original Certificate of Origin.

Presentation

Rule 9

For the purposes of claiming preferential tariff treatment, the importer shall submit to the customs authority of the importing Party at the time of import, a declaration, a Certificate of Origin including supporting documents (i.e. invoices and, when required, the through Bill of Lading issued in the territory of the exporting Party) and other documents as required in accordance with the domestic laws and regulations of the importing Party.

Rule 10

1. The Certificate of Origin shall, in accordance with domestic laws and regulations, be submitted to the customs authority of the importing Party within six (6) months from the date of issuance by the issuing authority of the exporting Party or the intermediate exporting Party in the case of back-to-back Certificate of Origin.
2. Where the Certificate of Origin is submitted to the customs authority of the importing Party after the expiration of the time-limit as stated in paragraph 1 for its submission, such Certificate of Origin shall be accepted when the failure to observe such time-limit results from force majeure or other valid causes beyond the control of the producer and/or exporter.
3. In all cases, the customs authority of the importing Party may accept such Certificate of Origin, provided that the

good has been imported before the expiration of the time-limit of the said Certificate of Origin.

Rule 11

A Certificate of Origin shall not be required for:

(a) a good originating in the territory of a Party which does not exceed US$ 200.00 FOB; or
(b) a good sent by post from the territory of a Party which does not exceed US$ 200.00 FOB, provided that the importation does not form part of one or more importations that may reasonably be considered to have been undertaken or arranged for the purpose of avoiding the submission of a Certificate of Origin.

Rule 12

1. Where the origin of a good is not in doubt, the discovery of minor discrepancies, between the statements made in a Certificate of Origin and those made in the documents submitted to the customs authority of the importing Party for the purpose of carrying out the formalities for importing the good shall not *ipso facto* invalidate the Certificate of Origin, if it does in fact correspond to the good submitted.
2. For multiple items declared under the same Certificate of Origin, a problem encountered with one of the items listed shall not affect or delay the granting of preferential tariff treatment and customs clearance of the remaining items

listed in that Certificate of Origin. Paragraph 1(c) of Rule 14 may be applied to the problematic items.

Record Keeping Requirement

Rule 13

1. For the purposes of the verification process pursuant to Rules 14 and 15, the producer and/or exporter applying for the issuance of a Certificate of Origin shall, subject to the domestic laws and regulations of the exporting Party, keep its supporting records for application for not less than three (3) years from the date of issuance of the Certificate of Origin.
2. The importer shall keep records relevant to the importation in accordance with the domestic laws and regulations of the importing Party.
3. The application for Certificates of Origin and all documents related to such application shall be retained by the issuing authority for not less than three (3) years from the date of issuance.
4. Information relating to the validity of a Certificate of Origin shall be furnished upon request of the importing Party by an official authorised to sign a Certificate of Origin and certified by the appropriate government authorities.
5. Any information communicated between the Parties concerned shall be treated as confidential and shall be used for the validation of Certificates of Origin purpose only.

APPENDIX 13. AKFTA

Verification

Rule 14

1. The importing Party may request the issuing authority of the exporting Party to conduct a retroactive check at random and/or when the importing Party has reasonable doubt as to the authenticity of the document or as to the accuracy of the information regarding the true origin of the good in question or of certain parts thereof. Upon such request, the issuing authority[8] of the exporting Party shall conduct a retroactive check on a producer's and/or exporter's cost statement based on the current cost and prices within a six-month timeframe of the specified date of exportation[9], subject to the following procedures:

   (a) the request of the importing Party for a retroactive check shall be accompanied with the Certificate of Origin concerned and shall specify the reasons and any additional information suggesting that the particulars given on the said Certificate of Origin may be inaccurate, unless the retroactive check is requested on a random basis;

   (b) the issuing authority of the exporting Party receiving a request for retroactive check shall respond to the

---

[8] In the case of Korea, the issuing authority referred to Rules 14 and 15, for the purpose of origin verification for the exported goods into the ASEAN Member countries, refers to the customs authority in accordance with its customs laws and regulations.

[9] With reference to the six-month timeframe, the issuing authority of the exporting Party can choose any six-month period, before or after the date specified, or any time in between as long as it does not exceed the period of six months.

request promptly and reply within two (2) months after receipt of the request;

(c) the customs authority of the importing Party may suspend provision of preferential tariff treatment while awaiting the result of verification. However, it may release the good to the importer subject to any administrative measures deemed necessary, provided that they are not held to be subject to import prohibition or restriction and there is no suspicion of fraud; and

(d) the issuing authority shall promptly transmit the results of the verification process to the importing Party which shall then determine whether or not the subject good is originating. The entire process for retroactive check, including the process of notifying the issuing authority of the exporting Party the result of determination on whether or not the good is originating, shall be completed within six (6) months.

While the process of the retroactive check is being undertaken, sub-paragraph (c) shall be applied.

2. The customs authority of the importing Party may request an importer for information or documents relating to the origin of imported good in accordance with its domestic laws and regulations before requesting the retroactive check pursuant to paragraph 1.

Rule 15

1. If the importing Party is not satisfied with the outcome of the retroactive check, it may, under exceptional circumstances, request verification visits to the exporting Party.

2. Prior to conducting a verification visit pursuant to paragraph 1:

   (a) an importing Party shall deliver a written notification of its intention to conduct the verification visit simultaneously to:

   (i) the producer and/or exporter whose premises are to be visited;

   (ii) the issuing authority of the Party in the territory of which the verification visit is to occur;

   (iii) the customs authority of the Party in the territory of which the verification visit is to occur; and

   (iv) the importer of the good subject to the verification visit;

   (b) the written notification mentioned in sub-paragraph (a) shall be as comprehensive as possible and shall include, among others:

   (i) the name of the customs authority issuing the notification;

   (ii) the name of the producer and/or exporter whose premises are to be visited;

   (iii) the proposed date of the verification visit;

   (iv) the coverage of the proposed verification visit, including reference to the good subject to the verification; and

   (v) the names and designation of the officials performing the verification visit;

   (c) an importing Party shall obtain the written consent of the producer and/or exporter whose premises are to be visited;

(d) when a written consent from the producer and/or exporter is not obtained within thirty (30) days from the date of receipt of the notification pursuant to subparagraph (a), the notifying Party may deny preferential tariff treatment to the good referred to in the said Certificate of Origin that would have been subject to the verification visit; and

(e) the issuing authority receiving the notification may postpone the proposed verification visit and notify the importing Party of such intention within fifteen (15) days from the date of receipt of the notification. Notwithstanding any postponement, any verification visit shall be carried out within sixty (60) days from the date of such receipt, or a longer period as the Parties may agree.

3. The Party conducting the verification visit shall provide the producer and/or exporter, whose good is subject to such verification, and the relevant issuing authority with a written determination of whether or not the good subject to such verification qualifies as an originating good.
4. Any suspended preferential tariff treatment shall be reinstated upon the written determination referred to in paragraph 3 that the good qualifies as an originating good.
5. The producer and/or exporter shall be allowed thirty (30) days from the date of receipt of the written determination to provide in writing comments or additional information regarding the eligibility of the good for preferential tariff treatment. If the good is still found to be non-originating, the final written determination shall be communicated to

the issuing authority within thirty (30) days from the date of receipt of the comments/additional information from the producer and/or exporter.
6. The verification visit process, including the actual visit and the determination under paragraph 3 whether the good subject to such verification is originating or not, shall be carried out and its results communicated to the issuing authority within a maximum period of six (6) months from the first day the initial verification visit was conducted. While the process of verification is being undertaken, paragraph 1(c) of Rule 14 shall be applied.

Rule 16

1. The Parties shall maintain, in accordance with their respective domestic laws and regulations, the confidentiality of classified business information collected in the process of verification pursuant to Rules 14 and 15 and shall protect that information from disclosure that could prejudice the competitive position of the person who provided the information.
2. Subject to the domestic laws and regulations, and agreement of the Parties, classified information may only be disclosed by the authorities of one Party to another, for the administration and enforcement of origin determination.

Denial of Preferential Tariff Treatment

Rule 17

Except as otherwise provided in this Appendix, the importing Party may deny claim for preferential tariff treatment or recover unpaid duties in accordance with its laws and regulations, where the good does not meet the requirements of Annex 3, or where the relevant requirements of this Appendix are not fulfilled.

Special Cases

Rule 18

When destination of all or parts of the good exported to the territory of a specified Party is changed, before or after its arrival in the territory of that Party, the following shall be observed:

(a) even if the good is already imported into the territory of a specified importing Party, the customs authority of that importing Party shall endorse the Certificate of Origin to the effect for all or parts of the good in case where the importer makes a written application for the preferential tariff treatment along with the submission of the original Certificate of Origin; and

(b) if the changing of destination occurs during transportation to the territory of the importing Party as specified in the Certificate of Origin, the producer and/or exporter shall apply in writing, accompanied with the issued Certificate of Origin, for a new issuance for all or parts of the good.

Rule 19

For the purposes of implementing Rule 9 of Annex 3, where transportation is effected through the territory of one or more intermediate countries, other than that of the exporting Party and the importing Party, the following shall be produced to the relevant government authorities of the importing Party:

(a) a through Bill of Lading issued in the territory of the exporting Party;
(b) a Certificate of Origin;
(c) a copy of the original commercial invoice in respect of the good; and
(d) other relevant supporting documents, if any, as evidence that the requirements of Rule 9 of Annex 3 are being complied with.

Rule 20

1. Notwithstanding Rule 9 of Annex 3, a good sent from the territory of the exporting Party for exhibition in another country and sold during or after the exhibition for importation into the territory of a Party shall be granted preferential tariff treatment on the condition that the good meets the requirements as set out in Annex 3, provided that it is shown to the satisfaction of the customs authority of the importing Party that:

    (a) an exporter has dispatched the good from the territory of the exporting Party to the country where the exhibition has been held and has exhibited it there;

(b) the exporter has sold the goods or transferred it to a consignee in the territory of the importing Party; and
(c) the good has been consigned during the exhibition or immediately thereafter to the territory of the importing Party in the state in which it was sent for the exhibition.

2. For the purposes of implementing paragraph 1, a Certificate of Origin shall be provided to the relevant government authorities of the importing Party. The name and address of the exhibition shall be indicated. As an evidence for the identification of the good and the conditions under which it was exhibited, a certificate issued by the relevant government authorities of the country where the exhibition took place together with supporting documents prescribed in sub-paragraph (d) of Rule 19 may be required.
3. Paragraph 1 shall apply to any trade, agricultural or crafts exhibition, fair or similar show or display in shops or business premises with a view to the sale of foreign good and where the good remains under customs control during the exhibition.

Rule 21

1. Customs authority in the importing Party may accept Certificates of Origin in cases where the sales invoice is issued either by a company located in a third country

or by an exporter for the account of the said company, provided that the good meets the requirements of Annex 3.
2. The exporter of the goods shall indicate "third country invoicing" and such information as name and country of the company issuing the invoice in the Certificate of Origin.

Action Against Fraudulent Acts

Rule 22

1. When it is suspected that fraudulent acts in connection with a Certificate of Origin have been committed, the government authorities concerned shall cooperate in the action to be taken by a Party against the persons involved.
2. Each Party shall provide legal sanctions for fraudulent acts related to a Certificate of Origin.

Customs Contact Point

Rule 23

1. Each Party shall designate a contact point for all matters relating to this Appendix.
2. When the contact point of a Party raises any matter arising from Annex 3 to the contact point of any other Party, the customs authority of the latter Party shall assign its own experts to look into the matter and to respond with its

findings and proposed solution for resolving the matter within a reasonable period of time.
3. The contact points shall endeavor to resolve any matter raised under Annex 3 through consultations.

Appendix 3 Explanatory Notes to Annex 3

1. RVC Calculation Formula

For the purposes of Rule 5 of Annex 3, RVC of a good specified in Appendix 2 shall be calculated in accordance with the formula provided for in paragraph 2 of Rule 4 of Annex 3.

2. Non-Qualifying Operations for Textile and Garment

Notwithstanding any provisions in Annex 3, a good from Chapters 50 through 63 shall not be considered to be originating in the territory of a Party if the following operations are undertaken exclusively by itself or in combination within each paragraph in the territory of that Party, whether or not both RVC and CTC criteria, are satisfied:

(a) simple combining operations, labeling, ironing or pressing, cleaning or dry cleaning, packaging operations, or any combination thereof;
(b) cutting to length or width and hemming, stitching or overlocking of fabrics which are readily identifiable as being intended for a particular commercial use;

(c) trimming and/or joining together of accessory articles, such as straps, bands, beads, cords, rings or eyelets, by sewing, looping, linking or attaching;
(d) bleaching, waterproofing, decating, shrinking, mercerizing, or similar operations for the purposes of having merely undergone the finishing operations; or
(e) embroidery which represents less than five (5) percent of the total area of the embroidered goods or embroidery which contributes less than five (5) percent of the total weight of the embroidered goods.

3. Agricultural and Horticultural Goods

Agricultural and horticultural goods grown in the territory of an exporting Party shall be treated as originating in the territory of that Party even if they are grown from seed, bulbs, rootstock, cuttings, slips or other live parts of plants imported from a territory of a third country.

4. Aquacultural Goods

Aquacultural goods raised in the territory of an exporting Party shall be treated as originating in the territory of that Party if they are raised from seedstocks such as eggs, frys, fingerlings, glass eels or oyster spats to be normally fed on initial feed such as rotifer or artemia.

ATTACHMENT

Original (Duplicate/Triplicate/Quadruplicate)

1. Goods consigned from (Exporter's business name, address, country)	Reference No.
	ASEAN-KOREA FREE TRADE AREA PREFERENTIAL TARIFF CERTIFICATE OF ORIGIN
2. Goods consigned to (Consignee's name, address, country)	(Combined Declaration and Certificate)
	Issued in $\frac{\text{FORM AK}}{\text{(Country)}}$
	See Notes Overleaf
3. Means of transport and route (as far as known) Departure date Vessel's name/Aircraft etc. Port of Discharge	4. For Official Use ☐ Preferential Treatment Given Under ASEAN-Korea Free Trade Area Preferential Tariff ☐ Preferential Treatment Not Given (Please state reason/s) .... Signature of Authorised Signatory of the Importing Country

5. Item number	6. Marks and numbers on packages	7. Number and type of packages, description of goods (including quantity where appropriate and HS number of the importing country)	8. Origin criterion (see Notes overleaf)	9. Gross weight or other quantity and value (FOB)	10. Number and date of Invoices

11. Declaration by the exporter	12. Certification
The undersigned hereby declares that the above details and statement are correct; that all the goods were produced in .... (Country) and that they comply with the origin requirements specified for these goods in the ASEAN-KOREA Free Trade Area Preferential Tariff for the goods exported to .... (Importing Country) .... Place and date, signature of authorised signatory	It is hereby certified, on the basis of control carried out, that the declaration by the exporter is correct. .... Place and date, signature and stamp of certifying authority

13. ☐ Third Country Invoicing ☐ Exhibition ☐ Back-to-Back CO

APPENDIX 13. AKFTA

OVERLEAF NOTES

1. Parties which accept this form for the purpose of preferential tariff under the ASEAN-KOREA Free Trade Agreement (AKFTA):

BRUNEI DARUSSALAM	CAMBODIA	INDONESIA
REPUBLIC OF KOREA	LAOS	MALAYSIA
MYANMAR THAILAND	PHILIPPINES VIETNAM	SINGAPORE

2. CONDITIONS: To enjoy preferential tariff under the AKFTA, goods sent to any Parties listed above:
   (i) must fall within a description of goods eligible for concessions in the country of destination;
   (ii) must comply with the consignment conditions in accordance with Rule 9 of Annex 3 (Rules of Origin) of the AKFTA; and
   (iii) must comply with the origin criteria in Annex 3 (Rules of Origin) of the AKFTA.
3. ORIGIN CRITERIA: For goods that meet the origin criteria, the exporter and/or producer must indicate in box 8 of this Form, the origin criteria met, in the manner shown in the following table:

Circumstances of production or manufacture in the first country named in box 11 of this form	Insert in box 8
(a) Goods wholly obtained or produced in the territory of the exporting Party	"WO"
(b) Goods satisfying Rule 4.1 of Annex 3 (Rules of Origin) of the AKFTA	"CTH" or "RVC 40%"

APPENDIX 13. AKFTA

(cont.)

Circumstances of production or manufacture in the first country named in box 11 of this form	Insert in box 8
(c) Goods satisfying the Product Specific Rules - Change in Tariff Classification - Wholly Obtained or Produced in the territory of any Party - Regional Value Content - Regional Value Content + Change in Tariff Classification - Specific Processes (d) Goods satisfying Rule 6	"CTC" "WO-AK" "RVC" that needs to be met for the good to qualify as originating; e.g. "RVC 45%" The combination rule that needs to be met for good to qualify as originating; e.g. "CTH + RVC 40%" "Specific Processes" "Rule 6"

4. EACH ARTICLE MUST QUALIFY: It should be noted that all the goods in a consignment must qualify separately in their own right. This is of particular relevance when similar articles of different sizes or spare parts are sent.

5. DESCRIPTION OF GOODS: The description of goods must be sufficiently detailed to enable the goods to be identified by the Customs Officers examining them. Name of manufacturer, any trade mark shall also be specified.

6. HARMONIZED SYSTEM NUMBER: The Harmonized System number shall be that of the importing Party.

7. EXPORTER: The term "Exporter" in box 11 may include the manufacturer or the producer.

8. FOR OFFICIAL USE: The Customs Authority of the importing Party must indicate (√) in the relevant boxes in column 4 whether or not preferential tariff is accorded.

APPENDIX 13. AKFTA

9. THIRD COUNTRY INVOICING: In cases where invoices are issued by a third country, "the Third Country Invoicing" box should be ticked (√) and such informations as name and country of the company issuing the invoice shall be indicated in box 7.
10. EXHIBITIONS: In cases where goods are sent from the territory of the exporting Party for exhibition in another country and sold during or after the exhibition for importation into the territory of a Party, in accordance with Rule 20 of the Operational Certification Procedures, the "Exhibitions" box should be ticked (√) and the name and address of the exhibition indicated in box 2.
11. BACK-TO-BACK CERTIFICATE OF ORIGIN: In cases of Back-to-Back CO, in accordance with Rule 7 (2) of the Operational Certification Procedures, the "Back-to-Back CO" box should be ticked (√).

BIBLIOGRAPHY

Arndt, S. and Kierzkowski, H., *Fragmentation: New Production Patterns in the World Economy* (Oxford University Press, 2001).
European Commission, *Impact Assessment on Rules of Origin for the Generalized System of Preference (GSP)* (2007).
Ganeshan, W. and Kawai, M., *Asia's Free Trade Agreements: How Is Business Responding* (Asian Development Bank, 2011).
Hayakawa, K., Hiratsuka, D., Shiino, S. and Sukegama, S., *Who Uses Free Trade Agreements?* (JETRO, 2007).
Hiratsuka, D., Isono, I., Sato, H. and Umezaki, S., "Escaping from FTA Trap and Spaghetti Bowl Problem in East Asia: An Insight from the Enterprise Survey in Japan" in Soesastro, H. (ed.), *Deepening Economic Integration in East Asia: The ASEAN Economic Community and Beyond* (ERIA, 2007), pp. 304–327.
Inama, S., *Rules of Origin in International Trade* (Cambridge University Press, 2009).
  "The Reform of the EC GSP Rules of Origin: Per Aspera Ad Astra?" *Journal of World Trade*, 45 (2011).
James, W., "Rules of Origin in Emerging Asia-Pacific Preferential Trade Agreements: Will PTAs Promote Trade and Development," *Asia-Pacific Research and Training Network on Trade Working Paper Series*, 19 (2006).
Kimura, F., "International Production and Distribution Networks in East Asia: Eighteen Facts, Mechanics, and Policy Implication," *Asian Economic Policy Review*, 1 (2006), 326–344.
Medalla, E. M. and Balboa, J., *ASEAN Rules of Origin: Lessons and Recommendations for Best Practice* (PIDS, 2009).

Takahashi, K. and Urata, S., "On the Use of FTAs by Japanese Firms," RIETI Discussion Paper, 08-E-002 (2008).
"On the Use of FTAs by Japanese Firms: Further Evidence," RIETI Discussion Paper, 09-E-028 (2009).
UNCTAD, *Market Access for Least Developed Countries* (2001).
UNCTAD, *Trade Preferences for LDCs: An Early Assessment of Benefits and Possible Improvements* (2003).
UNCTAD, *Trade Is Better Than Aid to Aid for Trade* (2008).

INDEX

absorption/roll-up principle, AFTA rules of origin and, 21–24
accumulation, ATIGA rules of origin revisions and, 38–39
across-the-board percentage criterion
  in ASEAN–Japan FTA, 52–56
  in ASEAN–Korea FTA, 51–52
  ASEAN Single List and, 24–27
  rules of origin and, xvi–xx, 19–20
actual domestic content.
  See also local content criteria
  cumulative rule of origin and criteria for, 19–20
addition methods, local ASEAN content criteria and, 12–15
administrative problems with rules of origin
  cost issues in, 57–75
  opacity of ASEAN rules, xvi–xx, 1–3, 2n.1, 10–11
  substance of administrative requirements, 88
  summary of, 93–95
ad valorem percentages, substantial transformation criterion and, 24–27
Agreement on Customs Valuation
  in ASEAN–Japan FTA, 52–56
  Cambodia and, 169n.7

Agreement on the common effective preferential tariff scheme for the ASEAN free trade area (1992), 97–108
agro-based products, product-specific rules of origin for, 27–34
aluminum products, product-specific rules of origin for, 27–34
apparel products, product-specific rules of origin for, 27–34
ASEAN–Australia–New Zealand FTA (AANZFTA), provisions of, 48–49
ASEAN Customs Agreement of 2012, 72–73
ASEAN Economic Community (AEC)
  revisions to rules of origin and, 93–95
  rules of origin and, xvi–xx
ASEAN Framework agreement for the Integration of Priority Sectors
  alternative PSROs for textiles in, 27–34
  development of, 24–27
ASEAN Framework Agreement on Goods in Transit, 73–75

401

INDEX

ASEAN Free Trade Area (AFTA) agreements
   absorption/roll-up principle and, 21–24
   alternative product-specific rules of origin under, 27–34
   ASEAN–China FTA and, 40–48
   ASEAN–India FTA, 49–51
   ASEAN–Japan FTA and, 52–56
   ASEAN–South Korea FTA, 51–52
   Common Effective Preferential Tariff scheme and, 1–3, 12–15, 97–108
   Form D certificate of origin requirements in, 60
   product-specific rules adopted by, 24–27
   rules of origin and, 93–95
   rules of origin principles and guidelines, xvi–xx, 17–19
   underutilization of, research concerning, 6–10
ASEAN–India FTA, provisions of, 49–51
ASEAN Industrial Cooperation (AICO) scheme, 3–6
ASEAN–Japan FTA, provisions of, 52–56
ASEAN Preferential Trade Agreement (APTA)
   regional value content rules, 27n.3
   rules of origin and, xvi–xx, 93–95
ASEAN Single List, formulation of, 24–27
ASEAN Subcommittee on Rules of Origin (SCAROO), Form D certificate of origin rejection decision matrix, 61t
ASEAN Trade in Goods Agreement (ATIGA)
   absorption/roll-up principle and, 21–24
   administrative requirements in, 88
   Annex 7, 200–205
   Annex 8, certification procedures, 206–223
   Appendix 8 concerning Form D certificate of origin requirements, 69–71
   cumulative rules of origin guidelines, 199
   customs administration and, 72–73, 165–174
   final provisions and amendments, 191–194
   Form D certificate of origin and, 57–72
   institutional provisions, 189–190
   loss of origin prevention and, 73–75
   non-tariff measures in, 157–160
   operational certification procedures in, 239–255
   provisions of, 114–133
   regional value content calculations, guidelines for, 197–198
   rules of origin provisions, xvi–xx, 1–3, 34–39, 86–95, 141–156, 224–256
   sanitary and phytosanitary measures, 183–188

402

INDEX

self-certification adoption, 78–80
standards, technical regulations and conformity assessment procedures, 175–182
tariff liberalization provisions, 133–141
textiles and textile products attachment, 195–196
trade facilitation provisions, 161–165
trade remedy measures, 188–189
underutilization of, 86–92
"ASEAN Way" of consensus and non-confrontation, 1–3
regional trade agreements and, 86–92
"ASEAN-X" concept, self-certification and, 82–85
Australia, ASEAN–Australia–New Zealand FTA and, 48–49
automotive products
ASEAN trade agreements and, 6
Form D certificate of origin problems and, 69
product-specific rules of origin for, 27–34

"blanket" certificates of origin, use in NAFTA of, 77–78
Brunei, self-certification program in, 78–80, 82–85
"buffet" policymaking, self-certification and, 82–85
build-down calculations
ASEAN FTA agreements, 89
in ASEAN–Korea FTA, 51–52

build-up calculations, in ASEAN–Korea FTA, 51–52

Cambodia
Agreement on Customs Valuation and, 169n.7
Information Technology Agreement and, 34–39
certificate of origin (CO)
in ASEAN–China FTA, 40–48
ATIGA data requirements, 228–256
ATIGA operational procedure for, 206–223
"blanket" certificates of origin, 77–78
customs administration and, 72–73
free trade agreements and, 1–3
issuance rates for, 3–6
loss of origin prevention of, 73–75
Certified Exporter status, self-certification and, 78–80
change in chapter (CTH)
ATIGA revised rules of origin and, 34–39
product-specific rules of origin and, 27–34
change in tariff classification (CTC)
in ASEAN–Australia–New Zealand FTA, 48–49
ASEAN–India FTA and, 49–51
ATIGA revised rules of origin and, 34–39
Form D certificate of origin and, 57–72

403

INDEX

change in tariff classification (CTC) (cont.)
  product-specific rules of origin and, 27–34, 86–92
  self-certification and, 78–80
change in tariff sub-heading (CTSH), product-specific rules of origin and, 27–34
China, ASEAN–China FTA, rules of origin in, 40–48, 257–259
Common Effective Preferential Tariff (CEPT) scheme
  agreement on (1992), 97–108
  AICO scheme and, 3–6
  ASEAN Free Trade Area agreement and, 1–3
  Form D certificate of origin rejection and, 60–61
  intra-ASEAN trade and, 6
  loss of origin prevention and, 73–75
  product-specific rules and, 24–27
  rules of origin for, 12–15, 17–19, 109–113
compliance costs
  Form D certificate of origin, 57–72
  rules of origin requirements, 3–6
conformity assessment, ATIGA provisions concerning, 175–182
consensus building, "ASEAN Way" of consensus and non-confrontation, 1–3
corporate income tax rates in ASEAN, 81t
  self-certification and role of, 80–81
cost calculations. *See also* direct method calculations; indirect method calculations
  in ASEAN–India FTA, 317n.5, 324–325
  ASEAN methodologies for, 12–15, 15n.1, 17–19
  ATIGA regional value content guidelines for, 197–198
  Form D certificate of origin compliance costs, 57–72
  for rules of origin, 86–92
  value-added calculation and, 91
cumulative rules of origin
  absorption/roll-up process and, 21–24
  in ASEAN–China FTA, 40–48
  ASEAN guidelines for, 19–20
  ATIGA guidelines, 38–39, 199
  Form D certificate of origin and, 71–72
customs administration
  absorption/roll-up principle and, 21–24
  ATIGA provisions concerning, 72–73, 165–174
  duty collections targets for, 86–87
  Form D certificate of origin rejection by, 60–61
  free trade agreements and, 1–3
  opposition to self-certification from, 78–80
  rules of origin negotiations and, 10–11, 93–95

INDEX

Customs Valuation Agreement (WTO), 91–92

deductive methods, local ASEAN content criteria and, 12–15
direct method calculations
  AFTA formula for, 16–17
  in ASEAN–Australia–New Zealand FTA, 48–49
  in ASEAN–India FTA, 49–51, 317n.5, 324–325
  in ASEAN–Japan FTA, 52–56
  for ATIGA rules of origin, 89
  local ASEAN content criteria and, 12–15
  regional value content, 29–31
document-based verification
  administrative barriers for, xvi–xx, 1–3, 2n.1, 10–11
  ATIGA provisions concerning, 228–256
  problems with, 93–95
dual certification regime, self-certification and, 77–78
dual rules of origin approach, ASEAN adoption of, 27–34
duty-free imports, rule of origin and, 1–3

e-ASEAN products, product-specific rules of origin for, 27–34
East Asia, ASEAN free trade agreements in, 3–6
electronics machinery
  ASEAN–Japanese trade agreements and, 3–6

product-specific rules of origin for, 27–34
ERIA research, Form D certificate of origin and, 57–72
European Union (EU)
  rule of origin reforms and, 1–3
  self-certification and, 77–78
ex-factory price, AFTA calculation of, 16–17
exporting countries
  ASEAN rules of origin and, 86–92
  ATIGA revised rules of origin and, 34–39
  Form D certificate of origin and, 57–72
  self-certification by, 76–85
  substantial transformation criterion and, 24–28
exports, management procedures for, 3–6

fisheries
  ATIGA provisions concerning, 145n.5
  product-specific rules of origin for, 27–34
Form D certificate of origin
  administrative costs and problems concerning, 57–72
  AFTA issuance requirements for, 60
  ASEAN Subcommittee on Rules of Origin (SCAROO) rejection decision matrix, 61t
  ATIGA Appendix 8 concerning Form D certificate of origin requirements, 69–71

405

INDEX

Form D certificate of origin (cont.)
  ATIGA establishment of, 58
  copy of, 59t
  loss of origin prevention and, 73–75
  rejection of documentation, reasons for, 60–61
  self-certification as alternative to, 76, 82–85
  specimen signature process for, 7–10
  treatment of minor discrepancies in, 70–71
  underutilization of ASEAN agreements and confusion over, 6–10
free on board (FOB) price
  AFTA calculation of, 16–17
  in ASEAN–Australia–New Zealand FTA, 48–49
  in ASEAN–Japan FTA, 52–56
  in ASEAN–Korea FTA, 51–52
  CEPT rules of origin and confusion over, 12–15
  product-specific rules of origin and, 27–34
free trade agreements (FTAs)
  absorption/roll-up principle in, 21–24
  advocacy of ASEAN rules of origin in, 40–43
  ancillary rules in, 40–44t
  ASEAN–Australia–New Zealand FTA (AANZFTA), 48–49
  ASEAN–China FTA, rules of origin in, 40–48
  ASEAN–India FTA, 49–51
  ASEAN–Japan FTA, 52–56
  ASEAN–Korea FTA, 51–52
  ATIGA trade facilitation proposals, 161–165
  comparison of rules of origin in, 41–43t
  Form D certificate of origin interaction with, 71–72
  rules of origin negotiations and, xvi–xx, 1–3, 88
  underutilization of ASEAN agreements, studies of, 6–10, 86–87
  utilization in East Asia of, t3–6t,

Generalised System of Preferences program (EU), rule of origin reforms and, 1–3
GSP Form A, introduction of, 7–10

Harmonized Tariff Schedule (HTS)
  in ASEAN–Japan FTA, 52–56
  in ASEAN–Korea FTA, 51–52
  ATIGA revised rules of origin and, 34–39
  rules of origin, xvi–xx
healthcare, product-specific rules of origin for, 27–34

imports
  customs administration and, 72–73
  free trade utilization and rates for, 3–6
  rules of origin requirements and, 1–3

INDEX

India, ASEAN–India FTA, 49–51, 313–329
indirect method calculations
  in ASEAN–Australia–New Zealand FTA, 48–49
  in ASEAN–India FTA, 49–51, 317n.5, 324–325
  in ASEAN–Japan FTA, 52–56
  for ATIGA rules of origin, 89
  local ASEAN content criteria and, 12–15
  regional value content, 29–31
Indonesia
  corporate income tax rates in, 80–81
  local ASEAN content criteria in, 12–15
  opposition to self-certification in, 78–80
  self-certification pilot program in, 82–85
  underutilization of ASEAN agreements by, 6–10
Information Technology Agreement (ITA) (WTO), ATIGA rules of origin revisions and, 34–39
intermediate products. see absorption/roll-up principle
investment incentives, free trade agreements and, 3–6

Japan
  ASEAN free trade agreements in, 3–6
  ASEAN–Japan FTA and, 52–56

Kyoto Convention, Annex K of, 24–27

labor costs, value-added calculation and, 91
Laos
  Information Technology Agreement and, 34–39
  local ASEAN content criteria in, 12–15
  self-certification pilot program in, 82–85
Less Developed Countries, utilization of free trade by, 6–10
local content criteria. *See also* actual domestic content
  absence of ASEAN definition for, 18–19
  AFTA calculation methods, 16–17
  CEPT rules of origin and confusion over, 12–15
  value-added calculation, 91
loss of origin, prevention of, 73–75

Malaysia
  product-specific rules of origin in, 37n.5
  self-certification program in, 78–80, 82–85
  underutilization of ASEAN agreements by, 6–10
member states
  ATIGA revised rules of origin and, 34–39, 139n.3

INDEX

member states (cont.)
    CEPT rules of origin and confusion over, 12–15
    customs administration variations in, 72–73
    Form D certificate of origin and, 57–72
    self-certification adoption by, 78–80
Most Favored Nation (MFN) status
    custom duty rates and, 1–3
    customs administration and, 72–73
    intra-ASEAN trade and, 6
    tariff rates in Japan and, 3–6
Myanmar
    Information Technology Agreement and, 34–39
    local ASEAN content criteria in, 12–15

New Zealand, ASEAN–Australia–New Zealand FTA and, 48–49
non-confrontation, "ASEAN Way" of consensus and non-confrontation, 1–3
non-originating materials
    in ASEAN–China FTA, 40–48
    in ASEAN–Japan FTA, 52–56
North American Free Trade Agreement (NAFTA)
    self-certification provision in, 77–78
    triple transformation requirement under, 24–27
    utilization rate for, 6–10

value-added calculations under, 89
numerator calculation, for ATIGA rules of origin, 89

Operational Certification Procedures (OCP)
    ASEAN–China FTA, 265–275
    ATIGA guidelines for, 239–255
    customs administration and, 72–73
    loss of origin prevention and, 73–75
originating material
    in ASEAN–Australia–New Zealand FTA, 48–49
    ASEAN–China FTA definition of, 40–48
    in ASEAN–Korea FTA, 51–52

percentage criteria. *See also* across-the-board percentage criterion; *ad valorem* percentages
    ASEAN–China FTA and, 40–48
    in ASEAN–Japan FTA, 52–56
    in ASEAN–Korea FTA, 51–52
    ASEAN Single List and, 24–27
    legacy of, 86–92
    rules of origin and, xvi–xx, 19–20
Philippines
    free trade utilization in, 3–6
    self-certification pilot program in, 82–85
phytosanitary measures, in ATIGA, 183–188
predictability, in rules of origin negotiations, 10–11

INDEX

pre-export examinations
  Form D certificate of origin and, 57–72
  self-certification and, 76–85
preferential trade agreements (PTAs)
  customs administration and, 72–73, 86–87
  percentage criterion calculations, 89–91
  rules of origin and, xvi–xx, 93–95
processing operations, product-specific rules of origin and, 27–34
production cost formula, AFTA calculation of, 16–17
product-specific rules of origin (PSRO)
  AFTA adoption of, 24–27
  alternative rules, in 2000–2009 period, 27–34
  in ASEAN–Australia–New Zealand FTA, 48–49
  ASEAN–China FTA, 259n.1, 259n.2, 259n.3, 260n.4, 262n.5, 276–307, 284n.6
  in ASEAN–China FTA, 40–48
  in ASEAN–India FTA, 49–51, 315n.1, 315n.2, 315n.3, 316n.4, 324–325
  in ASEAN–Japan FTA, 52–56
  in ASEAN–Korea FTA, 51–52
  ATIGA revisions and, 34–39, 145n.4
  change in tariff classification and, 27–34, 86–92
  individual country variations concerning, 34n.4, 37n.5

substantial transformation criterion and, 32

qualifying ASEAN national content, cumulative rule of origin and criteria for, 19–20
qualitative analysis, rules of origin, xvi–xx

regional trade agreements (RTA), growth in East Asia of, 86–92
regional value content (RVC)
  APTA and, 27n.3
  in ASEAN–Australia–New Zealand FTA, 48–49
  in ASEAN–Japan FTA, 52–56
  in ASEAN–Korea FTA, 51–52
  ATIGA formulae, 34–39, 90, 197–198t
  defined, xvi–xx
  direct method calculations, 29–31
  indirect method calculations, 29–31
  product-specific rules of origin and, 27–34
  value material calculation for, 88–92t
roll-up. *see* absorption/roll-up principle
rubber-based products, product-specific rules of origin for, 27–34
rules of origin (RoOs) (ASEAN). *See also* free trade agreements (FTAs)

409

INDEX

rules of origin (RoOs) (ASEAN). (cont.)
  absorption/roll-up process and, 21–24
  administrative problems with, xvi–xx, 1–3, 2n.1, 10–11
  AFTA principles and guidelines, 17–19
  alternative rules, introduction in 1995–2000 of, 24–39
  ancillary rules, table of, 40–44t
  in ASEAN–Australia–New Zealand FTA, 48–49
  in ASEAN–China FTA, 40–48, 257–259
  in ASEAN–India FTA, 49–51, 313–329
  in ASEAN–Japan FTA, 52–56
  in ASEAN–South Korea FTA, 51–52
  ATIGA provisions and guidelines, xvi–xx, 1–3, 34–39, 141–156, 224–256
  in Common Effective Preferential Tariff (CEPT) scheme, 17–19, 109–113
  cost issues with, 57–75
  cumulation rules for, 19–20
  free trade agreements and, 40–43
  function and classification, xvi–xx
  international comparisons in FTAs of, 41–43t
  percentage criteria for, xvi–xx, 19–20, 86–92
  preferential trade agreements and, 93–95

substantial transformation test, 24–27
value-based calculation, 12–19

sanitary measures, in ATIGA, 183–188
self-certification
  proposals and procedures for, 76–85, 93–95
  for trading companies, 82–85
Senior Economic Officials Meeting (SEOM), underutilization of ASEAN agreement studies and, 6–10
Singapore
  corporate income tax rates in, 80–81
  free trade utilization by, 3–6
  local ASEAN content criteria in, 12–15
  product-specific rules of origin in, 34n.4
  self-certification program in, 78–80, 82–85
small and medium-sized enterprises (SMEs)
  ASEAN rules of origin and, 86–92
  rules of origin and, xvi–xx
South Korea, ASEAN–Korea FTA and, 51–52, 89
specimen signature process
  Form D certificate of origin rejection and, 60–61
  proposed improvements for, 7–10
steel products, product-specific rules of origin for, 27–34

410

INDEX

"substantial transformation" standard, rules of origin and, xvi–xx
substantial transformation test
 definition of criterion, 32
 product-specific rules of origin and, 27–34
 rules of origin reform and, 24–27
substantive origin criteria, in ASEAN–China FTA, 40–48
subtraction-based calculations, for ATIGA rules of origin, 93

tariff liberalization
 free trade agreements and, 1–3, 2n.1
 substantial transformation criterion and, 24–27
tariff liberalization and classification
 in ASEAN–Australia–New Zealand FTA, 48–49
 ASEAN–India FTA and, 49–51
 in ASEAN–Japan FTA, 52–56
 ASEAN rules of origin and, 86–92
 ATIGA provisions for, 133–141
 Form D certificate of origin and, 57–72
 product-specific rules of origin and, 27–34
textiles and textile products
 alternative PSROs for, 27–34
 ATIGA attachment concerning, 195–196

product-specific rules of origin for, 24–27, 32–34
 substantial transformation criterion and, 25n.2
Thailand
 Form D certificate of origin rejections in, 61
 self-certification program in, 78–80, 82–85
 underutilization of ASEAN agreements by, 6–10
third-country material, CEPT rules of origin and confusion over, 12–15
trade facilitation
 ASEAN rules of origin as barrier for, 86–92
 ATIGA proposals for, 161–165
 ATIGA trade remedy measures, 188–189
trading companies
 corporate income tax rates and, 80–81
 customs administration suspicion of, 78–80
transparency, in rules of origin negotiations, 10–11

undetermined origin criteria, CEPT rules of origin and confusion over, 12–15
US–Central America Free Trade Area, 51–52
US GSP agreement, 89

value-added tax (VAT), self-certification and, 80–81

411

INDEX

value-based calculation
  absorption/roll-up principle and, 21–24
  in ASEAN–Korea FTA, 51–52
ASEAN rules of origin, 12–19
for ATIGA rules of origin, 93
Form D certificate of origin and, 71–72
value of materials calculation, proposals for, 93
value of non-originating materials (VNM), in ASEAN–Japan FTA, 52–56
value of originating materials (VOM), in ASEAN–Korea FTA, 51–52
Vientiane Agreement, ASEAN–China FTA and, 40–48
Vietnam
  free trade utilization in, 3–6
  self-certification pilot program in, 82–85
"wholly originating" principle, rules of origin, xvi–xx
wood-based products, product-specific rules of origin for, 27–34
working operations, product-specific rules of origin and, 27–34
World Customs Organization, absorption/roll-up principle and, 21–24
World Trade Organization (WTO)
  Agreement on Rules of Origin, 24–27
  Customs Valuation Agreement, 91–92
  Information Technology Agreement, 34–39

For EU product safety concerns, contact us at Calle de José Abascal, 56–1°, 28003 Madrid, Spain or eugpsr@cambridge.org.